THE HUNGARIAN VIZSLA

THE HUNGARIAN VIZSLA

by

Gay Gottlieb

With a special section on the working Vizsla in Britain
by Louise Petrie-Hay

Distributor:
NIMROD BOOK SERVICES
P.O. BOX 1
LISS HANTS GU33 7PR

ISBN 0 947647 - 09 - 0

First Published 1985

DEDICATION

to Sydney and our children

Typeset by: Della Woodman · Fareham · Hampshire

Printed by:

Published by:
NIMROD BOOK SERVICES
(Fanciers Supplies Ltd)
LISS, HANTS, GU33 7PR
ENGLAND

CONTENTS

ACKNOWLEDGEMENTS AND INTRODUCTION

I have long felt that there is a need for a work on the Hungarian Vizsla in Britain, given that there does not exist anything by way of reference to the particular aspects of our Vizsla. Now that this type of dog is increasing in numbers it would seem timely that there is a work which provides information for the novice coming into the breed. It is my wish to stimulate all Vizsla enthusiasts who would like to acquire a deeper understanding of the unique quality and versatility of one of the Hunt, Point, and Retrieve breeds.

In working up to the research and preparation of this book I tried to consider the particular needs of the British owner. Therefore I have written little on the Hungarian Vizsla abroad, or of our exports preferring to concentrate on the breed in this country although I have given a detailed account of imports and progeny thus tracing our foundation stock. Also unique to this work is the section on the working Vizsla in Britain, written by my friend and colleague, Louise Petrie-Hay, who is held in high esteem for her knowledge and contribution to the Hungarian Vizsla as a breeder in competition, and as a field trial judge. She has had vast experience of training this breed and at last we now have our own book of reference on how to train the Vizsla.

Part of the book is devoted to Imprinting, and Socialising. This required extensive research and I am most grateful to those who have written on the study of the subject which has taken place in America. The chapter on Showing and Handling pays particular attention to the requirements specific to the Vizsla in the British show ring.

All data is recorded up to the year 1984, therefore it is inevitable that recent events and results in the history of the Vizsla in Britain have not been included.*

I wish to thank all those who have provided encouragement, enthusiasm and support, and those who have so generously provided the many photographs. In particular may I thank Barbara Douglas-Redding for giving me her extensive breed notes dating back to 1965, they were invaluable material. Also my thanks to Sharon Seward for her patient researches of important data concerning the registrations at the Kennel Club. To Jackie Perkins for her graphic illustrations and to all who patiently read and corrected the manuscript for me.

London
December 1984

Gay Gottlieb

*The book was just going to press when the 1985 Crufts' results were known and the photograph of the successful *Paris* was included. Editor.

vi

LIST OF ILLUSTRATIONS

COLOUR ILLUSTRATIONS —
Appear after page xvi and show historical illustrations
as well as modern dogs.

EARLY HISTORY OF THE

HUNGARIAN VIZSLA

The photographs (Figs. 1—4) which follow were obtained from Hungary through Dr. Zoltan Tôth.

Figure 1 Karoly Thuroczy with his Vizsla *Trick*, 1860 (from *Nimrod* magazine, 1917).
Figures 1, 2, 3 and 4 courtesy Dr Zoltan Tôth

Figure 2 Witti yellow Hungarian Vizsla male (owner: Gyula Popovich from *Nimrod*, 1918) His name appears in every pedigree dated 1918 and for 16 years his progeny were inbred and those with white were culled.

Figure 3 Participants of the Hubertus Vizsla Competition in Isaszeg, Hungary, 1918.

Figure 4 Hanved 15 year-old male.
("Yellow" in colour, but note the white patches)

Figure 5 A retrieve in Hungary

COLOUR
ILLUSTRATIONS

Plate 1 Part of a Gothic Panel (15th century) from Christian Museum in Esztergom (Hungary) showing dog believed to be Vizsla. (Research Study: Dr. Zoltan Tôth) Corvina Press, Budapest.

Plate 2 **Top** An early hunting scene in Hungary.
Bottom Falconry with dog believed to be Vizsla.
Both are from *Illustrated Vienna Chronicle* **(1357) reproduced by kind permission National
Széchényi Library, Budapest**

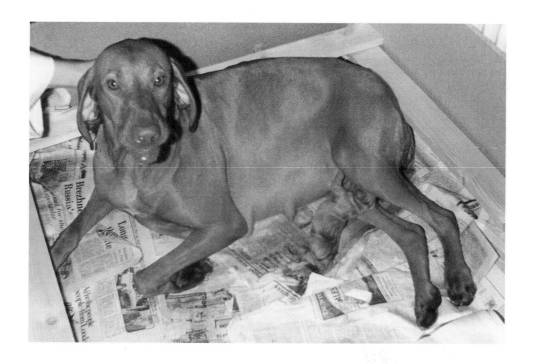

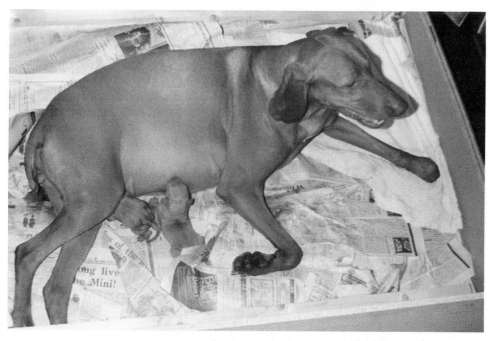

Plate 3   **Top** Motherhood — the first whelp
Bottom The Second Whelp — the maiden dam is very calm.

Plate 4   **Top** Newspapers removed all are feeding; the dam is content.
Bottom Tails have been docked and dew claws removed.

Plate 5 **Top** Sh.Ch. *Russetmantle Paris* at Crufts 1985 with the judge Mr. Leslie Page and the author.
Bottom Mrs. S. Gray's Ch. *Abbeystag Emilio*.

Plate 6   Matai Lurko (Angela Boys)

Plate 7 First Vizsla to win a Gun Dog Group – Mary Bradbrook's Sh.Ch. *Russetmantle Bee.*

Plate 8 **Top** *Waidman Brok* in the Field (Louise Petrie-Hay)
Bottom *Waidman Brok* at Woburn Game Fair on point.

Plate 9 "A Frosty Morning" (Mr and Mrs N Cox) *Calversam Barleybroth* and *Viszony of Vallota* (rear).

Plate 10 **Top** *Calversam Barleybroth* demonstrates the versatility, courage and fitness of the Vizsla. **Bottom** Barbara Douglas-Redding with *Wolfox Emla*, *Editha* and *Edwina*.

Plate 11 Nigel Cox on a Grouse Moor with *Viszony of Vallota.*

Plate 12 The author pausing on a picking-up day. Ch.*Russetmantle Troy, Waidman Brok, Waidman Che, Waidman Crumpet*

Plate 13 The only two Hungarian Wire-Haired Vizslas in Britain. *Aranyos Tizsu Dudus* (B) owned by Mr & Mrs Layton *Borostyanko Gulyas of Carric Temple* owned by Mrs. C. Appleton.

Plate 14 First Show Championship Dog in Britain.
Sh.Ch. *Waidman Remus* bred by Louise Petrie-Hay, owned by the author.　　(*photo: Diane Pearce*)

Plate 15 Joram de la Creste   (photo: Sally Anne Thompson)

Plate 16 The Hungarian Vizsla was bred as a hunting dog and is now a versatile shooting dog.

HISTORY and MANAGEMENT

Figure 1.1 Winners of a Field Trial in Hungary (c.1973)

CHAPTER 1

HUNGARIAN VIZSLAS HISTORY

EARLY ORIGINS

The origins of the Hungarian Vizsla are very difficult to trace but its history probably began in the 9th century when the warring Magyar tribes migrated from the Steppes of Asia. They led a nomadic life until eventually they settled in the Carpathian basin, now known as Hungary. It is thought that by tradition the Magyars, when not occupied with cattle breeding, hunted a great deal. On their travels they were accompanied by their horses, sheep, cattle, and camels as well as their hunting and herding dogs. It is believed that through the centuries the Hungarian herding breeds we see today evolved from these early Magyar herding dogs. It is thought that the Vizsla of today is descended from the hunting dogs which had been crossed with other native dogs, then subsequently with the Turkish "yellow dog" when they invaded and occupied Hungary during the 16th and 17th centuries.

The Turks occupation lasted for 15 years. During this time the Vizsla is mentioned in the correspondence of the day and by the end of the 16th century the name "Vizsla" had become generally accepted replacing the name "yellow pointer".

Vizsla, the plural being Vizslak, not Vizslas, means "to seek" in Turkish and it could be supposed that the name also originates from a hamlet in the Danube Valley that bore the same name in the 12th century. The Hungarian pronunciation of the 'i' in Vizsla is 'e' as in 'event' or as the 'i' in 'film'. The 'zs' is pronounced as the 's' in 'pleasure' or 'measure'.

Hungarian scholars believe that the progenitor of the breed is to be seen in some of the illuminations depicting hunting scenes in the 12th and 13th century, illustrated in the *Viennese Chronicle* written by the Carmelite Friars in 1357. This manuscript is the recognised illustrated record of Hungarian culture and it mentions the Vizsla by name.

Early Sporting Dogs
For centuries the breed was owned by the sporting nobility of Hungary. They used their dogs to scent and search for birds which were either netted or caught by falcons. There are letters reported to be in the Hungarian National Record Office in Budapest — one is written by Michael Komlossy in 1515, requesting a Vizsla, "suitable to net quails". Another written in 1563 by Kristoff Bathyani requested a dog (Vizsla) with a good nose, a retriever for quail.

3

In the 1700's, when firearms were introduced, the Zay family of Zaycegroe were known for their skill in breeding and training their dogs for hunting and working with the gun and their strain was much sought after by the aristocracy who valued the Vizsla for his pointing and retrieving ability. It is believed that our modern prototype was evolved by the selective breeding of the Zays to satisfy the needs of the sporting nobility of the day.

Development of the Standard Type Dog

Toward the end of the century, various breeds were brought into Hungary and were purposely bred to the Hungarian Vizsla. It was the fashion for the aristocracy to bring in "English gamekeepers". They brought their retrievers with them and inevitably they were used on the native bird dogs.

In 1880 Zoltan Hamvay imported the English Setter and Julius Barczy de Barczihaza brought in the Irish Setter. These dogs were bred to the Vizsla. It is also suggested that as well as other pointing breeds (the English Pointer for instance) other hound breeds were used, such as the Bloodhound, German Vorstehund, Balkan Beagle, the ancient Foxhound, Pannonion Hound and the Rumanian Copie. There is no evidence that the German Short-Haired Pointer or the Weimaraner were used at any time in this breed's history. The outcrossing was not done "under the blanket" but purposely to increase the hunting quality, thus strengthening the characteristics of the native Vizsla. It is believed that the first stud book was kept by these two breeders and around this time the first Field Trial for the Hungarian Vizsla was held.

Thus the breed existed approximately in its present form in the 18th century, then in the 19th century selective breeding improved its good properties, finally resulting in the present day Vizsla.

The Aim — A Multi-Purpose Dog

The Vizsla had always been owned by the nobility. He had been bred in the private kennels of the powerful barons and until 1946 when Hungary became a republic Hungary was a feudal state and the distinctive feature of the rural economy was the large number of big estates owned by the feudal lords, a class who had arrogantly ruled the land for centuries. The countryside differed widely from one district to another and some of the terrain the dogs had to work was the best shooting ground in Europe, well known for the abundance and variety of game it held. Thus a multi-purpose dog was required who would work fur and feather, and the versatile Vizsla could fulfil these requirements. He needed to be fast with the sort of nose that would permit him to find game in the thick cover of crops or high grasslands or in the vast plains of corn. He was called upon to find the giant hare, often hidden in the high tufts of grass on the open Putza of the central Hungarian plain, and to drive the hare towards the waiting guns. This same dog hunted out deer in the dense forests driving them into the clearing towards the guns. In the woods and thickets he had to point wood-cock and pheasant and on the banks of the lakes and rivers and in the marshland he must flush waterfowl, wild duck, goose and quail. He was also required to hunt and hold at bay wild boar and wolf — this was done with several dogs working together. The Vizsla flourished under these conditions and his natural retrieving ability on land and in the water added to his valuable qualities.

4

Figure 1.2 Matai Lurko Baying the dead wild boar. In many of the present-day pedigrees.

THE 20th CENTURY

The Austro-Hungarian Empire had extended its influence over a large area for many years, then with frequent border changes two-thirds of Hungary's pre-war 1914—1918 territory was annexed by the neighbouring states. As a consequence a considerable number of Hungarians (over 3,000,000) now lived in those countries, thus many Vizsla owners found themselves suddenly part of Czechoslovakia, Rumania, Italy, Germany, Poland and Russia. In addition a succession of wars and agricultural crises led to the emigration of about 1,500,000 Hungarians, the majority of whom reached North America eventually.

Two world wars and the Russian occupation almost spelled doom for the breed. Following World War I, numbers had declined and it was felt that the breed had lost its identity due to too much outcrossing with too many foreign breeds. A dedicated few searched the land far and wide for bird dogs resembling the old Vizsla. After this monumental task some dozen dogs became the foundation stock of all registered Vizslas in Hungary.

The First Vizsla Club in Hungary
The first Vizsla Club in Hungary was formed in 1924. Dr Kalman Polgar became the president. It had always been his dream to restore the breed. Another founder member was Captain Karoly Baba. He published a book on training, breeding and the care of the Vizsla. Other founding members and officers were:

Hon President	—	Count Lazslo Esterhazy
Treasurer	—	Mr Petocz
Registrar	—	Josef Stifft
Genealogists	—	Professor Balazs Otvos
		Professor Endre Felix
National Judge	—	Dr Elemer Markus
Supplies	—	Dr Janos Wirker

All the members owned Vizslas and all were devoted to restoring the breed. An initial *standard* was worked out and efforts were made to establish a strain and type. Through a very controlled breeding programme it became possible to breed out the colour variations and extensive white markings on the chest and feet which had begun to appear.

A great boost to the breed at this time was the win achieved by Captain K Babas' champion *Vegvari Betyar* who took first place over several prize-winning English and German Short-Haired Pointers at the incredible age of 13 years old. Her record was only surpassed by the National Champion *Kati* owned by Dr K Polgar who had earned the greatest number of awards and was best working Vizsla at 13 years old. She had borne 73 puppies in her lifetime. Lurko was also known for his successes in the field, in obedience trials and in the show-ring.

6

Effects of the Wars on the Breed

In 1935 the Federation Cynologique Internationale recognised the Hungarian Vizsla as a separate breed and the *Standard* was also revised. By 1944, 5,000 Vizslas had been registered and the breed seemed to have established itself again only to find that hardly a decade later 80%—90% of the breed were sadly affected by the ravages of the second world war and the Russian occupation of Eastern Europe in 1956—1958.

A piece called *My Hunting Pals* by Lorant de Bastyai describes vividly in detail his homecoming after the second world war:

> When I left the Hungarian Army and reached our country home, I found the empty house in an untidy condition, the furniture half broken lying huddled together, and my books were torn and slung around the room.
>
> There was no sign of my dear hawks and my Hungarian pointer dog was also missing. After learning from my friends in the neighbouring houses that they had given my birds their freedom and there was such a shortage of meat, I asked "How about my dog?" The answer was, "Perhaps retrieving pheasants and partridges on the Russian plains, perhaps in the German woods".
>
> Every normal human being, after tidying up the house would start to get new furniture, new curtains and so on. But not me. After I had put the broken furniture on the bonfire in our garden and half broken items which I could repair later back in the rooms with the remains of my books, my main thought was to get the hawks and the dog again.

Later he describes how he acquired his future Vizsla:

> I did not have to wait long for my future dog. One early summer afternoon, I was sitting in my drawing room with war damaged furniture still around, reading the daily post and Lurak, my hawk was on my fist. Suddenly the bird started behaving in an unusual way, giving a high-pitched warning call. "Pitt — pitt — fitch!" All the doors and windows were open in the warm summer weather and through one of these open doors the "strange thing" walked in, holding in its mouth a piece of meat longer than the head of this five month old Hungarian pointer puppy. She came in as if this had always been her home, and on the other end of the lead was one of my friends.

This little Vizsla — *Pacal* became his devoted companion.

In the era of the Russian occupation 1956—1958 over 188,000 Hungarians sought homes elsewhere, many taking their dogs with them. The old Hungarian families established themselves in European countries and thus the breed was dispersed widely. It is believed that some of the best stock left the country in this manner. If we look at any of our extended pedigrees all common ancestors come from Hungary or Czechoslovakia. From photographs of the breed in these two countries it is noticeable how, although the type remains the same, the conformation differs considerably. The Hungarian dogs appear to be lighter in bone and smaller than the Czechoslovakian dogs which appear heavier and to have more substance. This difference was quite noticeable in our basic English stock but it would seem today that we are producing Vizslas which do combine both quality and substance.

Among the many who fled the country after the Russian occupation, was Col Jeno Dus, director of the Magyar Vizsla Club. He managed to mimeograph the stud books and the minutes of all the club meetings. He buried these original documents near the Austrian border and escaped to freedom.

In these confused times many Vizslas were lost or went astray. (Some people lost their lives as did their Vizslas trying to get across the border.) In 1956 when Michael Kende was appointed the new director of the Magyar Dog Breeders Association, it was

Figure 1.3 Matai Panni   (taken in Hungary)

decided that those Vizslas which were of unknown origin should be registered if they were thought to be "very good" in appearance and showed "a good nose". These in turn should be bred with Vizslas having 2 or 3 generation pedigrees. The progeny could once more be bred to another one of unknown origin. All puppies were inspected closely. If it were agreed that their standard was good enough, they were registered and the parents entered in the stud book.

I should like to quote an extract from an interesting article written by Group Captain David, who left Hungary in 1958:

> I was HBM Air Attache in Hungary from May 1956—Sept 1958 and was invited by the Military Protocol Department in Budapest to attend a boar shoot in the Bakonyi forest in August 1956. The jaegermaester who accompanied me had a wonderful Vizsla bitch with him. The Vizslas fame as a hunting dog is well known behind the Iron Curtain. Their bravery is second to none. They are one of the few breeds who will face up to a wild boar to protect their masters.

Captain David bought one of this bitch's puppies. He continued:

> I named him *Betyar* because the Robin Hood like tribe of rascals (Betyars) used to operate from the Bakonyi forest.
>
> The puppy was about 5 weeks old and easily rested in my right hand at the time we came together. He is now nearly thirteen years old and has been a wonderful friend to have for all these years. His life has been adventurous. He was with me in Budapest throughout the Hungarian uprisings and the dreadful aftermath. He escaped from my house during curfew time and was shot by a Russian sentry who was guarding a gun post outside. The sentry was only doing his duty — shooting at something making a noise. The poor puppy managed to crawl back to my house and I found him nearly dead on the doorstep. Luckily the bullet had gone right through him and missed all the vital organs. He responded bravely to nursing and in two weeks was his old self again. He avoided any soldier in brown or khaki uniform after that. Indeed on one memorable occasion he chased three Russian soldiers down our road. He meant business. The Russians were scared and the local Hungarians highly delighted.

PRESENT DAY POSITION

The Vizsla has survived monumental disasters in Hungary, scarcely did he seem to have a chance to stabilise before new miseries befell him. But he is now well established in many countries as well as in his own. Hungary is now a socialist state. Much of the land is state owned with farm co-operatives. There are a number of private breeders scattered throughout the country and also a few of the state operated farms have kennels as a sideline. It is not an unusual sight in Budapest to see a Vizsla walking along with his owner out shopping, which means that he has adapted to the flat dwelling life. But although the very rich varieties of water fowl once found in the marshy regions and lakes, now survive only in nature reserves, there is still ample opportunity for the Vizsla to work. Shooting remains a popular sport and the forests of Hungary still harbour abundant numbers of red deer and wild pig, and the lowlands contain rodents, hares, partridge and pheasants. 82% of all hunting territory in Hungary is leased to hunting associations — individuals may not rent shoots — the remaining 18% is run directly by the state. Hunters associations are led by the National Association of Hungarian Hunters. The organ of the association the "Nimrod" contributes to the education and training of hunters to a great extent.

The Second World Congress of Breeders

In August 1982, the Second World Congress of Breeders of Hungarian Breeds, was held in Budapest. Those attending had the opportunity of visiting Hortobagy National Park, a reserve where they saw herds of horses, cattle, and sheep. Later they visited Lake Balaton, the largest lake in the European continent, they crossed the lake by ferry and drove to a state farm near Balatonfanyves where they met Miklos Farkashazi, now secretary of the Hungarian Vizsla Club. He had arranged a demonstration of the dogs working in a nearby field. The first exercise was to quarter, the second was three retrieves of planted seen game, two pheasants and a hare, and the third demonstration — the dogs had to track a hare that had been dragged along the

Figure 1.4 Matai Vadasz Retrieving at 4 months (taken in Hungary)

Figure 1.5 Mâtai Cseles at a Hungarian Show

Figure 1.6 Oportó Bitang, 3 year old dog owned and handled by Dr. László, President,
Hungarian Vizsla Club

ground – this they appeared to do with skill retrieving the hare to hand. They moved onto the water demonstration and here had to retrieve live and dead ducks, some achieved the live retrieves more successfully than others, it was felt that some dogs did not have enough drive. The last exercise was to test steadiness, all dogs had to be steady to shot, they all sat collectively, only one Vizsla broke, this was the second 'failure' for this dog that day. It was felt that he had a temperament problem, Miklos Farkashazi explained that due to this the dog would have to be eliminated from any breed programme. It was noted that many dogs in the demonstration had long tails, fewer dogs are docked now that the 1981 *Standard* does not ask for a docked tail.

When Angela Boys went over to Hungary in September 1972 she went to a show held in the International Fairground. 139 Vizslas were catalogued. There were two judges, one was M. Balazs (*Karoly*) and the other, none other than M. Dravenka (*Istvan*) who proudly told her that it was he who sent the first Vizslas over to England. Angela reports:

> Judging and showing is done in a very relaxed way with the judges walking about with a cup of coffee, stopping for a word with a spectator, kissing a hand, then back to the dogs. Each judge has a table and chairs under a striped umbrella, where he dictates his criticism of each dog to his assistant and then gives a copy to the exhibitor.

The placed dogs were good and Angela Boys admired two bitches who she would have bought if she could! She reports that though a lot were put down for being slab-sided, racy and oversized, colour was good – a rich dark gold, being much appreciated and the pale colours were put out.

Figure 1.7 Mátai Móka Winning Best of Breed in Budapest – bred by Miklós Farkasházi

She writes:

It is easy for one to criticise but I saw loose feet, loose elbows, cow hocks, roach backs, weak quarters with no second thigh and hawk eyes, yellow green.

Ingeborg Horvath returning to his country of origin for the second World Congress of Breeders in 1982, also comments on the show he attended, Dr Bud McGiven, American judge, handler and breeder of Vizslas, judged the show in Budapest, a great honour for him, approximately 35 people had gathered from all parts of the USA and some from Canada for this occasion — the first American judge to go over the Vizslas in their country of origin. Horvath comments:

Showing is very different from what we are used to, the dogs are paraded in the ring willy-nilly, some climbing over barriers. They are on wide leather collars and wide leather leads, they have not been trained to stack and Bud McGiven had some trouble seeing movement. No special effort is made to show respect for the judge by presenting themselves or the dogs with a modicum of cleanliness.

He also comments that he did not see any midgets or over-sized Vizslas, all appeared to be fairly uniform in size. Colour ranged from a fairly light sandy shade to a somewhat darker golden rust:

While I saw no great fronts or great rear angulation, all the dogs seemed to be in balance, that is, the quality of the front angulation matched the rear. It seemed to me that dogs are bred for the total picture not for 'great rear angulation' or 'super shoulder lay back', I think that some of us tend to lose sight of the whole dog and breed for parts.

Miklós Farkasházi was to have judged the breed in 1982 in England. His appointment was anticipated with great interest and he had a very good entry, but sadly he was unable to leave Hungary. Our Hungarian Vizslas have yet to be judged by anyone from its 'Country of Origin'.

Figure 1.8 A retrieve in the snow in Hungary.

CHAPTER 2

HISTORY OF THE BREED IN BRITAIN

FIRST REGISTRATION IN 1953

According to Kennel Club records the first registration of Vizslas was in 1953 although it has been reported that there were a pair of dogs in Hay-on-Wye before 1939. At the beginning of the war, a Mr Talgarth was offered a dog and bitch of Hungarian Retriever breed to save them from being put down. Owing to conditions, he accepted the bitch only — there were no papers — her wonderful nose and general keenness were commented on and there is little doubt that this was a Vizsla.

Early Imports

In August 1953 *Agnes* and *Ernest* were imported from Hungary by Mrs J Wyndham-Harris. They were a brother and sister bred by M Dravenka(*Istvan*)and born 1948. Mr Wyndham-Harris was in the Diplomatic Service, first living in Budapest, then in Paris. On the family's return to England, they brought these two dogs back with them as companions and gun dogs. The brother and sister were mated three times. In 1953 there were 6 puppies, 3 dogs and 3 bitches. *Boldro, Apollo, Boldrogrange Ann, Boldroville Adonis, Intrepid Anthony, Resourceful Annabelle, Wyndham Alexandra*. In 1954 there were 5 puppies, 4 dogs and 1 bitch — *Boldrowood Prince, Boldrowood Bountiful, Boldrowood Brigard, Brilliant Buda*, and *Boldrowood Princess*. 3 dogs and the bitch were exported to America to Mr Charles Hunt. Major R H Petty bought the bitch *Boldrogrange Ann* and in May 1955 *Ernest* and *Agnes* were transferred to Major R H Petty's ownership of the *Strawbridge* Prefix. In 1955 there were 2 dog puppies born, *Strawbridge Ficko* and *Strawbridge Pete*. *Pete* was later exported to America.

Import 1956

In August 1956 *Adalyn von Hunt* was imported from America by Major Petty. She was bred by Mr and Mrs C F Hunt and born in 1955. Major Petty was to play a significant role in the breeding of the early Vizslas. *Adalyn* was mated three times. In 1957 to *Strawbridge Ficko*. There were 8 puppies, 5 dogs and 3 bitches. These were *Strawbridge Amos, Angy, Alka, Antal, Apro, Arany, Arpad* and *Attila*. From this litter 3 were exported to America. In 1958 she was mated again to Ficko, this time 7 puppies, 3 bitches and 4 dogs. These were *Strawbridge Barna, Bella, Bruce, Ben, Boske, Buda* and *Rhett Butler*. *Rhett Butler* was exported to America. In 1960 she was mated to her son *Strawbridge Barna*. There were 4 dogs and 4 bitches,

Strawbridge Ceda, Cigany, Chicktosh, Cilla, Csana, Csibeza, Czinka. Czinka was sold to Mr and Mrs Hilbre-Smith, who had previously had two puppies from Mrs Wyndham Harris, and later she was transferred to Mrs Louise Petrie-Hay of the *Waidman* prefix. In 1965 *Czinka* represented the breed at the Game Fair and was also featured in *The Field*. She was typically Vizsla, both in conformation and character. When in the house she was very affectionate and quiet and when in the field she had the tireless enthusiasm and energy so well known to Vizsla owners. She died at thirteen years of age.

These two imported bitches, *Agnes* and *Adalyn,* produced 36 puppies between them, all were registered at the Kennel Club. 9 were exported to America and *Strawbridge Barna* went to Germany in 1967. Unfortunately there are no records or photographs to be found so it is not known whether these early Vizslas would fit the *standard* of today.

Alec MacRae and *Tardosi Gyongyi*
Earlier in the year of 1956, Mr Alec MacRae had imported *Tardosi Gyongyi* from Hungary. She was bred by Mr Lajos Dudas of Budapest in 1959. Alec MacRae had bought his first Vizsla in 1956 from Major Petty. He saw the litter advertised in *The Field* and went to see these "new" dogs. He says that from the first he was attracted by their appearance, friendly disposition and history. He bought *Strawbridge Buda* and became the first Vizsla owner in Scotland. He imported two Vizslas from Hungary thus bringing in new blood so badly needed by this time. He trained and worked his dogs up in Scotland on grouse, pheasant and wild fowl. He also field trialled his dogs proving a great stalwart of the breed. He is spoken of with affection by all who knew him. Mrs Lyndesay-Smith writes in the breed notes in 1967 that "Mr MacRae of Strathyre deserves all credit for the efforts he is making to popularise the breed".

Tardosi Gyongyi was called *Shian,* he mated her to *Buda* and later to his second import. The puppies carried his prefix *Creagan* which can be seen in many of the early pedigrees. When *Shian* was six years old Alec was over-dogged and he insisted on giving her to Louise Petrie-Hay. He drove down from Scotland with her, arriving at teatime. She did not appear to be worried when he left, she had a meal and settled in with the other dogs. But for the next month, when the front door was open, she would sit in the drive waiting for his return, every car that came had to be checked in case it was her master. In time she accepted the situation but her faithfulness to her master always remained.

Shian met her old master two years later at the Game Fair and was ecstatic with joy. Although not a hard man, Alec showed no great affection, but she would not leave his side until they parted at the end of the day. She was an excellent guard, both of the home and the car, a trait many Vizsla owners will recognise! She had tremendous drive and ability, she would work every type of country, face cover and could swim like an otter. Only her over keenness prevented her from becoming a field trial winner. She was an excellent brood bitch and would let no one near her puppies for the first ten days. Although no beauty she had a great heart and character, she was short on the leg and long in the back, but with plenty of bone and a very typical head. She certainly left her stamp on the breed. Mrs Virginia Phillips of the *Kinford* prefix bought her first Vizsla, *Creagan Anya,* from Alec MacRae. Later *Anya* was trialled

Figure 2.1 Creagan Anya(1964) (owner Mrs Virginia Philips)

successfully.

A Second Dog (1962)

In April 1962 Alec MacRae imported his second dog from Hungary. This was *Sibriktelepi Tigi,* a dog, bred by Mr J Farkas and born in 1961. The following year Alec MacRae field trialled him and he became the first Vizsla to win an award in a trial.

Virginia Phillips recalls that he was a charming dog and she liked him immensely. A super worker, tall, elegant and strong. He had a poor front and slack feet, but a noble head, excellent temperament and a good rich colour. He was mated to her *Creagan Anya* and the progeny included *Kinford Ficko, Lidi* and *Rica.*

Rica became one of Mrs Barbara Douglas-Redding's foundation bitches —*Wolfox Kinford Rica. Lidi* was first sold to Mrs Joan Matuszewka of *Monroe* Weimaraners, and later transferred to Miss Pauline Rankin of the *Zelten* prefix.   From *Anya's* second mating to *Tigi* came *Kinford Vlada,* one of Louise Petrie-Hay's foundation bitches.

Vlada went best of breed at City of Birmingham championship show in 1968 and won first prize in the any other variety open bitch class at Crufts in 1969. She was the dam of the first two show champions in the breed — Mr W Foster's *Kinford Zsuzsi* and my own *Waidman Remus. Waidman Ficko* was *Zsuzsi's* sire and *Waidman Fules* was Remus's. *Fules* worked well and looked good   In 1966 at the City of Birmingham Show he won the novice class, in 1967 he won the Any Variety Novice Class at Crufts and in 1968 he won the Gamekeeper Class at Crufts. When his training was finished he was sold to Wing Commander Stamford-Tuck of Battle of Britain fame.

A further Import (1963)

The next recorded import was in 1963. *Joram de la Creste* was imported from France by Mr Winter an American serviceman. He was bred by Countess de la Celle la Creste. It is said that he had been trained to do "manwork". Shortly after coming to this country his owner had to return to the States and the dog was given to an elderly couple living in Hastings. Louise Petrie-Hay saw an advertisement for his sale in *Dog World* under 'Bracque Hongroise'. She travelled down to see him and found him tied up in the garage by a heavy chain. She bought him and arranged that Joan Matuszewska should look after him, as she was unable to do so at the time. In 1964 the K.C. records his transfer from Mr Winter to Mrs Matuszewska. *Joram* was a handsome dog – this can be seen from photographs of him, and those who knew him remember his great quality and style. He gave a sense of nobility, power and elegance. His length of neck, straight topline and strong quarters, as well as his rich colour can be seen in some of our Vizslas today. He is in most of our pedigrees.

Mrs Barbara Douglas-Redding writes in her breed notes of 9th July, 1965 that at the Three Counties Show, *Joram de la Creste* was second in Any Variety Graduate Gundog. Later she writes:

> Southampton Championship Show gave us our first breed classes in the south. *Joram* went Best of Breed. Thirteen entries in the two classes were not too bad for a start. Our judge Mr L C James (deceased) was very interested and said kind things about our British dogs. We have a long way to go but interest is growing all the time.

Figure 2.2 Joram (courtesy Mrs L Petrie-Hay)

Figure 2.3 Five outstanding dogs 1965 — Left to Right: *Waidman Heros, Waidman Bor, Strawbridge Czinka, Waidman Zigi, Tardosi Gyongyi.*

Joram turned out to be a very complex character. He was not excitable nor fizzy, but his unpredictability became more and more evident. Virginia Phillips recalls that there were warnings not to touch him on the benches. Louise Petrie-Hay tells me that he would become aggressive at fairly regular intervals and that one had warning of this but as time went on it became more frequent. From evidence from those who knew him, it is agreed that he had suffered much deprivation in his early life and his experience of man - work had affected him. He had many tests done by different vets but there is no conclusive evidence pointing to either epilepsy or brain damage, given the absence of objective data. An aura of vagueness and myth remains about him to this day.

Late in 1967 Joan Matuszewska decided that *Joram* should be put to sleep as he was becoming unmanageable but Kathleen Auchterlonie persuaded her to let him be transferred to her care in Scotland. Sadly, after eight months Kathleen had to have him put down. This handsome dog was used at stud seven times. In 1964 he was mated to *Strawbridge Czinka*. This produced the first *Waidman* litter which included *Waidman Bor*. *Bor* was mated to *Tardosi Gyongyi* resulting in the *Waidman "F"* litter, which included *Fules*, *Ficko* and *Flook*. In 1966 he was mated to *Wolfox Kinford Rica*. From this mating *Wolfox Tallulah* was successfully shown by Barbara Doulgas-Redding and *Wolfox Topaz* by Dr Capel-Edwards who wrote various articles on the breed. *Topaz* represented the breed on television.

Rica died of leukaemia in 1970 aged 6½ years. Barbara writes that:

Rica was my constant companion and slept in an armchair at the foot of my bed. Strangely enough no-one else of all the ginger girls fancy adopting that vacancy and I am haunted by a chestnut ghost on its empty seat.

Figure 2.4 Kinford Ficko owned by Virginia Philips

In December of 1966 *Joram* was mated to *Creagan Agnes* belonging to Mr Evan Young, a very early owner and worker of the breed in Scotland with the prefix *Tintohill*. Two dog puppies in this litter, *Tintohill Buda* and *Betyar* will be seen in many of our pedigrees.

In 1967 Virginia Phillips used *Joram* on *Creagan Anya*. From the litter a bitch, *Kinford Nora* was to become the foundation bitch of Mrs W Foster's — *Gamelands* prefix. Again in this year *Joram* served Kathleen Auchterlonie's *Tintohill Astra*. Astra was Kathleen Auchterlonie's foundation bitch on which she built her successful working and showing kennel. A dog from this litter, *Saline Attila* was sold to Barbara Douglas-Redding and when mated to *Kinford Rica* produced Sh Ch *Wolfox Fabia*, also Sh Ch *Wolfox Flora*, and *Flavia* who went to Mrs Sheila Gray to become the foundation bitches of her *Abbeystag* kennels. *Saline Achilles* was worked by Kathleen Auchterlonie and became well known in the field trial world. *Saline Ayesha*, a bitch, was bought by Mrs Jackson to become the foundation bitch of the *Starleypoint* Vizslas in Scotland.

In 1967 *Joram* was mated to *Kinford Lidi* owned by Pauline Rankin and this litter produced *Atalanta Lass of Zelten* and Sh Ch *Artic of Zelten* — *Artic* won many tickets, there were times when Pauline and I stood side by side in the Open

Figure 2.5 Miss P Rankin's Sh Ch *Artic of Zelten*   (photo: CM Cooke & Son)

Dog Classes. One day it would be *Artic* winning and another *Remus*. We both enjoyed the amicable contest.

Pauline's dog had had an unfortunate accident and lost an eye playing with his litter mates when a puppy. In spite of this handicap, Bill Foster the allround judge, put him up and gave him his first C.C. Pauline Rankin had to publicly produce the vet's letter for the judge to verify the reason for his loss. Other judges followed suit and he was made up. All credit to them for he was a very fine dog in every respect.

Joram's last mating was in 1968 to *Tor Uaine Bracken* up in Scotland. This bitch was owned by Mrs Morrison and produced *Fruin Ransom* and *Reward*.

Concerning *Joram de la Creste,* I have questioned many breeders and in their recollections no known offspring has produced his alarming behaviour pattern. Given the small numbers of the breed in this country and the high integrity of the relevant breeders, this data is to be relied upon. In my view his behaviour would seem attributable to environmental and physical considerations, possibly the 'attack' training as part of the man work, since there is no evidence of his progeny inheriting his behaviour pattern and therefore one could conclude that it was not genetic. After considerable research I have not been able to produce documentary evidence of the early training, but owners believed this to be true.

GROWTH OF NUMBERS

The next import was not until six years later (in 1969). By this time a strong band of Vizsla enthusiasts both north and south of the border were breeding, working and enjoying their dogs. In 1964 there were 27 Kennel Club registrations and in 1965 there were about 300 Vizslas in the country. (Total Kennel Club registrations from 1954 to 1981 amount to 1,385.) Few were shown and the breed was still classified as a rare breed until 1971.

Figure 2.6 Sh Ch *Waidman Remus, Joram's* grandson, 1st dog Sh Champion in Breed (with the author).

Barbara Douglas-Redding writes at that time,

> What a thrill, now we have our own column alphabetically in *Dog World* breed notes, instead of being a Rare Breed for so many years.

She continues to say that,

> we have a lot to learn, especially about colour, conformation and working ability from our somewhat limited resources.

Until 1971 Hungarian Vizslas could only enter in rare breed classes or variety classes. There were very few actual breed classes. Those who did show at that time found it very disheartening as Barbara writes:

> This qualifying business for Crufts is almost a dead duck, trying your chances in the any variety classes provided by a few championship shows that are stuffed with the cream of established breeds.

Back in 1967 she wrote that the breed will have three representatives at Crufts — *Kinford Nora, Wolfox Kinford Rica* and *Wolfox Topaz*. And at Crufts 1968 there were 8 Vizslas entered in any variety sporting classes. 43 registrations were recorded this year at the Kennel Club.

HUNGARIAN VIZSLA CLUB

In 1968 on June 24th, the first AGM of the Hungarian Vizsla Club was held in Worcester. 25 founder members had applied to Kennel Club and they were duly issued with a licence. 13 members were present. Virginia Phillips was elected secretary, Mr Trist, treasurer and Louise Petrie-Hay was elected chairman.

Objectives

> The object of the club was to encourage high standards in breeding for working ability and conformation; to promote interest in training the Vizsla for field trials, as gundog, for obedience show and personal companion;
> To work actively to protect and advance the interests of the breed by encouraging sportsmanlike competition at field trials, breed shows and competitive obedience events;
> To urge members to breed only fully registered dogs that are within the Vizsla standard;
> To support research and educational work to reduce and/or eliminate undesirable or detrimental congenital traits from the breed;
> To conduct field trials, breed shows and obedience trials and training courses;
> Owners and/or handlers should be encouraged to attend working gun dog classes and obedience training classes.

FURTHER IMPORTS

Another import arrived in 1969 — *Szeppataki Csaba*. Imported from Hungary by Mrs K Auchterlonie and bred by M J Zelton in 1968. His Sire was *Kisufalui Dani* and his Dam, *Arokparti Erzsok Ledi*. Interesting to note that *Dani*'s, as he was known, great grandfather was *Sibriktelepi, Tigi*'s great-great grandfather. Kathleen Auchterlonie's beloved *Dani* was shown, worked and field trialled. He was a medium sized dog, goodlooking, heavier boned than some and a different type altogether than later imports from Hungary who were smaller in every respect. All who knew *Dani* were caught by his attractive personality. He enjoyed life and loved to work. Kathleen's only complaint was that she could not get him out of the water! He loved to dive deep down and would alarm her by remaining below too long! Barbara Douglas-

Figure 2.7 Sh Ch *Chantilly Jester,*
owned and handled by Heather McCabe

Figure 2.8 Sh Ch *Galfrid Sofia of Russetmantle*

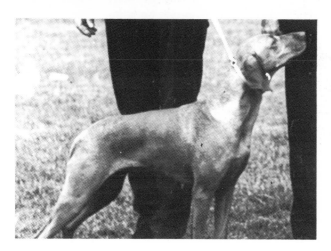

Figure 2.9 Important Dogs from Abroad —
Top: *Warhorse Lwow* (Mrs Henderson, USA)

Middle: *Bingo Vom Wurmbrand-park*

Bottom: *Bella Vom Wurmbrand-park*

Redding wrote in her notes:

> **Dani is very strongly coupled up, short-backed dog, plus well angulated with a splendid muscled up second thigh. He is already working well.**

All the puppies from his first litter to *Tintohill Astra* went to working homes. From his second mating to *Astra,* a bitch *Saline Coire* became one of Miss Angela Boys' foundation bitches, establishing her *Galfrid* prefix. This bitch was mated to Sh Ch *Waidman Remus,* the first *Russetmantle* Vizsla. Out of the litter Sh Ch *Galfrid Sofia* of *Russetmantle* became one of this kennel's foundation bitches. Another well known and loved Vizsla, Mrs Heather McCabe's Sh Ch *Chantilly Jester* was sired by *Dani* when mated to *Saffron Flora* in 1972. Interesting to note that *Saffron Flora* had the same sire on both sides and was outcrossed to *Dani.*

In 1970 there were four imports. The first was *Warhorse Lwow,* imported from America by Mrs B Henderson, bred by Messrs Warhol and E Minde, born in 1966. This Vizsla called *Horse* was brought over by the Henderson family. They lived briefly in England and then moved to Ireland. He was a gentle, good tempered dog. In the States he did well in the show ring and also won his companion dog certificate. Unfortunately he was crippled severely by a motor accident and was in plaster for weeks. He went to Barbara Douglas-Redding as the Hendersons were travelling between England and Ireland at this time. Barbara wrote:

> **I took this poor old cripple in after a bad motor accident. He had had to cope with two quarantines plus hook worm in Hawaii. A super dog. I loved him. The dear old sweetie naturally was a bit disoriented to start with but we soon got over that.**

Horse adored life at Maison-Redding, and all the ginger girls! It is said that he would have worked and probably would have done well in the show ring over here, but after his accident he could not even exercise but none of these trials and tribulations affected his sweet nature.

Horse sired two litters. In 1970 he was mated to Mrs Henderson's *Wolfox Editha.* From this litter *Starbeater Phoenix* was to become another of Miss Angela Boys' foundation bitches for her *Galfrid* prefix. A daughter from this bitch, *Galfrid Leda,* became a foundation bitch for the *Russetmantle* Kennel and she produced Ch *Russetmantle Troy,* one of the 5 champions in the breed to date.

Horse's second mating in 1971 was to *Abbeystag Wolfox Flavia,* Sheila Gray's bitch. Out of this litter, three pups were exported to Norway.

Bingo and Bella vom Wurmbrandpark Arrive
The next imports to arrive were brother and sister, *Bingo* and *Bella vom Wurmbrandpark.* They were imported from Austria by Lord Ashcombe, bred by Gunther Wanivenhaus. They were born in 1969 and were a year old when they came out of quarantine and went to live on Lord Ashcombe's estate outside Guildford. Whilst in quarantine *Bingo* mated *Bella* but the resultant pups were destroyed. A year later they were sent to Louise Petrie-Hay for training but unfortunately the freedom they had enjoyed on the estate, where game including deer abounded, made it impossible to produce reliable, steady dogs suitable for the sort of shooting which

they would get.

Lord Ashcombe decided that they should stay at the *Waidman* Kennels and they were transferred accordingly. They were shown two or three times and won the dog and bitch ticket at the National Gundog Championship Show in 1972, *Bingo* gaining the best of breed award. Judge Ivan Swedrup's critic of *Bella* at Birmingham Championship Show describes her as strongly built, good size and type with good legs and feet. All who knew her found her to have a sweet temperament. Many comment that she was an elegant bitch and a rich russet gold.

Bingo was a handsome dog. Mr Swedrup's comments perhaps do not do him justice "Strong, big, well shaped dog of good type." Barbara writes, "I had a pre-conceived idea that Austrian Vizslas were rather larger and coarser than their Hungarian counterparts. This is certainly not the case with these two. They are elegant and aristocratic to a degree, with beautiful conformation".

Sadly, *Bingo* died of leukaemia in 1976. Having been his constant companion for the seven years of their lives, *Bella* was quite unable to understand or accept his absence. Her unhappiness was unbearable and Louise Petrie-Hay had her put to sleep shortly afterwards.

Bella had only one litter, her heats were irregular and she never came into season again She was mated to *Waidman Nagy* (by *Waidman Kosikin* ex *Tardosi Gyongyi*). *Waidman Brok* was a dog puppy from this litter and he features in many pedigrees today. He was regularly worked and has been successfully trialled. He has sired many of the working and showing Vizslas today. When put to Sh Ch *Swanside Czarina* that litter produced Sh Ch *Swanside Czorna,* one of the top winning bitches in her day — sadly she produced no progeny. *Brok* was the first Vizsla to gain the highest place in a field trial open to all the hunt, point and retrieve breeds. This was in January 1975 in a novice stake.

Waidman Brok

I spent many happy days picking up with Louise Petrie-Hay with our Vizslas. Although an old man (sadly he died in 1984), *Brok* would work solidly all day and was absolutely trustworthy — if he said a bird was there, it was. He would veer off down a hedge, working on his own, pretending his deaf old ears could not hear the whistle. Young *Troy* (8 years old) and *Brok*'s sons and daughters, respecting his grey hairs, would never dream of picking up a bird that was *Brok*'s. From early morning until nightfall his old legs would not falter. No-one could resist his old grey face and his pleading eyes to come for a day's shooting.

His litter brother *Waidman Buda* went to Virginia Phillips and *Waidman Bogar* was sold to Mr M Farmer, who, in his first year of field trials entered him in four and *Bogar* was placed in all of them.

Other well-known Vizslas

Bingo was mated seven times. Much of his progeny are to be seen in the ring and in the field today. When mated to Roger Simkin's lovely bitch Sh Ch *Swanside Czarina* (his foundation bitch of the *Swanside Vizslas*) she produced 2 show champions *Swanside Zsigmund* and *Swanside Miklos. Miklos* went to Major George Wilkinson's *Andesheim* Kennels to be trained for a while, and *Ziggy* was sold to Richard Houghton

Sh Ch *Swanside Czarina* handled by Roger Simkin.

Mrs M Rice's Sh Ch *Swanside Czorna*, daughter of *Czarina* and *Brok*.

Bingo's and *Czarina*'s illustrious sons.

Sh Ch *Swanside Miklos*
handled by Minecke Mills-de-Hoog

Mr Richard Houghton's
Sh Ch *Swanside Zsigmund*

Figure 2.10 Four Top Dogs

of the *Peckers* prefix.

Swanside Zsigmund gained his title in no time at all. When put to Ch *Galfrid Tara*, Ch *Peckers Perchance* was a bitch from the first mating and Sh Ch *Peckers Parody* from the second.

Swanside Miklos later went to the well known GSP *Wittekind* Kennels owned by Mrs Minecke Mills de Hoog. He gained his title and became the only Vizsla to go through to reserve best in show. This he did at the National Gundog Championship Show in 1975. *Miklos* died in his third year. He was mated twice, first to *Galfrid Leda of Russetmantle* and then to Sh Ch *Galfrid Sofia of Russetmantle*. This mating produced *Russetmantle Kushba*, owned by Mrs Heather McCabe, *Kushba* gained her junior warrant and title by sixteen months. Dearly loved by Heather, her short life came to an end at 15 months old. She was run over.

Another of *Bingo*'s matings was to *Elia Amira* (by Sh Ch *Futaki Lazslo* ex *Saline Caroline*) and a bitch from this litter *Golden Claret*, became the foundation bitch for the Swindells and their *Czassa* prefix. She was mated to her brother and produced Sh Ch *Czassa Calista*.

The fourth import in 1970 from Hungary, *Starleypoint Komosreti Atok,* was brought in by Mrs Jackson in Scotland. He was bred by Kelner Janosonn and was born in 1969. This dog suffered badly in quarantine as no other import appears to have hitherto. He lost weight appallingly and his hind action was severely affected. He was used for stud seven times.

In 1971 *Saline Ayesha*, Mrs Jackson's foundation bitch, was mated to *Dani*, a dog pup, *Starleypoint Vilmos* went to Miss Boys' Kennel and was mated to *Braewater Heidi*.((*Heidi* was bred by Mr Brockbank of the *Braewater* prefix in Scotland). A bitch from this mating, *Galfrid Fecske,* was exported to Australia where she became a show champion. *Vilmos* is now living in luxury in Monaco and has an international reputation as an escapologist!

Starleypoint Kati also came from this litter. She was shown by Mrs Jackson at Crufts in 1972 and 1973. *Atok* was mated to *Kati* in 1972 and from this litter a dog, *Starleypoint Ulles* was sold to Mr Maitland-Smith who worked and trialled him successfully. He was placed third in the first Hungarian Vizsla Society Field Trial in 1973. Mr Maitland-Smith recently moved to Canada taking *Ulles* with him. From a repeat mating in 1975 a bitch, *Starleypoint Victoria* became Mr and Mrs Farquhar's first Vizsla for their prefix *Istvan*.

1971 Imports

Two imports were brought in in 1971. *Napketai Vadasz Elod,* imported by Mr P A Wright, was born in 1966. In Australia he was mated to Australian Champion *Galfrid Fecske* and from that litter Australian Champion *Kingsbury Erica* CD, CDX was produced. *Erica* belongs to Mrs F Harris of the *Kingsbury* prefix, who is secretary of the Vizsla Club of Australia.

The second import was *Sir Wigglesworth Witherspoon,* imported from America by Mrs B Robinson. He was bred by Mr Janis Futaki, born 1970. This dog came over as a companion dog with his family. He returned when the family went back to America. He was not used for stud over here. It is interesting to note that he was small and a solid dark russet and had a very good temperament.

Meanwhile 1971 was a memorable year for the breed. In 1970, Barbara Douglas-Redding writes in her breed notes, "Well, here it is, with Crufts 1971 catalogue in my left hand I write that there are four breed classes for us with challenge certificates, to be judged by Mrs Violet Yates". She continues:

> This has been achieved by sheer slog and the loyalty of a handful of owners who have bred, registered and supported in every possible way over the last few years. Now we must never let this wonderful breed get into the doldrums from idleness in accepting them but doing nothing constructive towards their future in the field, shows and as companions. It's up to every one of us. Don't forget they have been here since 1953.

I would like to add that Barbara Douglas-Redding herself contributed more than most. She always had a "good one" and she bred good ones repeatedly. She did a lot of winning but was always ready to encourage newcomers in the breed. It was a hard slog in those days. I remember standing endlessly in those enormous any variety classes at open shows and rarely was my *Remus* pulled out, but one or two good wins somehow kept one going. Margaret Foster's *Kinford Zsuzsi* was rarely beaten. She won an enormous any variety not classified class in 1970, making her eligible for the Big Ring in the gundog group and she was pulled out fourth. Barbara writes to me in 1982 that, "My old dears, like me, are ancient. *Fabia* 12½ years, *Aguila* 11½ and terribly white. The puppies? *Beren* and *Claudia* rising 10 years. Time flies on and I get less delicious daily".

Thus in 1971, Hungarian Vizslas were awarded six sets of challenge certificates for the first time in England at Crufts, Welks, SKC, Birmingham National, Leeds and LKA. Crufts had fourteen entries that year. Margaret Foster who was contributing to the breed notes at this time wrote that "A great deal of interest was shown in our breed at Crufts. A delighted Mrs Gottleib won the dog challenge certificate with *Waidman Remus* and *Kinford Zsuzsi* won the bitch ticket and BOB. *Zsuzsi* was again in the final six in the gundog group." These two Vizslas were to be the first dog and bitch show champions in the breed over here. *Kinford Zsuzsi* bred by Louise Petrie-Hay, was by *Waidman Ficko* and *Kinford Vlada*. *Waidman Remus* also bred by Louise Petrie-Hay was by *Waidman Fules* and *Kinford Vlada*. Those two were mated in 1972 and from this litter a bitch and a dog were exported to Australia where they became show champions. Another dog from this litter, *Gamelands Zorro*, belonged to Margaret Rice. He gained his title and was campaigned in Scotland and England.

REGISTRATION OF THE HUNGARIAN VIZSLA SOCIETY

1970–1971 were unhappy years for the club. Disharmony had reached the stage when the original members felt the club was not carrying on the spirit in which it was originally founded, which was to give advice and assistance to owners of working Vizslas. And so, on November 29th 1972, the Hungarian Vizsla Society was approved and registered under that name. So it came about that the small band who originated

Figure 2.11 Sh Ch *Futaki Lazslo* (imported 1971)   (photo: CM Cooke & Son)

Figure 2.12 Matai Sari of Galfrid a Hungarian import owned by A Boys.

THE HUNGARIAN VIZSLA

the Club resigned and started up the Society, leaving the club in the hands of new-comers to the breed. In spite of attempted reconciliations over the years, as yet the two remain firmly separate, although there are many Vizsla owners who are members of both.

1972 IMPORTS

In 1972 there were three imports, one from America and two from Hungary. Mr and Mrs Gray imported *Futaki Lazslo* from America. He was bred by Bela Hadik and born in 1971. Barbara Douglas-Redding writes:

> I don't know whether the name Bela Hadik means much to Vizsla folk over there. It certainly does to some of us who have owned and bred for some years. He was of course extremely well known in the USA as a prominent breeder of show and working stock. Born in Budapest in 1905 he left Hungary in 1945 after serving in the Hungarian Cavalry in World War II. It was he who produced the breed's first Dual Champion, *Futaki Daroz*, in America. His *Futaki* line has since then produced bench champions, field champions and three of the four dual champions over there. He died in New Hampshire February 16th 1971.

Lazslo came from this very illustrious kennel and was a useful addition to Sheila Gray's *Abbeystag* line. He had much to contribute to the breed. He came from a Hip Dysplasia clear line and had a breeder's letter himself. He was a medium sized dog and a very good type who did well in the field and in the show ring, gaining his show champion title. He passed on his good qualities. He sired two of the five present champions, Ch *Abbeystag Bruna* (dam *Abbeystag Wolfox Flora*) and Ch *Abbeystag Emilio* (dam Sh Ch *Abbeystag Wolfox Flavia*). All credit to Sheila Gray who trained her dogs herself — no mean feat! Barbara Douglas-Redding's Sh Ch *Abbeystag Claudia of Wolfox* was also by *Lazslo*. She recalls seeing *Lazslo* for the first time just after he had come out of quarantine, saying that, "He was in splendid condition both physically and mentally. He is a very smart show boy and a lovely colour". Interesting to note that he has great similarity in type and size to American *Warhorse Lwow* CD. Sadly he died in 1980, a great blow to Sheila Gray. He is greatly missed for he was part of her family of Vizslas and was a sweet-tempered, friendly dog, as are all the dogs from this kennel.

The Galfrid Vizslas
The second and third imports this year were both imported by Miss Angela Boys. *Matai Sari of Galfrid* came from *Matai* kennels of Miklos Farkashazi and was born in 1970. Angela Boys went over to Hungary to look at the Vizslas in their country of origin. She was introduced to many breeders and she especially liked the *Matai* Vizslas owned by Miklos Farkashazi, chairman of the Hungarian Kennel Club and a well known judge and authority of the breed in Hungary and abroad. Angela bought two bitches. They were mated in Hungary and whelped in quarantine over here. *Sari* was the first to arrive. She produced 7 puppies by *Matai Lurko* CACIB and trial winner. All the pups were healthy and *Sari* handled the state of affairs without turning a hair. Her temperament was excellent, she was very sweet natured and a good gundog. She had been partly trained in Hungary and after she came out of quarantine she went to Major George Wilkinson's *Andersheim* kennels where her training was finished. She

returned to Angela Boys and although not possessing the qualities to go to the top as a show dog, she was entered in one or two shows and was placed. She was in the Crufts 'personality parade' in 1975. She was trialled a few times and won a certificate of merit at one. She worked regularly until eventually she was lent to Mr & Mrs Slim whose old Vizsla had died at the beginning of the season. Sadly she was with them only five months before she died of cancer of the liver at the age of seven. *Sari* was loved by all who knew her. She was a great ratter and Angela Boys describes how many a time she would dive into a nearby trout stream and retrieve a fish to hand. Her name is in many of our modern pedigrees, and she contributed much to the breed.

Sari had five litters, one in Hungary, one in quarantine and the other three while with Angela Boys. From the litter born in quarantine, 2 were to feature in field trials — *Galfrid Gaspar, Galfrid Gelert* and *Galfrid Gerda*. *Gaspar*'s name appears in many pedigrees, siring progeny who worked and showed. He gained his junior warrant. He was consistently in the cards when shown but never gained his title. He sired Sh Ch *Galfrid Jade* when put to his mother *Sari*. When put to *Saline Coire of Galfrid,* Sh Ch *Galfrid Mia* was one of his offspring. When mated to Sh Ch *Windover Ondine* of *Galfrid,* three from this litter went abroad, one to South Africa, another to France and a third to Malaya. There was a small bitch out of this litter called *Galfrid Otis*. She was given to Major George Wilkinson as a present and she became the 'apple of his eye' There was an occasion when this little grand-daughter of *Sari*'s was entered in one of the Society's Field Trials.

A part of the Judges' report for the day states:

> *Otis* worked well despite her size and the fact that the heather was making a right mess of her undercarriage which was red and sore. Later on *Otis* was going over to retrieve a snipe that had been shot. An obviously wounded hare got up and went off across the heather and down along a narrow ditch out of sight. George Wilkinson was told to send his bitch for this hare as it obviously had priority over the dead snipe. He was a little bothered as he did not think *Otis* could carry a hare. 'Try her' was all the sympathy he got. She was put on the line and followed it well. The last we saw of her she was way down the hill going toward a bit of woodland. A long pause. George Wilkinson sensibly refrained from calling her as the wind was far too strong. In the distance, the little Vizsla could be seen carrying the hare, head high and trying not to trip up over its tangling legs. A very proud handler went to meet her and relieve her of her burden. It was an excellent bit of tracking and showed courage and determination.

Owing to such bad conditions it was not possible to get a result. It was felt that the dogs and handlers had aquitted themselves so well the Vizsla Society placed first, second and third and the final placing at the end of the day was a win for *Galfrid Otis.*

George Wilkinson wrote in the 1979 Vizsla Society newsletter:

> It is with the deepest regret that I have to report the death by accident of my Hungarian Vizsla *Galfrid Otis*. She was in all a great character and the cause of her death was, to my deepest sorrow, through her devotion to me and my own absent-mindedness. In addition to her prowess in the field, she was my constant companion and guard. No one dare enter my car without my being present. She was gentle and sweet natured with my small grandchildren. She was just reaching the peak of her form and one looked forward to many years of shooting and trialling with her.

Her litter brother *Galfrid Gelert* was sold to Trevor West and trained by George Wilkinson. Trevor West became a familiar figure at field trials gaining many wins with his Vizslas. *Galfrid Gerda* was sold to me and was my first brood bitch. She was trialled a few times winning a certificate of merit at one. She was mated once to Sh Ch *Waidman Remus* and produced four puppies, one bitch went to Holland another, *Flax*, was trained by George Wilkinson and was sold to a working home as was *Gerda* eventually.

From *Sari*'s mating to *Galfrid Pej*, *Galfrid Tara* went to the *Russetmantle* kennels. Later she was sold to Richard Houghton of the *Peckers* prefix and he made her up and later qualified her. When *Tara* was put to Sh Ch *Swanside Zsigmund*, she produced Ch *Peckers Perchance* in her first litter, and Sh Ch *Peckers Parody* in her second.

The second bitch to join the *Galfrid* kennels in 1972 was Hungarian import *Faradpusztai Charlott of Galfrid*, bred by Sarley Janosne and born in 1969. *Chitri*, as she was called, was a disappointment to Angela Boys. She is convinced to this day that this bitch was not the one she was expecting to arrive in England. *Chitri* had three litters. She was in whelp by *Matai Bitang Tucsok* and had her seven puppies in quarantine without any trouble. One of the dog puppies was *Galfrid Hugo* who was to go to Mrs Doraine Larner of the *Yelrehta* prefix. He was campaigned in the show ring by Doraine and by Eddie Bundy and later on by the professional handler Marjorie Williams, gaining his title and a best of breed in the year 1978 at Crufts under Mr D Page. When put to *Halstock Fair Maid of Yelrehta*, a bitch from that litter, *Yelrehta Gemini* also gained her title. Another bitch *Yelrehta Maria* went to Mr and Mrs J Swindell of the *Czassa* prefix.

From *Chitri*'s mating with Sh Ch *Waidman Remus*, *Galfrid Iro* went to Spain where he was shown and worked successfully. A litter brother, *Galfrid Imre* went to Holland where he gained his title.

Chitri and *Sari* were both small bitches but *Chitri* did not have the style nor the warmth or working ability of *Sari* although she was another excellent ratter! Her coat was light and she had a rather broad ribcage. She became grey very early in her life.

BREED TYPE

In 1972 and 1973 breeders were particularly concerned over height and size in the breed because the recent imports and their progeny were smaller than most of the stock already in this country.

I remember standing next to Angela Boys in the ring, she with *Gaspar* and I with *Remus*, both were within the *Standard* but *Gaspar* was at the bottom and *Remus* at the top of the scale. The late Arthur Westlake was judging. He stood in front of us with his cowboy hat to one side, "Now that's the Hungarian type — smaller, and that's the large English type." I felt as if I were handling an elephant. *Gaspar* won the class as the judge explained, "I am judging to the Hungarian standard"!

Barbara Douglas-Redding writes:

Size is a subject that is looming up. Every now and again oversize and too tall Vizslas are cropping up from the same bloodlines that produce specimens of the correct size. It will take more years to sort these faults out considering the progeny from stock imported in the last three years. My mind boggles as to how it can be coped with.

Well, I would say we are still attempting and we are still having problems, an uneven litter is not unusual, for example, 4 puppies at 7 weeks weighed:

Dog	—	14 lbs 6 oz	Bitch	—	13 lbs 4 oz
		13 lbs			12 lbs 6 oz

In the Hungarian Society Newsletter of October 1975, Virginia Phillips writes in an article called *Food for Thought*:

There has been much written recently in the national press on the subject of dog foods and suggestions made that in some households, the dogs are fed on better and more balanced fare than the children. Old established breeders in this country are rather disturbed about the conflicting impressions gained by British visitors to Hungary about the size and stamp of present day Vizslas. A few years ago our stock recently imported from Hungary appeared to fulfil their requirements on size, shape colour etc and be fitted to perform the all round job for which they were intended. Nowadays, size varies considerably, heightwise and in the amount of bone and the shapes of the heads show wide discrepancies.

On Size

One can appreciate that there are likely to be differences between American bred dogs and ours over here and obviously different methods of feeding and rearing as well as preferences for certain characteristics would influence their lines. It is still interesting to note that a recent Hungarian author reported that the wartime breeds are still feeling the effects of widespread undernourishment experienced during the Second World War, and that pups are frequently weaned on Semolina and thereafter do not have the benefit of our carefully prepared and balanced foods with their mineral and vitamin additives. Could the present smaller size of some recent Hungarian imports be attributed to their rearing or is it a result of a deliberate breeding policy?

Barbara Douglas-Redding writes:

Last week I measured *Beren*. He's just about 25", the top male limit. I forbade him to think of growing another hair's breadth. At Birmingham National 1974, Dr Esther Rickards, the judge, had some difficult classes to judge which she herself admitted was because of the size variations. She looked at my *Beren* and said, "He's biggish isn't he?" I replied, "He's just up to the top limit the last time I measured him and I've not dared since." Her charming reply was, "Don't dear, don't."

Margaret Foster in her breed notes in 1974 wrote:

I think all judges of our breed should bear in mind the standard which is now official. This states the lowest height for bitches is 21" and the highest for dogs 25"; I am told there is a dog now winning in the ring who is 3" below the standard. Someone remarked to her "I see you are getting miniatures in the ring now!"

On Colour

There are some interesting comments on colour. Barbara Douglas-Redding writes:

> Here are a few translations on the colour theme to occupy you. They are taken at random mostly
> from Hungarian sources. In this country we register Vizslas as 'Russet-gold', but the following
> give food for thought; dark sandy, yellow with gold sheen, dark tan, dark yellow, sedge yellow,
> rather dark sandy yellow in several different shades — dark brown and pale yellow are
> objectionable — chestnut, like a chestnut horse, roast bun, bread roll and crust of bread!

In 1968 an article in *Country Life* written by M S Lampton called "A Gundog from
Hungary — the Magyar Vizsla", comments on colour:

> The colour is officially described as yellow, this is not as we know it in Labrador Retrievers but
> a deeper shade reddish golden or bracken colour. Brown or pale fawn are unacceptable colours.

At Welks 1972 Mr Udvardy of Hungary, an FCI judge of all Hungarian breeds visited
our benches. He commented that like USA he wanted a fairly rich russet colour free
from paler shoulder flashes. Returning to the question of size he felt that many of the
Vizslas he saw at Welks were oversized, too tall to fit in with the Hungarian standard,
also there were too many straight shoulders. He thought some of the exhibits he saw
were somewhat light in bone for real field work.

Barbara Douglas-Redding comments,

> well over here in our shooting world they are used as what the Americans term, 'bird-dogs', and
> really nothing larger than a hare is their expected lot in Great Britain as opposed to coping with
> bigger game in other parts of the world.

Figure 2.13 Mrs Gray's Sh Ch *Abbeystag Wolfox Flora*. Dam of the first champion in the breed,
Ch *Abbeystag Bruna*.

On Eye Colour

At one of the Birmingham championship shows in 1972 Mrs De Casembroot was worried by the number of pale eyed exhibits present. Barbara Douglas-Redding felt that the light eye fault which had been increasingly noticeable in some of our youngsters over the last 18 months is a thing we might try to correct somehow. From all accounts, this was not just incidental to Great Britain but was popping up in the Vizsla world everywhere, including the country of origin. She also came to the conclusion that the pattern of lightness is not always settled in the change from the early blue to what should be nice warm sherry, fitting in harmony with the coat colour by the time the pups have left home and so it is only the show stock seen in the ring who give indications of this and that trend.

In 1980 Angela Boys records in her breed notes that Mr Froggat had a large entry of 47 Vizslas at LKA and that, "There were a lot of young puppies out winning". Mr Froggat said he noticed a lot of light eyes. "Dare I point out," Angela comments, "that many puppies have light eyes until they reach maturity. The eye that will darken has a dark rim to the iris and is totally different to the staring hawk eye, a serious fault and fortunately rare in the breed in England."

S M Lampson, in his article in *The Field* comments on the eye. "The eyes of the Vizsla, unlike those of most more familiar breeds may be pale yellow although if dark they are quite in order!"

Barbara Douglas-Redding writes:

One of Sheila Gray's pups by the Late *Warhorse Lwow* **CD** is now just over a year old. To start with, she had one green eye and one brown. This lasted for ages. Now both eyes are the correct colour, so live and learn and refrain from making snap judgements at an early age. Let us not get too worried about heads and colours yet, but concentrate on trying to get our conformation and movement right plus of course keeping correct working temperament well to the fore. Colour fanatics in other breeds in the past have done great disservice to their breeds in the long run.

She also quotes USA Professor Phil Wright, a well known breeder of Vizslas as saying:

I was fortunate enough to see [in Hungary] at a hunting training session, the top winning show Vizslas and a goodly number of dogs which both show and hunt extensively. There is not a shadow of doubt in my mind that the Vizsla in Hungary is primarily a hunting dog. I did not see a large Vizsla in Hungary. The dogs I saw in several towns and villages as well as in Budapest were almost entirely of the golden rust colour, reddish or rust-tint, yes, but Irish Setter red, no! I also say that many show dogs are veering away from the real type of the breed, tall dogs, straight shoulders, poor feet, funny gait and rosy red colour are becoming common in shows. They could not back it up in the field.

Barbara Douglas-Redding comments:

I found this all very interesting reading. Although we have quite a variation in sizes over here in Britain, I do think that conformation generally has improved out of all recognition in the past 20 years. Most of you will not have seen the early imports or their progeny.

THE VIZSLA IN COMPETITION

November 1973 saw the first field trial run for the breed. It was a novice stake organised by the Hungarian Vizsla Society and took place in Northumberland. *Windover Ripp*, owned and handled by Mr F W Berry gained a first. *Saline Caroline*, owned and handled by Mr E Greig, got second place and *Starleypoint Ulles*, Major Maitland-Smith's dog came in third place.

In the same year, two more bitches were imported from the *Matai* kennels in Hungary. Mr Alan Heyman visited Miklos Farkashazi and bought *Matai Vica* and *Matai Pirok*. *Vica* was born in 1973 and she was the first to arrive in England. Six months later *Pirok*, who was six months younger than *Vica*, arrived.

Vica was trained by Mr John Parke, friend and shooting companion of Alan Heyman's. John described her as an exceptional worker. He trained her in four months. He was given *Pirok*, or *Heidi* as she was known, and she took a little longer to train — 18 months! Both Vizslas were shot over and trialled very successfully. These two bitches were also small, very much the same type as Angela Boys' two imports.

Vica was mated to *Futaki Lazslo* when she was 2½ years old. She had 8 puppies but there are no recorded registrations of these pups. John Parke had a bitch from this litter and was over the moon with her working ability. He found her very easy to train and he works her regularly.

His bitch *Heidi* was not bred from. He describes her as "a funny little thing". He felt she had been mistreated in quarantine, resulting in her deep distrust of anyone but him. Nevertheless this "funny little thing" managed to win field trials!

In the 1974 October edition of the Hungarian Vizsla Society newsletter reporting the results of the field trial on the Marshland Estate, the ground kindly offered by Alan Heyman for the trial, Mr J Parke's *Matai Pirok* was first, Alan Heyman's *Matai Vica* was second and Trevor West's *Galfrid Gelert* was third. It is reported that *Pirok* was beautifully handled, she ranged freely but was under complete control and all the time was working to find game. John Parke is to be doubly congratulated as the day before he won the Weimaraner Club's novice stake running against German Shorthaired Pointers, Weimars and a large Munsterlander. This was the first time that a Vizsla had been placed first in a stake for all breeds which hunt, point and retrieve. *Heidi* won another field trial in 1977.

I remember a field trial on the Marshland Estate in 1975 for other reasons. It was a beautiful land and a fine day for once. We all started off with such high hopes as always but handling dogs and in this case Vizslas is an activity that can be a great leveller. Apart from the first 3 placings, there were no others.

Angela Boys wrote in the breed notes reporting the field trial:

Sheila Gray had come over from Dorset with her home bred Sh Ch *Abbeystag Bruna* who unfortunately met one of the many hares as did George Wilkinson's *Galfrid Otis*, and so did Virginia Phillips' good looking *Waidman Buda*. Louise Petrie-Hay stopped *Waidman Brok* on another but he played with his retrieve. Gay Gottlieb's *Galfrid Gerda* failed on the water test as did my own *Matai Sari*, both of them keen water dogs. Why do they do this to us? Having gotten my own *Gaspar* through the day without a runner on which he usually runs in, at the very end he failed on his retrieve — a dead cock pheasant — at which he took one look and walked away. We all have the "should have been here last week" Joyce Grenfell situations. "Never done that before" we say weakly, but there is always another day and everyone enjoyed it. One by one we were eliminated that day but as each disappointed handler joined the waiting group, all were able to sympathize.

Figure 2.14 Galfrid Gaspar and Sh Ch *Galfrid Jade* (Photo: Diane Pearce)

Figure 2.15 Import *Mocsarkereso Vac of Galfrid.*

Change in the Vizsla Club

In 1973 members of the Hungarian Vizslas Club received notices of resignation from the chairman, Bill Foster, and the secretary, Margaret Foster. The reason for the resignations was "owing to certain actions by some members of the club to which we cannot remain impartial". Thus, there was yet another change in the history of the club. Major J L Houghton was elected chairman and Roger Simkin (*Swanside*) became secretary. A year later Major George Wilkinson took on the job of chairman since Major Houghton wished to retire. The new treasurer was Mr Lambert. George Wilkinson, keen on working and trialling his dogs, energetically fostered and provided the means for further working trials and until 1980–1981 the Club and Society held at least two field trials each a year. All who were interested in trialling their Vizslas supported both. In spite of this, frequently there were not enough entries to fill the card of twelve running, so GSP, *Weimar*, and *Great Munsterlander* owners would be invited to join us.

New Blood Brought to the *Galfrid* Vizslas

There was one import in 1977 and one or two others who were not registered. *Mocsarkereso Vac of Galfrid* was imported from Hungary by Miss Angela Boys. Bred by Istvan Kass in 1976. Her dam was *Matai Vadasz* and her sire, *Morcos Pushztai Bori*. Gaining many RES, CCS, and 2CC's, she is a gentle companionable, bitch. She has a good front and shoulders beautifully proportioned head, being a medium sized Vizsla with a lot of scope. She brought a new line to the *Galfrid* kennel. She was mated to *Galfrid Gaspar* in 1977 and to *Galfrid Odo* twice (in 1979 and 1981). From the first litter *Galfrid Fergus*, a very handsome dog, was always in the cards. He was exported to South Africa in 1981 and became a champion soon after. In 1982 she was mated to *Galfrid Sean* (Sh, Ch *Galfrid Sofia of Russetmantle*'s brother). *Galfrid Rudi* won the dog CC at Leeds Championship Show at the age of fourteen months, and his litter sister *Rosa* gained her first championship certificate at Crufts in 1984 and gained her title later in the same year. Her fifth litter was by *Galfrid Job* in 1983.

In the 1977 Society Newsletter, Louise Petrie-Hay writes:

> **Congratulations to Michael Farmer. Not only was the field trial at Loton the first of our trials he had ever attended but it was also the first time he and *Bogar* (*Waidman Brok*'s brother) had run in a trial — he was placed second. Then he went up to Ford in Northumberland and was lucky enough to get a run in the novice stake run by the GSP Club where competition was very hot and the card filled with GSP trial at Burton le Coggles and although 5th reserve on the card was fortunate to get a run owing to a number of withdrawals. This time he won. Not bad for his first season! And I am delighted to report that he intends to continue next year. His example should give heart and encouragement to many Vizsla owners who have really good working dogs but just not the bravery of Mr Farmer to have a go in a trials.**

In 1977 in order to encourage the novice to 'have a go' the Hungarian Society held their first 'get together'. It was conceived by the society to encourage and help all those Vizsla owners who wished to work their dogs, a day together with other nervous novices and some not so novice, organised and planned to encourage everyone to attempt the basic exercises of hunt, point, and retrieve. The day is constructed in such a way that there is no competition. Every handler is given every opportunity to do his best in the most relaxed, friendly atmosphere. During the course of the day,

Figure 2.16 Sh Ch *Prins* imported from Holland.   (photo: Dave Freeman)

the Vizslas are released from any discipline or the pressures of performing and join in the 'race'. Owners and dogs alike throw inhibitions to the wind. It is a most delightful and comic occasion — 40 Vizslas romping through the high summer grass, somehow the amusement it affords still allows us to admire our lovely breed.

1977 also saw the first demonstration at the Game Fair by breeds which hunt, point, and retrieve. The Vizsla has been well represented every year since then, the club and the society providing information for interested visitors to the breed stand.

The First Open Qualifying Field Trial
In 1979 the Hungarian Vizsla Society was granted a Kennel Club licence to run it's first open qualifying field trial. By 1980 the Hungarian Vizsla Club had changed hands again. Major George Wilkinson felt he should retire and the secretary, Mrs

Dorothea Hunt, joined him. Mr Richard Houghton was elected chairman and Mrs Sharon Seward became secretary. Mrs Jackie Perkins (of the *Gardenway* prefix) was to replace her as secretary later on.

There were 153 registrations recorded in this year.

THE 1980's

In 1981 Dutch, Lux and Swiss Sh Ch *Prins* was imported from Holland by Mrs Kwieschke and Mr R Finch. Born in 1975 and bred by S Middleton his sire was *Kamp Milo-cinnamon Magyar* VD, Beulaker and his dam *Luizza*. *Prins* came out of quarantine in fine fettle. He was first shown at Manchester Championship Show and won RES, CC, under Richard Houghton. He then went on to gain his Show Champion title in a matter of months, handled by Dick Finch, eminent judge and breeder and exhibitor of the 'Hansom Weimaraners'. *Prins* also won high placings in the veteran stakes in 1982. He was a very handsome and elegant dog, different in type to our present Vizslas, of which few could hold their own at his age. He has a noble bearing, fine head and well proportioned body, very showy, covering the ground with a beautiful stride. *Prins* was mated to Mr M Eliot's *Russetmantle Pepper* in 1983 and there were 9 puppies in the litter, 6 dogs and 3 bitches.

There were 173 registrations recorded in 1982. Thus by now the breed had gathered an increasing number of enthusiasts, both in the field and in the show ring. Entries had reached up to 45—50 at some championship shows. 1973 Crufts had 7 exhibitors, in 1983 there were 27! Sheila Gray writes in her report in the Hungarian Vizsla Society newsletter on Crufts 1982:

> **Our steward Mr J Lamb called the first class together, both he and the judge Mr R Finch were looking smart complete with bowler hats!**

She also comments on the excellent entry awaiting Mr Miklos Farkashazi at Ardingly show ground at the Hammersmith Gold Medal Show:

> **Imagine how we felt on arrival to find that Mr Farkasházi had not been allowed to leave Hungary, most of us came many miles for a true Hungarian breeders opinion.**

Working Tests
The Society also ran their first working test, 13 Vizslas entered, John Churchill's *Laser Duite* (by *Waidman Brok* and *Calversam Amber*) was best overall winner gaining the Marion Trophy. Mary Bradbrook also won a working test with *Russetmantle Bee* (by *Russetmantle Crisp* and *Russetmantle Ash*) at 10 months old this year. She also won the bitch championship certificate and best of breed under Mr Braddon at Leicester Championship Show and then went on to be pulled out in the last four in the Gundog group. *Bee* gained her title and won the Gundog group at S.K.C. — the first Vizsla ever to achieve this honour — in 1984.

Figure 2.17 John Powell on the Hungarian Vizsla Club Show Stand at Crufts with Bronze Vizsla loaned by A Boys.

1983 seemed to consolidate the earlier efforts of many to encourage everyone to get their Vizslas working, those who had tried working tests the year before had a try at field trailling this year. Sue Cowburn's *Peckers Penny* — bred by Richard Houghton (by *Swanside Little Trooper* and Ch *Peckers Perchance*) has been shown successfully, — she had also been picking up for a couple of seasons. *Penny* gained certificate of merit at her first trial, and she won the second at the Hungarian Vizsla Society all aged stake held at Sansaw. What an achievement — trained and handled by Sue. I think many of us who witnessed her receiving the award, 'had a tear in our eye'.

Sue Harris who also shows her Vizslas successfully, won the novice stake at Apley Park with her *Perdita's Puzzle of Szajani,* (by *Waidman Brok* and *Starleypoint Victoria*) for the second time, and her young puppy *Szajani Csipke* (by *Czassa Camboge* and *Perditas Puzzle of Szajani*) gained a certificate of merit and best puppy award. Richard Houghton trialled his Sh Ch *Peckers Perchance* for the first time, and she won a certificate of merit, making *Stella* the first champion made up in a trial. My Ch *Russetmantle Troy* won his second certificate of merit at this trial, held by the Large Musterlander Club at Westerham. Sylvia and Nigel Cox were also to be congratulated, as their young *Viszony of Vallota* won the all-aged stake run by the German Shorthaired Pointer Club in Norfolk, and in 1984 made history by winning an open qualifying stake.

All three show champions made up this year, Perkins' Sh Ch *Russetmantle Grebe of Gardenway,* and in 1984 *Grebe* won a novice working test and a best in show at an open show, Sh Ch *Gardenway Bula,* and Neill's Sh Ch *Saline Judi* are working Vizslas, they have all been shot over during the season.

Vizsla Club's First Open Show

The Hungarian Vizsla Club held their first open show in the spring of 1983, it was a very well organised happy event. It was well supported by many Vizsla enthusiasts. The judge, David Layton, (*Midlander*) well respected as judge, trainer, and breeder of the German Short-haired Pointer, had a good entry of 55 to go over, he made Mrs Bugden's *Russetmantle Glade of Duncarreg* (by Ch *Russetmantle Troy* and Sh Ch *Galfrid Sofia of Russetmantle*) best in show and still not out of puppy!

By the end of 1983 there were 38 show champions in the breed in Britain, five of those are champions, two dogs and three bitches.

In conclusion, the breed in Britain today, although still a minority, is increasing in numbers. But the Hungarian Vizsla remains a dog for the conoisseur and with our limited resources he can never become the 'National dog of Britain', as he is in Hungary.

CHAPTER 3

THE STANDARD

The *standard* outlines the necessary features of a particular breed, although the functional principles of the dog remain the same, each breed is unique in its appearance. The *standard* provides the blueprint and it is to this prototype that all breeders should refer. Thus, an image of the Hungarian Vizsla is provided as a fundamental reference for all who wish to advance the breed. Many breeders will have their own idea of their "ideal Vizsla", but does it fit the *standard*? The *standard* must be studied and learned, in order to understand how the structure of a dog suits its function. The judge must also know how to interpret the *standard* for it is he who judges the physical and mental attributes in the ring and their level of excellence in the field.

Viewing the dog as a whole, the parts should fuse together in unity, and to understand the uniqueness of any breed it is important to know how each element works correctly in relationship with the others. A breeder cannot hope to breed a good dog without knowing the points that make it a good dog, a judge cannot judge a dog without knowledge of the points that deserve appraisal.

There are basic features that must be considered, such as **type, balance, conformation, style, soundness** and **temperament**. To understand more of the breed essentials and characteristics it is important to examine the *standard* in great detail. This should give a deeper appreciation of the particular features of the Hungarian Vizsla.

THE BRITISH KENNEL CLUB STANDARD
FOR THE HUNGARIAN VIZSLA

The breed *standard* of the Hungarian Vizsla was approved April 1973 by the Kennel Club and revised in 1975. The points are as follows:

CHARACTERISTICS

The Hungarian Vizsla should be lively and intelligent, obedient but sensitive, very affectionate and easily trained. It was bred for hunting, for fur and feather on open ground or in thick cover, pointing and retrieving from both land and water.

Although there are more Vizslas in the show ring today than ten years ago we have not reached the point at which the breed has a show type and a working type, as has happened in some gundog breeds. It is difficult to maintain these two aspects, one reason being time, another that to keep a show dog in top condition needs particular

1 — Nose
2 — Muzzle
3 — Stop
4 — Forehead
5 — Occiput
6 — Pole Joint — 2 verts
7 — Neck — 7 verts
8 — Withers — 8 verts
9 — Back — 5 verts
10 — Loin — 7 verts
11 — Croup — 3 verts
12 — Tail
13 — Upper thigh — femur
14 — Lower thigh — tibia & fibula
15 — Hock

16 — Pastern
17 — Canon Bone
18 — Stifle
19 — Tuck up
20 — Belly
21 — Brisket
22 — Elbow
23 — Forearm — radius & ulna
24 — Pastern
25 — Knee
26 — Forearm
27 — Upper-arm — humerus
28 — Chest
29 — Throat
30 — Lip

Key to Fundamental Points

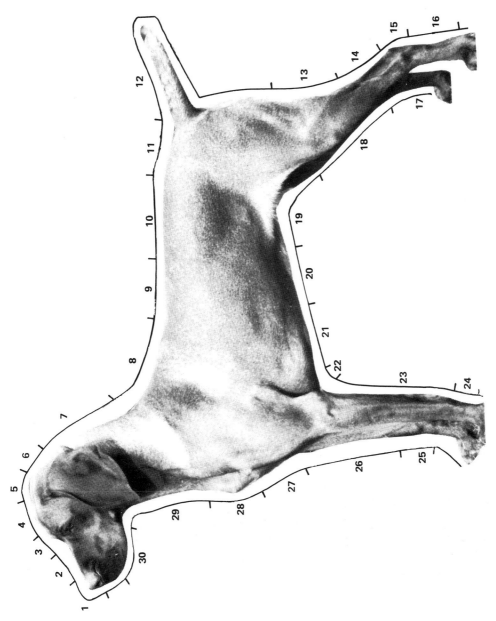

Figure 3.1 Fundamental Points of the Hungarian Vizsla

exercise and feeding; if he is working as well he will inevitably lose some condition and weight and can be overmuscled. Above all, a gundog needs to have an early training pattern, too much physical strain on soft bone can create faults in the dog's conformation. The basic reason for a bad front is bad breeding but the condition can be aggravated by working a dog too early.

Vizsla owners who work and show their dogs are to be commended, since it is they who will not allow the natural rudiment of the dog to change. If we do not deviate we may not have the supreme champion or the greatest field trial dog, but the beautiful Golden Pointer will remain a "many sided hunting dog" or a "many sided dog".

GENERAL APPEARANCE

A medium sized dog of distinguished appearance, robust but lightly boned

---

We can breed robust and heavy dogs, slight and very light boned dogs, some like Whippets and some like Bloodhounds, but the correct type is "robust and not too heavily boned". A light boned Vizsla could be a weedy one. If compared to the Weimaraner and German Shorthaired Pointer, it should be understood that there are substantial differences, one being this particular aspect of his conformation.

HEAD AND SKULL

The head should be gaunt and noble. The skull should be moderately wide between the ears with a median line down the forehead and a moderate stop. The muzzle should be a little longer than the skull and although tapering, should be well squared at the end. The nostrils should be well developed, broad and wide. The jaw strong and powerful. The lips should cover the jaws completely and should be neither loose nor pendulous. The nose should be brown.

We have many types of heads in the breed, in particular one being narrow with little stop, the eyes being close together and small, the muzzle tending towards snipeyness with little lip; another conforms nearer to the *standard*, but can easily tend toward a heavy head, the skull being too wide and an exaggerated stop, a muzzle too short and blunt, too much lip and throatiness giving a bloodhound look.

The muzzle measurement in the *standard* is an incorrect translation. It should read, "the muzzle a little shorter than the skull". I have noticed that the nose can turn a dark brown when the bitch has puppies but it soon reverts to its natural pigmentation when the pups are weaned. The description of the lips can be misleading for they must not be tight and should be generous — a very important characteristic of the

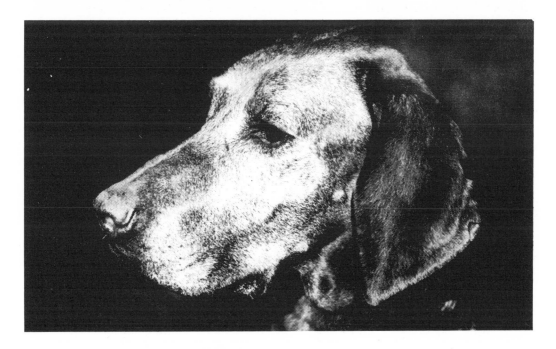

Figure 3.2 Examples of Characteristic Heads
Top: Young Bitch
Bottom: Old (Grey) Bitch   Photos: Diane Pearce

breed since this is important to retrieving gently to hand. The Vizsla must have a soft mouth.

EYES

Neither deep nor prominent, of medium size, being a shade darker in colour than the coat. The shape of the eyes should be slightly oval and the eyelids should fit tightly. A yellow or black eye is objectionable.

Eyes are the feature one's attention ultimately settles on when looking at this dog. The Vizsla eye can show his gentleness and devotion, his boldness, strength and soft-ness of character that should be part of his nature. The size of the eye when correct gives the open, honest expression necessary in this breed. If the eyes are too small or too close together this characteristic is lost.

We do have some pale eyes which are a fault, but frequently by the time the dog is two years old this is a problem no longer. We have judges who complain, "What is happening to the breed, the eyes are too light", and often this means that a judge who does not know the breed intimately, never having bred a litter or owned a puppy, may not know that the Vizsla puppy eye goes through various colour changes, from blue when born, to green, to yellow or light brown to hazel then to a shade darker than the coat. It can take up to two years to reach the correct colour. Thus we have many youngsters in the ring who will not have the correct eye colour on the day, but will no doubt change as they mature.

EARS

The ears should be moderately low set, proportionately long with a thin skin and hanging down close to the cheeks, should be rounded 'V' shaped not fleshy.

What a wealth of feeling ears can express in this breed. When the Vizsla is standing alert and interested they give the head a frank aspect. When he is seeking or giving affection the ears can fold close to his head giving him a simple look, especially if he is one of those who is able to smile! If he is worried by a noise behind him and listening intently he can raise his ears while wrinkling the brow, the ears still hanging limp. When the ears hang correctly they should frame the head, and should not fold outwards or inwards.

The ears should reach to the corner of the mouth easily. A puppy's ears can meet in front of the muzzle! If they do not reach the corners of the mouth very early on they probably will not grow to the correct length. Ears always seem to grow shorter, not longer! It is often found the shorter ear goes with a narrower head.

MOUTH

Sound white teeth meeting in a scissor bite, full dentition is desirable.

A bad mouth is rare in the breed so far. There should be 42 teeth in a dog's jaw, 20 in the top jaw and 22 in the lower.

When puppies are 3—4 months old, their mouths can look a mess. Some teeth are loose, some stick out, some have already fallen out, the gums look swollen, the mouth looks awry. As all the milk teeth fall out and the new ones take their place, the mouth usually corrects itself in a very short time. It can be worrying if one has no knowledge of this. In some cases a puppy may not lose all his milk teeth. As the second teeth appear, the puppy can have a double tooth or several double teeth. Best to leave them and in time the problem will correct itself. It is said that an overshot mouth will never be corrected but an undershot can, if not too exaggerated.

FOREQUARTERS

Shoulders should be well laid and muscular, elbow straight pointing neither in nor out, the forearm should be long.

In common with the other hunt, point and retrieve breeds we have a problem with fronts. No sooner do they seem to improve than the faults appear again. Looking at photographs of Vizslas in Hungary and America, especially Hungary, their shoulders seem no better than ours. It is not for the want of trying to improve this point. It may be a result of lack of experience and knowledge of conformation in this country, but frequently the Vizsla which has the better front does not conform with the type that we all strive for. He is often the narrow, tucked up sort that is not typical, nor should be, of the breed.

One wonders whether well laid and muscular shoulders do not cancel each other out. In many cases a muscular shoulder can also create a loaded shoulder. We can increase the outside muscles without damaging the structure, but since the muscles beneath the blade run hand in hand, if they are increased and thickened, the blade will be pushed out at the top, which will either widen the front or rotate the blade on the curve of the ribs, bringing the point in and turning the elbows out. Thus we have not one problem but a complex set of inherited faults to correct and at the same time must try to breed to type. Tom Horner in an article called "It Seems to Me" in *Dog World* wrote that:

> In sharp contrast to the long legged Terrier, the conformation of the forehand in Spaniels, Setters, Pointers and Retrievers is such that in each of these breeds the dog stands with his forelegs much more under them than do the Terriers. Both groups require the long sloping shoulder blades to enable them to carry their heads correctly but the great difference lies in the length and placement of the humerus or upper arm, that little bone which joins the bottom end of the shoulder blade to the elbow and about which too many breed standards have little or nothing to say. In the long-legged Terriers the upper arm is short and steep, in the gundogs it is much longer and more sloping so that the angle between it and the shoulder is much smaller than in the Terriers and Pointers, and the elbow is placed much further back on the ribcage than in the case of the Terriers.

The advantage of a strong erect pastern is that a straight leg will bear more weight

49

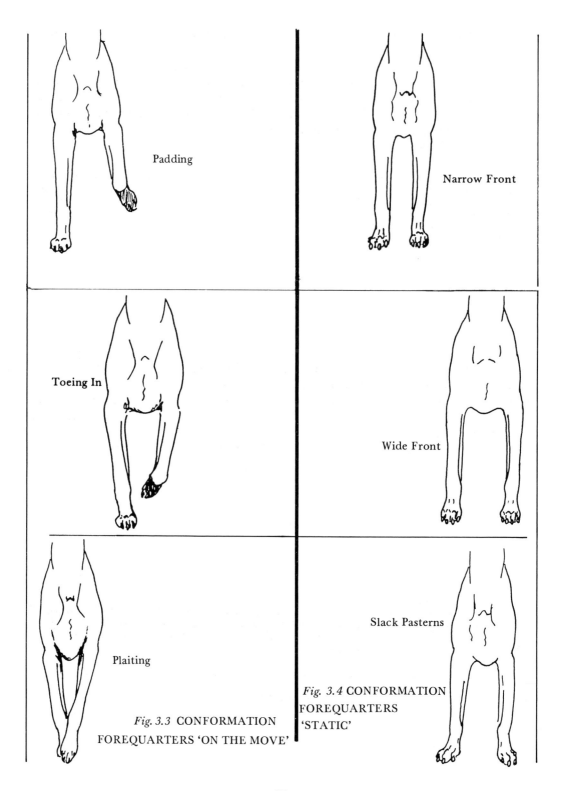

Padding

Narrow Front

Toeing In

Wide Front

Slack Pasterns

Plaiting

Fig. 3.4 CONFORMATION
FOREQUARTERS
'STATIC'

Fig. 3.3 CONFORMATION
FOREQUARTERS 'ON THE MOVE'

also some of the work is taken off the muscles. The slight 'give' in the joint absorbs the shock of the foot striking the ground. Sloping or slack pasterns are not desirable; the dog will tire quickly. Often flat feet and slack pasterns occur together. If these are due to lack of muscle then they can be corrected by regular exercise on a hard surface. In many cases the cause is due to the front assemblance being incorrect. If this is so the dog could have a 'fiddle front'. No amount of muscle formation could correct this fundamental fault.

A final quote from Tom Horner:

> Few points add more to quality in a gundog or any other breed than a really well placed pair of shoulders. Even a really big ribbed dog can have a good forehand provided his shoulders and upper arms are of the right length and in the right place. Very few dogs have real quality unless their shoulders are about right, so that good shoulders and upper arms are points well worth striving for in any breed programme. Well sprung ribs well carried back and reaching down to the elbow are a must in all gundogs.

The Neck (Not mentioned in the British *Standard*)

A muscled neck enables the Vizsla to give a well balanced appearance. However muscled he is throughout, until he is mature enough to hold his head up at the correct height, he will have too much weight on his forehand. He needs to spread the load evenly over the hindquarters, in order to take as much weight as possible on the front end. Otherwise he would be very good at handstands but not quite so good at driving his body forward from the quarters! Thus we have the term "well balanced" or "unbalanced".

The line of the neck should slope gracefully over the wither so that there is no definite line of demarcation. In most cases a long neck goes with a good shoulder, whereas a short neck goes with an upright shoulder.

BODY:

Back should be level, short well muscled, withers high. The chest should be moderately broad and deep with prominent breastbone. The distance from the withers to the lowest part of the chest should be equal to the distance from the chest to the ground. The ribs should be well sprung and the belly should be tight with a slight tuck-up beneath the loin. The group should be well muscled and almost parallel.

In the main, toplines in the breed are not a problem although there are one or two dippy ones and some roached, frequently indicating a shy temperament and not a structural fault. If the shoulder placement is incorrect, the elegant smooth topline from occiput to the tip of the horizontal tail is lost, the topline will be broken as the dog stands, walks or trots.

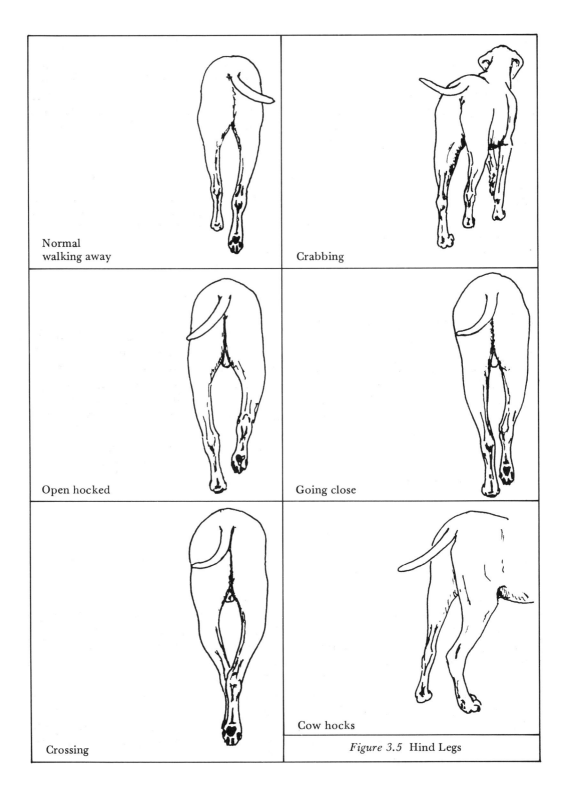

Normal walking away

Crabbing

Open hocked

Going close

Crossing

Cow hocks

Figure 3.5 Hind Legs

If a puppy does not start off with a good deep chest (or a good depth of brisket) which reaches well down to the elbow tip when viewed from the side, and, if the breastbone is not fairly prominent, as likely as not the chest will never be deep enough or "drop" as far as it should and the dog will look shelley. A familiar sight in this breed is a narrow and shallow chest, deep enough but too much tuck-up giving a leggy look to the dog. A gundog needs plenty of heart room the ribs being neither too barrelled nor slab sided. He needs plenty of "body" if he is to do a good day's work. Rather his proportions be too generous than too slight.

HINDQUARTERS

Should be straight when viewed from the rear, the thighs should be well developed with moderate angulation, the hocks well let down.

Surely this should read, "thighs should be well developed, *stifles* with moderate angulation". The thighs need to be well developed. Without good muscle no dog could work for long nor could he find the drive to give impulsion to the rest of his body. It is a poor dog who has no thigh and probably a weedy one too. Too high on the hock and too little angulation gives a straight leg; this dog could sprint well and pull but could not push well. The Vizsla needs to send his body forward with plenty of impetus. As quoted from *The Dog in Action* by McDowell Lyon, "'Longuns' for early speed, 'shortuns' to keep going".

Cow hocks are not necessarily a problem in the breed; they are certainly a fault since the back will lose efficiency in the loss of the straight forward line because the leg is crooked. A close mover is also faulted, again because of the interference of the drive forward due to the weakness of the pastern, as weight is applied the pastern will tune inward.

FEET

Feet tight, compact, well rounded with strong full pads.

The difference between a cat foot and a hare foot is purely in the length of the third digital bone. In the hare foot the third digital bone is longer than the same bone in the cat foot. The hare foot allows increased leverage action and therefore speed, since the Vizsla does not need "speed" (as does the greyhound), so much as endurance in the field, the cat foot is the most effective, the shorter more compact foot is less subject to injuries and its reduced leverage action lessens the strain on the ligaments.

Pads are very important in a good foot, if the heel pad is thick and well built up which it should be, the legs will receive much less shock from rough or hard going and will increase endurance by shortening the leverage action.

Splay feet are a very bad fault, although they may be improved by good road work. But in any breeding programme it is inadvisable to include an animal with this fault. Since endurance is so vital in this breed, good feet should be considered one of the most important points of all.

Dew claws should be removed, damage can be caused by catching them on an obstacle, and a very painful injury can result. Aesthetically, the leg looks much cleaner without these unsightly appendages sticking out of the inside.

GAIT

Graceful and elegant with a lively trot and ground covering gallop.

This is the most graceful and elegant golden dog if the conformation is correct and fits the *standard*. The trot will be a lively trot, daisy clipping as he goes. The gallop can look both flowing and effortless. Watching a Vizsla quartering ground using his nose, searching at a gallop, the quickness of his turns gives the sense of power and endless energy that his well built body affords.

McDowell Lyon's *The Dog in Action* is an essential book to read for those who are truly interested in movement. He writes 21 pages just on the gait.

R H Smythe in his book, *Judging Dogs* confirms the need for an open mind and fascination for more and more facts:

> There is a general belief held even by a few judges that, if a dog is sound in conformation, has a good shoulder, elbows and front, and has sound hips, and stifles and sound hocks, it cannot help but travel sound. Unfortunately this is not always the case. Moreover, a few dogs with quite poor conformation may occasionally travel sound, or at least much better than certain other dogs which on grounds of conformation, one would expect to go better than they actually do.
> There is a reason for this, and it lies not in the anatomical layout but in the dog's nervous system. The fault lies in lack of, or faulty synchronisation of the muscles of the body and particularly of those controlling the limbs.

Added to which a dog may have the perfect conformation, impeccable synchronisation of the muscles of the body but still not move correctly. This fault may be due to a dog's temperament. He can be inhibited in every way by his lack of initiative, drive and character. If psychologically he is insecure and unhappy, he is not likely to allow his body the freedom it needs to move correctly.

TAIL

Should be of moderate thickness, rather low set, with one third docked off. Whilst moving should be held horizontally.

A good set of tail with correct dock gives the Vizsla a well balanced look. In the American book *Your Vizsla* by Stauss and Cunningham it reads:

Tail length was once a serious problem because the breeders and veterinarians did not check the standards' one third off stipulation. Tails are now uniform with the gently curving arch upward so necessary for seeing the dog in the field in tall grass!

We would agree with C Bede Maxwell in her book *The Truth About Sporting Dogs* (also an American book) which states that:

Many Vizslas are ring posed with boxer-pegged tails, but one notes some drop to the proper position in gaiting. It is one of the several troubles for handlers that while American field trail fashion wants tails up, the natural construction of purebreds favours the straight or the down as per the breed *standards*. .My hope is that Vizslas with that inbuilt protection against 'selective breeding' may escape any alteration in the anatomical construction of thier hinderparts. My own practise in the rings is to ask the handler to correctly position the tail of any mishandled dog.

Docking tails is a very controversial subject. Mutilation (for that is the word), for the sake of aesthetics is offensive to many. Most in the breed would agree that the dock gives the dog a smarter outline but those dogs that are seen with long tails (though docked, some tails do grow on) do not appear particularly out of place.

For those who regularly work their dogs, docking is another matter and necessary; a torn damaged tail can be very painful and takes a long time to heal, often opening up the following season. This opinion in the working fraternity runs high when anti-docking suggestions are posed.

COAT

Should be short and straight, dense and coarse and feel greasy to the touch.

The Vizsla coat must be one of the easiest coats to manage, needing little or no brushing except when moulting, since the fur is so short there is very little mess. The sheen on the coat is attained by good food and good exercise. It is a single coat, although it appears thin and sparse on the underside of the dog, it is surprisingly thick if correct. When a Vizsla is as keen as he should be, he will not be deterred by any type of cover. Many will not believe this until they have witnessed a dog disappear into low blackthorn or brambles and come out unscathed, in spite of a thorn or two stuck in him.

Due to the density and greasiness of the coat, water rolls off as it does off a duck's back, unless the coat is soaked. Even then it dries quickly. The Vizsla seems acutely sensitive to the touch, he loves nothing better than being stroked. It fills him with delight. His coat is a pleasure to feel and though it is greasy, it does not seem so.

COLOUR

Russet gold. Small white marks on chest and feet, though acceptable, are not desirable.

As always, colour is in the eye of the beholder. To describe a colour is nigh impossible. Our Vizslas do vary in colour. We have some almost too dark, some definitely too light, even some too gingery, but there seems agreement in the breed that the *standard* colour is the one we all like and wish to see.

In general the dogs that are shown display a uniform colour.

Quoting from *Your Vizsla* again:

> Coat colour in America originally came in two predominant shades — a light sandy yellow-tan, and deep red, almost as dark as the coat of the Irish Setter. The lighter coloured coat generally was found on large, big-boned dogs, while the darker colour seemed to be seen more often on the smaller, more compact dogs. . . The darker reddish colour seems to be dominant, for the majority of the breed now carry this coat.

In general this can not be said of the Vizsla here but could so easily happen. *Your Vizsla* continues saying that: "Some of the finest specimens in the breed carry the 'Esterhazy saddle'or stripe, as it is known in Hungary today."

Our Vizslas certainly have it to some degree. It is a darker shading of the coat colour over the back; it slopes downwards over the shoulder and from there it narrows and goes back to the tip of the tail.

Too much white is rarely a problem, maybe this is because most conscientious breeders will put a puppy down at birth if it has too much white. One or two puppies in a litter may appear to have too much on the chest (5cm is allowed) or four white feet; but it can disappear after several days if the white is not pure and the skin is not bright pink beneath.

An aging Vizsla usually starts to go white under the chin, then over his face; his feet will go white at the same time. As he reaches old age he may go completely white giving a red roan effect.

WEIGHT AND SIZE

Weight 48½ to 66 lbs
Height at Withers: Dogs — 22½ to 25 inches   Bitches — 21 to 23½ inches

Faults — Undue lightness of bone, size too large or too small, bad colouring, too much white, spotted or black nose, entropic or ectropic eyelids, pendulant lips, mouth overshot or undershot, coarseness of head, thin coat or defective teeth.

If your Vizsla conforms to every word of the *standard* but is too large or too small, it will make little difference if he is a pet or a working dog. It will make a difference however if you wanted to show or breed him. Any consistent winner may be used for breeding and the progeny used in other breeding programmes, therefore a stud or bitch who is too short or too tall could change the height of the breed radically in no time at all if consistently bred from.

There is no point in mating a short animal to a tall one, hoping the puppies will be the correct size. Genes do not work that way. The only answer is to mate the right size bitch with the right size dog. Even then the litter may not be even!

Finally, the *standard* is the only blueprint we have to try and follow. It could be too easy to interpret the *standard* to fit our wishes rather than fit the dog to the *standard*. Lyons' *Dog in Action* puts forward as a positive start to a positive breeding programme the following advice:

If we like dogs for the sake of owning them or the pleasure of using them, we should want the individual to have the requisites of a functionally sound animal.

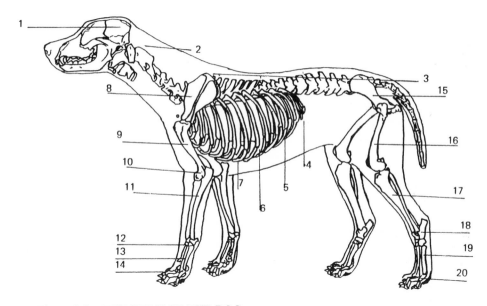

Figure 3.6 **SKELETON OF THE DOG**

HEAD, NECK and TOPLINE

1 Skull	Back — 7 vertebrae	Tail — 26 vertebrae
2 Neck — 7 vertebrae	Loin — 7 vertebrae	
3 Withers — 8 vertebrae	Croup — 3 vertebrae	

FOREQUARTERS

4 Floating Ribs — 1 pair   10 Point of Elbow
5 Joined ribs — 3 pairs   11 Forearm — radius and ulna
6 Connected to sternum — 9 pairs   12 Pastern Joint — 7 bones
7 Breast Bone — sternum   13 Pastern — 5 bones
8 Shoulder Blade — scapula   14 Toes — phalanges
9 Upper Arm — humerus

HINDQUARTERS

15 Pelvis   18 Hock Joint — tarsal bones — 5
16 Upper Thigh — femur   19 Hock — metatarsal bones — 5
17 Lower Thigh — tibia and fibula   20 Toes — phalanges

BREED STANDARD OF THE HUNGARIAN VIZSLA (BRITISH 1972)

CHARACTERISTICS—The Hungarian Vizsla should be lively and intelligent, it should have an excellent nose, should be obedient but sensitive, very affectionate and easily trained. Should be capable of hunting for fur and feather on open ground or in thick cover, pointing and retrieving from both land and water.

GENERAL APPEARANCE—A medium sized hunting dog of distinguished appearance, robust but lightly boned.

HEAD AND SKULL—The head should be gaunt and noble. The skull should be moderately wide between the ears with a median line down the forehead and a moderate stop. The muzzle should be a little longer than the skull and although tapering should be well squared at the end. The nostril should be well developed, broad and wide. The lips should cover the jaws completely and should be neither loose nor pendulous. The nose should be brown.

EYES—Neither deep nor prominent, of medium size, being a shade darker in colour than the coat. The shape of the eye should be slightly oval and the eyelids should fit tightly. A yellow or black eye is objectionable.

EARS—The ears should be moderately low set, proportionately long with a thin skin and hang down close to the cheeks, should be rounded 'V' shape, not fleshy.

MOUTH—Sound white teeth meeting in a scissor bite full dentition is desirable.

FOREQUARTERS—Shoulders should be well laid and muscular, elbows straight pointing neither in nor out, the forearm should be long.

BREED STANDARD OF THE HUNGARIAN VIZSLA (AMERICAN 1983)

The following proposed revised Standard for the Vizsla has been submitted by the Vizsla Club of America, Inc.:

GENERAL APPEARANCE—That of a medium sized short coated hunting dog of distinguished appearance and bearing. Robust but rather lightly built; the coat is an attractive solid golden rust. This is a dog of power and drive in the field yet a tractable and affectionate companion in the home. It is strongly emphasized that field conditioned coats, as well as brawny or sinewy muscular condition and honorable scars indicating a working and hunting dog are never to be penalized in this dog. The qualities that make a "dual dog" are always to be appreciated not depreciated.

HEAD—Lean and muscular. Skull moderately wide between the ears with a median line down the forehead. Stop between skull and foreface is moderate, not deep. Foreface or muzzle is of equal length or slightly shorter than skull when viewed in profile, should taper gradually from stop to tip of nose. Muzzle square and deep. It must not turn up as in a "dish" face nor should it turn down. Whiskers serve a functional purpose; their removal is permitted but not preferred. Nostrils slightly open. Nose brown. Any other colour is faulty. A TOTALLY BLACK NOSE IS A DIS-QUALIFICATION. Ears, thin, silky and proportionately long, with rounded-leather ends, set fairly low and hanging close to cheeks. Jaws are strong with well developed white teeth meeting in a scissors bite. Eyes medium in size and depth of setting, their surrounding tissue covering the whites. Colour or the iris should blend with the colour of the coat. Yellow or any other colour is faulty. Prominent pop-eyes are faulty. Lower eyelids should neither turn in nor out since both conditions allow seeds and dust to irritate the eye. Lips cover the jaws completely but are neither loose nor pendulous.

BREED STANDARD OF THE HUNGARIAN VIZSLA (HUNGARIAN 1981)

CHARACTERISTICS—Medium-size, short-haired, yellow gundog of elegant appearance. It is rather lightly than heavily built, reflecting a harmony of beauty and strength. Balanced, intelligent, with vivid temperament. History writers consider the Pannion hound as one of the ancestors of the Vizsla. The yellow gundog of the Turks also played a significant role in the development of the breed. Some writers, however, date back its first appearance to several years earlier. Latest researches indicate that the 'sloughi' was among the common ancestors. The first present-form specimens of the breed appeared in the early 18th century. In conformity with the modernization of hunting habits in the 19th century, other gundogs had been used in their improvement and finally there emerged a separate yellow national dog. The breed recovered after the war to develop into its present form, characterized by the following:

It is trained easily and quickly. Its character does not tolerate rough treatment. Inherited qualities, excellent memory and good reasoning power, make it the gundog of modern times. In spite of its great passion for hunting, it likes house keeping as well. Because of this and also because of its distinguished manner many people keep it as a companion dog. It is widely known for its excellent ability for acclimatization and is an untiring worker even in immense heat. Out of its inherited traits, the following are deemed necessary: excellent scenting powers; staunch, figurative pointing; distinct trailing and retrieving qualities, love of water work and excellent response to handling.

HEAD—Dry, noble, proportioned. The skull moderately wide, slightly domed. A slight median line, extending from the moderately developed occipital bone towards the forehead, divides the top of the head. The bridge of the nose is always straight. The foreface is well arched, neither pointed nor wide, ending in a well developed nose with nostrils well open.

BODY—Back should be level, short, well muscled, wither high. The chest should be moderately broad and deep prominent breast bone. The distance from the withers to the lowest part of the chest should be equal to the distance from the chest to the ground. The ribs should be well sprung and the belly should be tight with a slight tuck up underneath the loin. The croup should be well muscled and almost parallel.

HINDQUARTERS—Should be straight when viewed from the rear, the thighs should be well developed with moderate angulation, the hocks well let down.

FEET—Rounded with toes short, arched and well closed. A cat like foot is desirable, hare foot is objectionable. Nails short, strong and a shade darker in colour than coat, dew claws should be removed.

GAIT—Graceful and elegant with a lively trot and ground covering gallop.

TAIL—Should be of moderate thickness, rather low set with one third docked off. Whilst moving should be held horizontally.

COAT—Should be short and straight,dense and coarse and feel greasy to the touch.

COLOUR— Russet gold, small white marks on chest and feet should not be faulted but are not desirable.

WEIGHT AND SIZE—Weight: 48½–66lbs; Height at withers: DOGS 22½–25inches, BITCHES 21–23½ inches.

FAULTS—Undue lightness of bone, size too large or to small, bad colouring, too much white, spotted or black nose, entropic or ectropic eyelids, pendulant lips, mouth over shot or undershot. Coarseness of head. Thin coat, defective teeth.

NECK AND BODY—Neck strong, smooth and muscular, moderately long, arched and devoid of dewlap, broadening nicely into shoulders which are moderately laid back. This is mandatory to maintain balance with the moderately angulated hind quarters. Body is strong and well proportioned. Back short. Withers high and the topline slightly rounded over the loin to the set-on of the tail. Chest moderately broad and deep reaching down to the elbows. Ribs well sprung; underline exhibiting a slight tuck-up beneath the loin. Tail set just below the level of the group,thicker at the root and docked one-third off. Ideally, it should reach to the back of the stifle joint and be carried at or near the horizontal. An undocked tail is faulty.

FOREQUARTERS— Shoulder blades proportionately long and wide sloping moderately back and fairly close at the top. Forelegs straight and muscular with elbows close. Feet cat-like, round and compact with toes close. Nails brown and short. Pads thick and tough. Dewclaws, if any, to be removed on front and rear feet. Hare feet are faulty.

HINDQUARTERS—Hind legs have well developed thighs with moderately angulated stifles and hocks in balance with the moderately laid back shoulders. They must be straight as viewed from behind. Too much angulation at the hocks is as faulty as too little. The hocks are let down and parallel to each other.

COAT—Short, smooth, dense and close-lying, without woolly undercoat.

COLOUR—Solid golden rust in different shadings. Solid dark Mahogany red and pale yellow are faulty. Small white spots on chest are not faulted but massive areas of white on chest or white anywhere else on the body is a disqualification. Occasional white hairs on toes are acceptable but solid white extending above the toes is a disqualification. White due to aging shall not be faulted. Any noticeable area of black in the coat is a serious fault.

Measuring the straight line linking the tip of the nose and the inner corners of the eyes, the foreface is always less than 50% of the total length of the head. The fang is proportionately long, the jaw is well-developed, well muscled. The teeth are powerful, the incisors close like scissors. The expression is vivid, intelligent, the eyes are slightly oval. The eyelids are tight. The colour of the eyes harmonize with the colour of the coat: the darker the eyes, the more desirable. The ears are of medium length set slightly back at medium-height and are flat against the cheek, cover the ear-holes well and end in a V-shape rounding off towards the tip.

NECK—Medium length, well muscled,slightly arched, free from disturbing dewlaps. Set on the trunk at medium height.

TRUNK—Powerful, proportioned, slightly longer than with the quadratic breeds. The withers, pronounced, well muscled. The back is short, straight; the line tight with the upper line slightly rounding off towards the base of the rump. The chest is moderately wide and deep, reaching down to the elbows. The ribs are moderately arched. The shoulders are well muscled, the shoulder blades slant, the movement is free.

LIMBS—The forelegs are straight, strong boned, the elbows close to the body. The hind legs are well muscled, moderately angulated; hocks slightly low set. The toes are strong, well-rounded, compact. The paws are slightly oval, the nails are strong, the pads tough.

TAIL—Slightly low set, medium thick, narrowing towards the tip. It forms aesthetic entity with the body when only three-quarters of the original length is left. usually, one quarter is docked. If, however, the fine-lined tail is carried standardly, ie. close to the horizontal plane, docking is not mandatory.

SKIN—The skin is tight, free from wrinkles or folds. The skin is pigmented, the nose is flesh-coloured, the lips, the eyelids and the nails are brown. The pads are slate-grey.

AMERICAN 1983
Continued

GAIT–Far reaching, light footed, graceful and smooth. When moving at a fast trot, a properly built dog single tracks.

SIZE–The ideal male is 22 to 24 inches at the highest point over the shoulder blades. The ideal female is 21 to 23 inches. Because the Vizsla is meant to be a medium-sized hunter, any dog measuring more than 1½ inches over or under these limits must be disqualified.

TEMPERAMENT–A natural hunter endowed with a good nose and above-average ability to take training. Lively, gentle-mannered, demonstrably affectionate and sensitive, though fearless with a well developed protective instinct. Shyness, timidity or nervousness should be penalized.

DISQUALIFICATIONS–Completely black nose, massive areas of white on chest, white anywhere else on the body, solid white extending above the toes, any male over 25½ inches or under 20½ inches and any female over 24½ inches or under 19½ inches at the highest point over the shoulder blades.

HUNGARIAN 1981
Continued

COAT–The hair is laying flat close to the body; it is short, with rough feeling. The belly is slightly haired. At the ears the hair is shorter and more silky. The tail is covered with longer hair.

COLOUR–Various shades of sandy or dark sandy. Smaller white spots on the chest and on the feet are not faulted.

GAIT–Far-reaching, vigorous, smooth. While hunting, the gait is a balanced, steady canter.

HEIGHT–The ideal height for males: 56–61cm, 22–24 inches
for females:
52–57cm, 20½–22½ inches
4cm deviation from the above is permitted in either way, if it does not disturb harmony. Static and dynamic balance as well as symmetry are considered much more important than proportions measured in centimetres.

TYPEFAULTS–All those structural faults or significant defects that disadvantageously influence the harmony of movement and continuous work. Major faults are: extremely light or rough structure, significant deviation from the *standard*, disproportioned build, within this short but high structure over-size individuals with hindquarters. Faults of the head are considered of major importance, such as; disproportioned, either too wide or too narrow skull and forehead; pointed, hollow or cone-shaped head, hound head, overly expressed stop, short pointed muzzle, ram's nose. Important faults are, peundulous lips, loose skin on the head, small disproportionate, close, deep-set, or protruding light-coloured eyes; loose lids, expressionless, ill-intentioned look. Too low or too high set, narrow, twisted ears. Irregularly closing teeth, undershot overshot, over 2mm; wry mouth, buck-tooth, scale, yellow teeth, bigger dewlaps on the neck.

TRUNK—Slack muscles, loose back and narrow pelvis; short, sway-back or steep hind-quarters; sagging or sunken withers; chest either not properly deep or chest too wide; flat ribs. With females, sagging belly after whelping.

LIMBS—Set of the legs deviating from the *standard*; angulations; loose, not closed, long paws.

TAIL—Tail set high, carried considerably higher than the horizontal.

COAT—Thin,silky, extremely short; fine or thin, like the mouse-hair; and any deviation from the short hair.

COLOUR—Dark brown, rusty and pale yellow shades are not desirable. The darker stripe on the back (the king stripe), which is usually due to nourishment conditions, is not considered a significant fault. White spots around the throat, or marks are faulted only if larger than 5cm in diameter.

DISQUALIFICATIONS—Considerable devi-ations from the breed characteristics. Deviation from the *standard* height of more than 4cm in either way. Parti-colour, spottiness, bigger spots on the chest white feet. Pointed foreface, narrow greyhound-like or rough, hound-like skull. Light-coloured eyes, grey or contrasting coloured eyes. Ectropy, entropy, strong ram's nose; pink, slate-grey, black or spotted nose and black pigmented lips, or eyelids. Undershot; overshot more than 2mm; wry mouth, pendu-lous lips, salivation, strong dewlaps. Colours lighter than wax-yellow or brown colour. Shy, weak-nerved, albino, cryptorchid or monorchid dogs. Seriously constrained faulty gait. Dysplasia of the hip-joint.

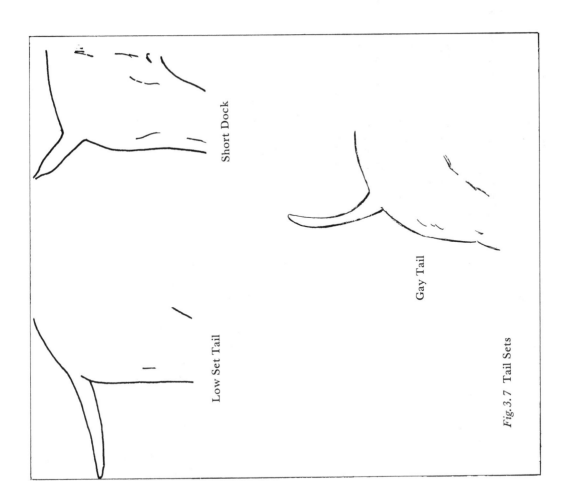

Low Set Tail

Short Dock

Gay Tail

Fig.3.7 Tail Sets

COMPARISON OF THE BRITISH, AMERICAN AND HUNGARIAN STANDARDS

Over the years the British, American and Hungarian breed *standards* have been altered and minutely changed, always with improvement in mind. Originally both British and American *standards* were based on the Hungarian Vizsla *standard* since that is the breed's country of origin. Referring to Ingeborg Hovarth's visit to Hungary in 1982, he writes:

> This brings me to the most important part of the trip, "The Official International Conference of the Breeders of Hungarian Breeds', where Miklos Farkashazi went over the new Hungarian *standard* which has been accepted as the official International Vizsla Standard by the FCI (Federation Cynologique Internationale).
> There have been no changes in their basic features of the *standard*. The last revision ten years ago was found not to have been specific enough and did not take into consideration the use of the Vizsla at the present and in years to come. The new *standard* is very much like the old original *standard*, but it keeps in mind the modern use of the dog.

If the British were to adopt the 1981 Hungarian *standard* it would mean some radical alterations.

These would be made in the first place under the heading DISQUALIFICATIONS. Disqualification in Hungary means disqualification from breeding not showing. In Hungary, in order for a dog to be allowed to be bred, it must first attend a 'breeders display' at a regular dog show, where a panel of judges goes over the dog and decides whether it is worthy of passing its genes along to the next generation. Should a dog get disqualified, the Hungarian Kennel Club (Magyar Ebtenyesztok Orszagos Egyesulete) or MEOE will not register the puppies and no official pedigree will be issued for the dogs. Thus disqualification has a very real and practical purpose in Hungary.

Disqualification in order of importance, first and foremost is for reasons of poor temperament, a shy, spooky dog will not be allowed to be bred. Disqualification can be affected secondly for faulty movement due to structural faults, and thirdly for a dog which suffers from hip dysplasia. Any dog is automatically disqualified if found to have this defect, many dogs are now being x-rayed. There are many other disqualifications listed, but it is doubtful whether the Hungarian terms of disqualification could ever become acceptable over here.

There would be changes under the heading TAIL. The tail, if carried correctly, i.e. in a horizontal plane, does not need docking. The Vizsla tail originally was never docked. The docking came in with the vogue for German Shorthairs. Thus, now there is a return to the original standard. It is believed the dog needs a longer tail for field work, for swimming, balance, and fast changes of direction.

A third change would affect the "NAME OF BREED". "Vizsla" is a very old Hungarian word which was first used to describe the dog at the time of the development of the first firearms. As there are no other types of Vizslas in the world (ex. German Vizsla, English Vizsla etc.) there is no need for the specification "Hungarian" in the name. Thus, the breed is simply to be known as "Vizsla".

All three standards for HEIGHT are shown here so that they may be compared:

BRITISH

Dog: H 22½″ — 25″
Bitch: H 21″ — 23½″   No disqualification over or under.

AMERICAN

Dog: H 22½″ — 24″   Any dog measuring more than 1½″ over or under
Bitch: H 21″ — 23″   these limits must be disqualified

HUNGARIAN

Dog: 22½″ — 24″   Any dog measuring more than 1½″ over or under
Bitch: 20½″ — 22½″   must be disqualified

Ten years ago the Hungarian standard raised the height allowance, it has now been returned to the original lower height with a deviation of 4cm (approx. 1¾″) either way. Static and dynamic balance as well as symmetry are considered much more important than proportions measured in centimetres.

The American 1960 *standard* was changed in 1965 specifically to limit the size of their Vizslas, it was not uncommon for winning dogs to measure 26″–27″. The newly revised American *standard* of 1983 has lowered the limit from a deviation of 2″ down to 1½″ (approx) similar to the Hungarian disqualification mark. So, in effect America asks for the same height as Hungary. The British *standard* for the Hungarian Vizsla asks for the tallest of all and neither puts a limit on deviation nor allows any officially. Unofficially I always understood that 2 inches were allowed either way. I feel that these differences in our *standard* must be considered with a view to adjusting it.

Let us now look at the 3 *standards* in comparison with one another, noting the differences. The American (A), British (B) and Hungarian (H):

GENERAL CHARACTERISTICS (*H*) 'yellow gundog, rather lightly than heavily built'. (*A*) also asks for these characteristics, whereas (*B*) asks for 'lightly boned'. I would suggest that it is not an apt description.

HEAD

Ingeborg Horvath reports:

There has also been a great deal of emphasis placed on the Vizsla head. It should be of noble appearance with a pleasing, intelligent expression. It is essential for the Vizsla to have a warm loving gaze, as this is very characteristic of the breed. The length of the muzzle should be slightly shorter than the length of the skull.

(A) asks for 'lean and muscular', compared to (B), 'gaunt and noble'. Gaunt is a strange translation, its meaning is given in the dictionary as, 'famished, slim and haggard'; lean would be more appropriate.

Due to mis-translation,(A) and (B) have always asked for the muzzle a 'trifle longer than the skull'. (A) have adjusted their new standard to 'muzzle is of equal length to the skull viewed in profile'. (B) still needs to be changed, although I doubt

any Vizsla could be found with a head whose proportions were otherwise.
The Hungarian *standard* reads:

> Measuring the straight line linking the tip of the nose and the inner corners of the eyes, the foreface is always less than 50% of the total length of the head'.

This is a very clear specific measurement.

EYES There is a difference between the (**B**) and (**A**) *standards*, the former asks for 'a shade darker than the coat', and the latter, 'colour portion harmonizing with the colour of the coat, the darker the eye more desirable'. All *standards* object to the pale or yellow eye.

NECK The British Standard omits the neck altogther! (**A**) and (**H**) ask for 'medium length, no dewlap and well muscled', but (**A**) lays down that it should be 'arched' and (**H**) that it should be 'slightly arched'. An arched, muscled neck could look out of proportion and over exaggerated in this breed thus the definition of (**H**) seems preferable. (**A**) describes the neck, 'broadening nicely into the shoulders which are well laid back', which is more explicit than (**H**) which states that it should be set on the trunk at medium height'!

FOREQUARTERS AND BODY None of the *standards* mention the humerus, leaving an incomplete description of the forequarters. Nor are the pasterns mentioned, should they be sloping or erect?

In describing the topline (**B**) wants the 'croup well muscled and almost parallel', (**A**) would like it to be 'slightly rounded over the loin to the "set on" of tail, with the back short, and (**H**) wishes for the 'upper line slightly rounding off towards the base of the rump'.

The British *standard* is the only one that gives the dimensions 'the distance from the withers to the lower part of the chest be equal to the distance from the chest to the ground'. Although (**H**) states that the trunk should be powerful, slightly longer than with the quadratic (square) breeds'. This was one of the changes in (**H**) that was discussed by Miklos Farkashazi:

> The Vizsla is not square, but slightly longer in the body than in height. The dog should not look like a pointer, nor should it ever become as strong and as fast a dog as the English Pointer. This difference between the Vizsla and the Pointer should be maintained.

HINDQUARTERS (**A**) asks for 'moderate angulation at stifles and hocks', whereas (**B**) and (**H**) ignore the stifle.

(**H**) desires that the 'Hindlegs are well muscled, moderately angulated, hocks slightly low set', (**B**) that the 'Hocks well let down', and (**A**) is very explicit, stating that:

> Too much angulation at the hocks is as faulty as too little. The hocks which are well let down, are equidistant from each other from the hock joint to the ground.

64

FEET (**B**) states that nails must be short, strong and a shade darker than the coat, (**A**) that nails should be brown, whereas (**H**) only asks for them to be strong.

GAIT (**B**) asks for a 'lively trot and a ground covering gallop' whereas (**H**) requires that 'while hunting, the gait is a balanced steady canter'. (**A**) includes in the standard the requirement that 'when moving at a fast trot, a properly built dog single tracks'.

TAIL The British *standard* has always stated that the tail 'whilst moving should be held horizontally'. (**A**) now specifically states that the tail is to 'reach the back of the stifle joint and be carried at or near the horizontal. An undocked tail is faulty', clearly the American Vizsla will continue to have his tail docked for a few more years. (**H**) now states that if the tail is held correctly, docking is not mandatory (a difficult decision to make when a dog is three days old). The length of dock has also changed to ¼ taken off whereas the British and American *standards* ask for a third to be removed.

Clearly the new departure from the original Hungarian *standard* will require much reflection. Any undocked import will cause confusion in the ring since the long tail will not conform to the British or American *standards*.

COLOUR The three *standards* agree that while marks or spots on chest and feet are not faulted, only (**B**) states that it is undesirable. Rusty is one of the shades objected to by (**H**) and the darker stripe on the back called 'the king stripe', which is usually due to nourishment conditions, is not considered to be a significant fault.

In conclusion, whether (**B**) and (**A**) *standard* adopts the rigid restrictions of the (**H**) 'disqualifications' is questionable. Whether docking eventually becomes optional is questionable, but the most obvious difference between the British Hungarian Vizsla, the American Hungarian Vizsla and the Hungarian 'Vizsla' is that the British *standard* asks for the tallest dog.

There is much food for thought in the update 1) Hungarian and American *standards*. The British *standard* has not been revised since 1972 and it is not as extensive or as detailed as the standard of the other two countries. The adjustments that have been made are not to fit the Vizsla but for the dog to conform to the *standard* — a far sighted decision to make.

Under the heading "General Appearance" the American *standard* in 1983 has included the clause:

> **It is strongly emphasised that field conditioned coats, as well as brawny or sinewy muscular conditions as well as honourable scars indicate working and hunting dogs and such a Vizsla must not be penalised. The qualities that make a 'dual dog' are always to be appreciated, not depreciated.**

This is a progressive positive and important statement that should contribute to the advance to any gundog breed should its message be heeded.

REVISION OF THE BRITISH STANDARD

In 1983 the British Kennel Club instructed that all standards must conform in specific wording, titles and headings. All breed organisations were invited to reassess their standards in order that the Kennel Club may appraise them.

The following is the rephrased example of the standard submitted by the Hungarian Vizsla Club.

PROPOSED NEW BREED STANDARD FOR THE HUNGARIAN VIZSLA – THE HUNGARIAN VIZSLA CLUB

1. **Temperament**
   Good natured, very affectionate. A loyal and protective companion.

2. **Characteristics**
   Lively, intelligent, enthusiastic worker with an excellent nose. Sensitive dog, easily trained, adaptable and eager to please. Bred for hunting fur and feather, pointing and retrieving from land or water.

3. **General Appearance**
   Medium sized dog of distinguished appearance, robust with good quality medium bone.

4. **Head & Skull**
   Head lean and noble. Skull moderately wide between ears with median line down forehead and moderate stop. Muzzle a little shorter than skull, tapering but well squared at end. Nose brown, nostrils well developed broad and wide. Lips covering jaws completely, neither loose nor pendulous.

5. **Eyes**
   Neither deep nor prominent, of medium size, a shade darker in colour than coat. Slightly oval in shape, eyelids fitting tightly. Yellow or black eye undesirable.

6. **Ears**
   Moderately low set, proportionately long with a thin skin and hanging down close to cheeks. Rounded 'V' shape. Not fleshy.

7. **Mouth**
   Jaws strong and powerful. Sound, strong, white teeth meeting in perfect regular and complete scissor bite. Full dentition desirable.

8. **Neck**
   Strong, smooth amd muscular. Moderately long, arched and devoid of dewlap. Broadens into shoulders.

9. **Forequarters**
   Shoulders well laid. Upper arms (shoulder to elbow) long. Elbows well back and set close to body. Foreleg straight, pasterns strong and erect. Loaded or straight shoulders are bad faults.

10. **Body**
Back level, short, well muscled, withers high. Chest deep (reaching to elbows), moderately broad (about a hand's width behind elbows, to allow freedom of movement of upper arm). Prominent breastbone. Distance from withers to lowest part of chest equals distance from chest to ground. Ribs well sprung and belly tight with slight tuck up beneath lin. Croup well muscled.

11. **Hindquarters**
Hindleg parallel when viewed from rear, thighs well developed with moderate angulation, hocks well let down.

12. **Feet**
Turning neither in nor out, rounded with toes short, arched and tight. Cat like foot is required, hare foot undesirable. Nails short, strong and a shade darker than coat, dew claws should be removed.

13. **Gait**
Graceful and elegant with a lively trot and a ground covering gallop.

14. **Tail**
Moderately thick, rather low set, one third docked off. When moving carried horizontally.

15. **Coat**
Short, straight and dense, feeling slightly greasy to the touch.

16. **Colour**
Russet gold. Small white marks acceptable (though not desirable) on chest only.

17. **Weight/Size**
Weight 48½–66 lbs (106.7–145.2k). Height at withers: Dogs 57–64 cm (22½–25"). Bitches 53–60cm (21"–23½").

18. **Faults**
Any departure from the foregoing and in particular: Bone too light/heavy. Over/under sized. Colour too dark/light. Too much white or white anywhere but chest. Discoloured nose. Entropic/ectropic eyelids. Overshot/undershot mouth. Coarse or heavy head. Defective teeth.

19. **Note**
Male animals should have two apparently normal testicles fully descended into the scrotum.

A NOTE ON TEMPERAMENT

From the first moment I saw a Hungarian Vizsla I was captivated by the breed and I am still. To me he remains the proud creature that I met fifteen years ago, standing in the sunlight, his russet-gold coat rich against the spring green. He was alone in a field, alert and agile, every muscle tense, head held high, nose twitching, aware of nothing else but the sights and senses in his dog world. He relaxed and threw himself on the ground and rolled, pressing his shoulders deep in the grass, pushing his muzzle forward into the daisies. Finally, he lay still on his back, his legs in the air while he gazed at the passing clouds. This joy and zest for living culminated in one last ecstatic fling before he sprang to his feet effortlessly and stood proudly as before. He caught sight of us laughing at him. He ran towards us wagging his tail with delight. I never cease to appreciate this breed's ability to move me and then reduce me to laughter by its ridiculous antics.

Months later, I saw more Hungarian Vizslas at a field trial. It was a cold, wet, foggy day. The rain poured relentlessly, soaking dogs and handlers through to the skin. I had driven through the countryside since dawn, anticipating a glorious, clear autumn day, expecting all the excitement of a shoot with the added thrill of watching Hungarian Vizslas competing — nothing could have been further from my imaginings. There was no game to be seen, visibility was nil, small groups of sodden competitors huddled gloomily under the scant shelter provided by the bare trees. But as the green clad figures trudged from field to field hoping for sight, sound or scent of pheasant, the Vizslas trotted by their sepulchral side, ever alert and ready to work, no sodden mud or lack of game could suppress their eagerness, not rain or wind halted them. I watched a small Vizsla bitch work through a field of kale so high there was no sign of a russet-gold coat, but as she quartered back and forth the foliage bent, indicating her methodical search for game. Another Vizsla, on point, could not be distracted. He knew there was game in the hedge, and there was. While he stood rigid, raindrops fell from his ears, nose and belly. The pheasant shot, he bounded off into the fog to retrieve it and returned with his prize, carrying it gently to hand, shivering with cold and excitement. *

This breed is a pleasure to own if his temperament suits you and yours suits him. He needs to be part of your life and your world. He loves to feel he is one of the family. Whether he is in the house or out walking with you, he is not a dog that remains out of sight for long. He rarely wanders far and his eyes seek you out wherever you are. He may appear to be asleep by the fire, but if you move, he will be wide awake, prepared to go where you will. His idea of comfort and relaxation may not fit in with his owner's plans for him, for it is difficult not to spoil him. He expects to sit by you on the settee, his brown eyes gazing at you in rapture as he rests his head on your shoulder. If you ask him to remove himself, he cannot believe you mean it and will stubbornly hide his head under your arm or beneath a cushion. Happy to sleep in your bedroom, kitchen or the kennel, but happiest of all to have company at all times.

His faithfulness is never questioned, such is his devotion to his family and his territory, it can lead to over-possessiveness. He is a creature of contrariness and fancies, his sensitivity and stubborness difficult to understand and deal with. It can affect his behaviour in every aspect be he pet or gundog. He can cringe if spoken to harshly whilst firmly persisting on having his own way until you have asserted yourself in a particular manner which he finds acceptable. But woe betide you if you do it by force. He can fold up completely as his stubborness increases and it can undo months of effective training.

---

*Steadiness is not included in the Standard, but it is vital in this breed, as it is in any Gundog.

He can be terrified by a fly, he may hide behind your chair at the sight of a curtain billowing in the breeze, the smallest kitten can dominate him, but he will guard your property, and the fiercest of meter ladies will flinch if she dares to approach your car.

He finds it difficult to accept that not everyone likes to have his wrist held in his mouth, however gently, a habit all Vizslas seem to have in common. Some Vizslas can become too persistent, insisting on asserting themselves to a point where they can get out of hand. He needs discipline and if not corrected his assertion can lead to aggression. So from early on, he must know who is "boss". Once that is established he accepts it totally and would rarely challenge it except in fun.

At his best, he should be well-muscled and well-covered but not fat. Nothing is hidden on this short-coated breed. Every fault and blemish can be seen. He should be an agile dog, lithe and speedy. He can jump and leap like a deer, using his powerful quarters. His sure-footedness can be alarming, watching him leap from rock to rock or racing up and down sheer cliffs without a slip.

This breed can work all day never seeming to tire. He is a strong swimmer and should love the water.

He has a delightful, whimsical side to his nature. He can stalk a butterfly or a bee, pointing as it settles on a flower, discerning it as an insect and not game will tiptoe past! What pleasure watching puppies stalking and pointing summer moths as they flitter in the light shed from the lamp in a kennel.

He will sit quietly watching a water wagtail darting backwards and forwards, or a house martin building his nest. He can merge with the stillness of the trout by the weed awaiting its passing nymphs. He can move through reeds and rushes with almost no sound, lowering himself into the water with hardly a ripple, swimming so skillfully along the water's edge, even a moorhen will not know he has passed by.

Walking six adult Vizslas through the woods after a thaw, the drips as they fall sounding loud on the autumn leaves, the mist lurking about the trees, the silence and loneliness made twelve dark eyes dart from side to side and behind us. I was glad of their company and they of mine as we crept out of the wood and walked quickly home for tea.

The Hungarian Vizsla is not a popular breed, and most who own one would agree that he is not for those who have never owned a dog before. He needs a good deal of understanding and tolerance; he will stretch your patience beyond its limits sometimes, but roar at him in a temper and he will creep towards you as if beaten and will take time to forgive you, but he will never forget.

A good Vizsla will work for you in any capacity. He needs to use his brain. He is highly intelligent at his best, his awareness and alertness, his responsiveness to command and ease with which he can learn allows him a varied range of activities — hunting, working trials, trialling, showing, whatever you wish, but none of these is possible unless you can come to terms with his temperament. His desire to please and his longing to hear his owner praise him, his intense wish to be involved with whoever is handling him can be the key in early training. A compromise can often be the trick, instead of direct confrontation, as long as he respects you. Over-handling and too much discipline without giving him a chance to succeed in any direction can augment a certain stubbornness that is part of his nature. Reward by hand and voice will get you everywhere; severe treatment, nowhere.

He will learn a lesson very quickly and as quickly become bored if pressed to repeat it over and over again. If this is understood, many a confrontation can be avoided. Little and often suits his nature rather than long spells of discipline, or he will start to flout authority and use his clowning antics to amuse himself and you. His enthusiasms are irresistible and will constantly extricate him from unmentionable misdemeanors.

Because of the ease with which he learns, too much pressure can be put on him too early and this can cause him to become over-anxious and excited. If his wish to do his best for you continues without being recognised you can cause him to develop into a dreadful fawning, clinging insecure animal who will be useless to himself and you and a nuisance to all. Firmness, calmness, gentleness, and a soft voice taking him step by step from one lesson to the next, never allowing ambition to push the pace, getting him to feel the joy of your pleasure, knowing he has done well, will pay such dividends as he gets older, that he will be ready for more and so will you.

The Hungarian Vizsla is a gundog first and foremost. To work should be his natural instinct. His complicated personality is best suited to this purpose. If he is not worked, it is very necessary that his owners provide him with a varied and full life as an alternative. He is not the sort of dog who should be pampered or sheltered.

It is not easy as an amateur to undertake the task of training any of the hunt, point and retrieve breeds, for the whole exercise is quite complicated from the handler's point of view as well as the dogs. But training classes are available in various parts of the country and there are now several good books on how to train the hunt, point and retrieve breeds.

Some owners have discovered the shyness and feyness of the Vizsla is not for them, but for those who have been able to understand and enjoy all his ways, he can be the most affectionate, lively and fascinating of companions.

Bred right, treated right, worked right, he can hold his own in any company.

THE WIREHAIRED VIZSLA

There are two Wirehaired Vizslas in Britain today. Both were imported from Hungary by Douglas Appleton. The first to arrive was *Aranyos Tisza Dudas*, bred by Sipos Istuanne in 1978, now owned by Mich and David Layton of the well known *Midlander* prefix. She is trained and handled by David and has been shown in any variety not classified classes with some success. Wherever she goes she draws much attention since no-one can resist her gentle eyes and be-whiskered face. She now has a mate imported in 1983 called *Boros Tyanko Gulyas of Carric Temple*, bred by Tumay Janson and born in 1980. It is hoped that they will produce the first litter of wirehaired Vizslas in Britain.

The Wirehair is registered as a Hungarian Vizsla by the British Kennel Club. It is the same in Hungary although there are two separate breed *standards*. Everything that has been mentioned about the Shorthaired Vizsla also applies to the Wirehaired variation with the exception of hair. It was bred in the 1930's by foresters and game-keepers who interbred the Vizsla with the Wirehaired German Pointer. In Hungary greater emphasis is laid on the hunting performance than elegant appearance, although neither dogs with too loose or those with too short coats are permitted for breeding purposes. Many who have seen the Wirehaired working abroad are impressed by its drive and hunting ability.

The Wirehaired Vizsla's Coat

Desirable is a coat of thick, rough hair of about 3 to 4cm in length with considerable underwool. The hair is correspondingly shorter on head and legs, only the eyebrows and whiskers can be bushy whereas on the ears the hair is quite short and soft. With this weatherproof coat the Wirehaired Vizsla is of course more suitable for work during the cold periods. To lie quiet and wait on cold foggy mornings, or frosty autumn mornings, or to fetch wild duck out of icy water and then sit for hours in a boat must certainly be more bearable in a suitably warmer coat. Due to his good temperament, his intelligence and the many hunting qualities, he can stand up to competition against any old and well known breed.

The Longhaired Vizsla

The Longhaired Vizsla is not recognised as a separate breed in Hungary nor in any other country. There is no separate breed *standard* and in Britain they are registered as Hungarian Vizslas, as they are pure bred, although the coat varies from the *standard*, None have been seen in the show ring in Britain, but there are one or two in the field, but none have been trialled. They are not culled in this country as they are elsewhere. When they have appeared in litters from time to time, they are such delightful and attractive puppies they have not been difficult to sell. The 'Furries' look like an Irish Setter (it is said that an Irish Setter and a Vizsla were crossed a few generations back in Hungary). The coat is Vizsla colour and soft and fine.

Figure 3.8   Head of Wirehaired Vizsla

Fig. 3.9 The Vizsla enjoys the water as well as retrieving over all types of terrain (photo: Dr.S. Gottlieb)

CHAPTER 4

FEEDING AND EXERCISING THE VIZSLA

Feeding and exercising are so closely connected in this breed, that it is difficult to discuss one without the other. Good feeding and good exercise will produce excellent condition, whether your Vizsla is a pet, a show dog or used as a gundog, he needs the very best. A healthy Vizsla must be alert and lively, well muscled and lean. He must have no excess fat. Since his coat is so short, every ounce he takes off or puts on shows. This can certainly present a problem for some Vizslas can be picky eaters, and others never seem satisfied. The back bone should not show nor the ribs when standing, but if the ribs show slightly when he is bending that can give an indication that he is looking right. If he is too fat, those bulging sides are a sign of too many tit-bits! A dip just before the root of the tail can also indicate overweight. A healthy Vizsla of course has a glossy coat, bright eyes and a willingness to work, exercise and play.

DIET

No two people feed their dogs the same way. Each owner evolves his own formula, having found the one that suits his dog, if his condition is perfect, it is well worth sticking to it. A Vizsla does go off condition for no apparent reason. If he is working, this is bound to occur since he will be using so much energy one day and the following he may have little exercise. But it can still happen even though he is eating regular meals and taking regular exercise. It is no mean feat to keep a dog permanently in peak condition.

Some owners swear by dry dog foods, some by semi-moist foods and some by canned foods or meat by-products. Some will only feed raw meat, others would never dream of it. But one thing is certain; a gundog must have food that will give him plenty of stamina. A Vizsla could not work all day if he were only fed on tit-bits from the table, nor for that matter if he were fed on the most expensive fillet steak. He must have a correctly balanced diet and that means protein, carbohydrates, and fat, all being energy providers.

1. **PROTEIN** is the essential constituent of muscle. The main foods that provide this are all meats, eggs, cheese, milk and fish.

2. **CARBOHYDRATES** provide food most rapidly converted into energy, but excess is quickly converted into and stored as fat. The main foods that provide this are cereal and biscuit.

3.**FAT** is burned much more slowly than carbohydrates and is thus a reserve fuel. It is a source of vitamins A and D, essential for sound bone and tissue structure.

So whether it be a complete diet that is fed, and there are many on the market, or diet of meat and biscuit with other additives, the Vizsla needs a high quality, high protein diet since he uses up so much energy and he needs to be a dog full of vitality.

So, let's consider quantities and here I am going to give the quantities and the type of food that I feed. I do not expect every one to agree with it, but it is the method that I have found suits all my dogs, the old and the young and it also suits me! I feed a high quality, complete dry food. I also add meat and good stock to that, which provides extra protein that I feel this type of dog needs, so they get beef, chicken, lamb, turkey, fish or tripe, or whatever I can find that is cheapest at the time. This is partly because to be in top condition for those who are showing, breeding and working, that extra protein is vital. It also encourages them to eat the boring processed food, although I have one or two who would eat Charlie Chaplin's boot-laces anytime! A fastidious eater prefers to have his palate tantalised by apple cores or lettuce leaves or even a little grated carrot, or Camembert cheese is never to be sniffed at! The quantities of feed given to an adult Vizsla are:

1½ lbs of complete food a day
and
1½ lbs of extra protein a day

If I were feeding a non-complete diet, that is, meat or some sort of protein and biscuit, plus the additives necessary, vitamins and minerals, the quantities would be the same as above.

If you mean to have your adult Vizsla a perfect specimen it is essential that he is correctly fed from birth, first by the dam, then by the breeder who weans him onto his first solid food and then by the owner who, on acquiring the new puppy should follow the diet sheet provided to the letter. Even if the feeding programme does not seem to be the best, it is only fair to the puppy and his digestive system to follow the diet his tummy knows and accepts until he is totally established in his new surroundings. Then if his diet needs changing, do it gradually, step by step. Never change two foods at the same time, for if the puppy is upset and he is sick or has diarrhoea it is impossible to know which new food has caused it. So slowly, slowly. Do not be too eager. Better still, if you respect the breeder, perhaps his way may be the best! When you need to try something new, give it at just one meal. If the puppy is upset do not give it again. Try after a week or two when he may be able to cope with it. Go back to the food you know agrees with him and then when there is no sign of upset, try another food. If you do need advice on feeding ask someone you respect and whose own dogs look fit and stick to their recommendations. If you seek help from several, you will not know where you are and your puppy certainly will not know where he is.

The puppy's diet has to have the correct amount of proteins, carbohydrates, fats, vitamins and minerals as do the adults, but in his case these foods need to be palatable so that he will eat the correct amount. They must be the right consistency so that his tender young stomach can digest them. Since his baby teeth cannot really deal with chewing and breaking up food and later on as the first teeth fall out and the second teeth begin to appear, the mouth can be very sore and the puppy may go right off his food. Therefore his food needs to be fairly soft until his adult teeth have come right through. The puppy will certainly need other bones or objects to gnaw on (preferably not the human hand or chair legs etc). As you prepare the food be guided by him and you will see what consistency suits him best.

By the time the puppy is four or five months old, he will probably be on three meals a day. I say probably because all puppies are different. Some drop the third meal quite early on, others continue until about six months old. If they seem to be bored by the cereal and milk meal, drop it, remembering to increase the quantities of the two remaining meals. As the puppy grows, and at this time of his life his growth rate is enormous, obviously his food must be increased, and it is helpful to decide on a particular day each week to add another ounce or two.

Figure 4.1 Two healthy youngsters (bred by Mrs J Perkins) (photo: Diane Pearce)

Sample Diet for a Puppy from 3–6 Months

1st Meal   Cereal or biscuit meal, or minced morsels plus Complan or powdered or cow's milk (to begin with, it is best to dilute cow's milk)

2nd Meal   Complete food or biscuit meal (softened with stock or hot water, meat raw or cooked and cut into small pieces)

3rd Meal   Complete food or biscuit meal with meat (prepared as above)

He can now have Bonios or a good hard biscuit last thing at night.

To this feeding programme I would add vitamins, e.g. Canovel, for the first six months, but it is always sensible to be advised by your vet.

It cannot be emphasised too strongly that regular meals are important. As a baby cries if his meal is late, so a puppy needs the same attention.

A Vizsla eating on his own often seems to be a problem. He becomes choosy, especially when a puppy or young adult. As he matures, the problem seems to resolve itself. If a dog is eating in competition with others the problem rarely arises. Of course this does not include a sick dog. It is difficult to recognise whether the Vizsla with his sensitivity feels the tension and worry of the owner or whether he genuinely is not hungry at times. But there is no doubt that a vicious circle can develop. The more the owner worries and fusses, the less likely the dog is to complete his feed.

I have a Vizsla who will not eat until all six others feeding with her have licked their bowls clean. She waits until one of them cannot resist the temptation of taking a quick nibble of hers then she leaps to the bowl and finishes it off as if she were starving! This pattern has continued for two years!

If a Vizsla puts on too much weight, it is simple enough to cut the amount he is being fed. But if he is too thin and will not eat the correct amount, that is much more of a problem. I find it is unwise to leave food down. It does not help to stimulate the appetite. If the dog does not eat his meal take it away and three or four hours later put fresh food down — if you can afford it! Old fly blown food does not stimulate the appetite. I find it better policy to feed my dogs twice a day, firstly because one enormous meal seems a lot to give all in one go. Secondly, having had another breed that was prone to bloat, it was always recommended to feed two meals a day, and thirdly, if there are one or two finicky ones they seem to prefer a small amount at a time.

If I do have a poor eater, there are various ploys I have up my sleeve to encourage the appetite. Cheese sprinkled over the food or good tasty stock often does the trick. Pieces of delicious shoulder of lamb raw or cooked mixed in the food some cannot resist. This is expensive but ideal. There is a lot of fat on this cut and can put those few ounces on in no time. A teaspoon or two of Marmite well mixed in can be tempting. Sainsbury's Yeast Extract has saved many a Vizsla from looking like a toast rack. It contains vitamin B which also helps to stimulate the appetite as do yeast tablets, obtained from any chemist. Many a time have I sat handing out minced morsels and Bonios to a Vizsla who has gone off peak form. Many dogs find tripe irresistible and therefore worth trying.

I do not allow my dogs to have bones. I know they are supposed to be good for the teeth, but I find the problems they cause are not worth the worry. They create endless arguments between the Vizslas who normally get on very well together. I have been so brainwashed by warnings from vets as to the possible dangers of pieces of small bone causing obstruction, resulting in life-saving operations or having had a dog with a chicken bone wedged across the roof of his mouth piercing the skin, I believe them absolutely and do not want to take risks. If you feel that it is essential that you give your Vizsla a bone, never give cooked bones, the reason being that they break easily and a dog will swallow the splinters. A large uncooked shin bone is the least likely to splinter although if determined, an adult Vizsla can break one up.

As you will have noticed, a dog will slink off with a bone, he will even bury it if he does not want to eat it straight away. If he is allowed to take it off and deal with it somewhere on his own, all well and good. But if you expect him to eat his bone in your house, in your human world, gnawing it by your fireside, you are asking him to deal with a confusing issue. Bones seem to be part of his primitive animal world. They can stir up feelings of aggression in some dogs, whatever breed. Many a time he will growl to protect his bone. On the one hand his animal instincts are being induced by you but on the other he has to deal with them in a way that is alien to him.

If you deal with him and his bone when he is a puppy he may be able to accept that he has to be civilised. If you give him the bone and then firmly take it away, dig some of the marrow out and give it to him, then return the bone talking to him all the time. He may learn that you are giving him a treat that only you can. Since he cannot reach the marrow, he will appreciate the help. But if your dog remains 'chancy' over a bone, it is not sensible to allow him one. Never allow your Vizsla to get you in a position where you are afraid of him. This particular issue is such a one unless you are absolutely sure of yourself.

Obviously it is important that your dog has something that he can gnaw on. There is nothing harmful in a large beef hide bone or other items like this that are on the market. They do not seem to produce such strong reactions as does the real thing.

EXERCISE

A working Vizsla is well on his way to attaining his full potential. Work satisfies his need to use his intelligence, his gundog instincts, his powerful body, his wish to serve his master and his need to enjoy a close relationship with a human. If he does not work then it is obvious that his needs should be satisfied by other means.

He needs space to run, freedom to play, greenery to root about in, good scents, fresh air to sniff and plenty of room to stretch his long legs. He needs at least an hour of energetic exercise a day. He should be taken out for a walk. A dog does not exercise himself by pottering about in the garden on his own. A Vizsla's sparkling coat and good condition is all to do with feeding and exercise and very little to do with what grooming aids you use. A poorly muscled, miserable, fretting, shy Vizsla

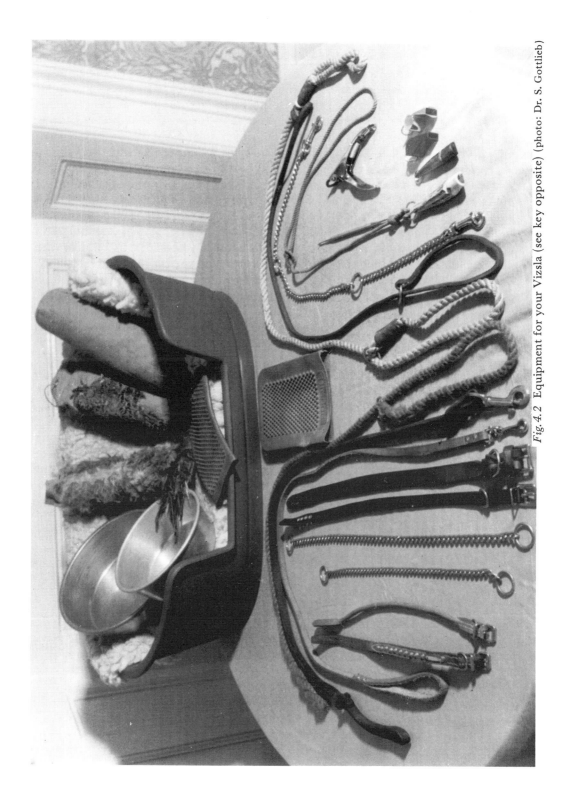

Fig. 4.2 Equipment for your Vizsla (see key opposite) (photo: Dr. S. Gottlieb)

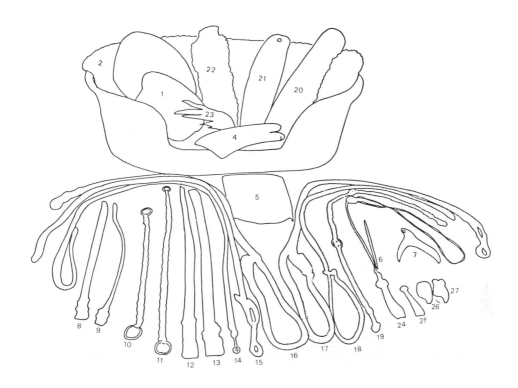

EQUIPMENT FOR YOUR VIZSLA
FOR THE PUPPY, FOR THE ADULT, FOR WORKING, FOR SHOWING, AND GENERAL CARE

All these items listed I have selected as the most practical over the years. Of course, it is a matter of individual preference and each owner will know what suits him and his dog best.

KEY: See Photograph

1.   **BOWLS**
     Two metal bowls, one for food and one for water, which should be available at all times. Plastic bowls are not advisable for this breed, the Vizsla has strong sharp teeth and although he is not generally a "chewer" a plastic bowl is tempting.

2.   **RUG**
     This type of soft covering is warm and easily machine washed, it is also almost indestructible.

3.   **BOX**
     This type of bed although not so aesthetic as a basket, will last much longer, easily washed and indestructible. They come in different sizes, the medium or large is ideal for the Vizsla.

4 & 5 **RUBBER GLOVES**
     These two rubber gloves, one with a thumb and the other without, are recommended for removing hair and dirt as well as toning up the muscles.

6.   **RASP**
     For scraping the teeth. Can be obtained from the vet, dentist or good pet shop.

7.   **NAIL CLIPPERS**
     This type are the best on the market, more expensive than most but well worth the extra money. The Vizslas nails are very strong and need sturdy well-made clippers.

COLLARS
8 & 9 LEATHER PUPPY COLLARS
Two small light collars with buckles, either one of these are ideal for the puppy's first venture out. I do not recommend a slip lead and collar because the puppy can choke easily and become frightened, his movements are very erratic and it is difficult for the handler to anticipate which way the puppy is going from one moment to the next.

10 & 11 CHOKE CHAINS
Some Vizslas never need a choke chain but there are others who definitely benefit from correction sterner than the word 'Heel'. A choke chain must only be used by the handler who knows how it functions. A puppy of three months old needs correction and discipline it is often kinder to use a choke chain correctly, than the alternative which is to berate the dog incessantly, meanwhile allowing him to do just as he wishes.

12 & 13 BENCHING COLLARS
The black webbing collar is smart and light. The handmade unstitched leather collar is of the highest quality soft leather and very strong.

LEADS
14 & 15 LEATHER LEADS
The smaller of these two leads is for the puppy collars. A little light lead which does not need to be tough is all that is necessary for the first few months. The larger lead is good quality soft leather, hand made with no stitching. The spring clip is very strong and allows for quick release. It is used in conjunction with the choke chain for obedience training.

16. SLIP LEADS
A light cotton and nylon lead for the well trained Vizsla used when a dog has to be "on a lead" but could manage perfectly well without one. Would not be practical for a dog who pulls!

17. WORKING SLIP LEAD
This lead is expensive, made of nylon rope and fine leather. It is tough weather proof and washable ideal for the gundog out in all weather conditions. A leather lead is not advisable to use if it is likely to get wet, it becomes soggy and slippery to hold.

18 LIGHT SHOW SLIP LEAD
There are many different types of show lead on the market. This lead suits a gundog and it is strong enough to check a dog, easy on the hands and looks workmanlike.

19 BENCHING CHAIN
Essential equipment to go with the benching collar. The chain is long enough to allow the dog freedom to lie down. The two clips are on swivels so that the dog is less likely to get tangled up. One clip is attached to the collar and the other to the bench ring.

DUMMIES
These dummies are all used for the initial gundog training in early retrieving work. All can be home made.

20 THE CANVAS DUMMY OF MEDIUM WEIGHT

21 THE CANVAS DUMMY WITH PHEASANT WING
This dummy familiarizes the gundog with the feel of feather (but not the scent).

22 THE CANVAS DUMMY WRAPPED IN A RABBIT SKIN
It can be sewn round or kept in place with rubber bands. The soft fur familiarizes the dog with the feel of fur (not the scent).

23 A PHEASANT WING
This little wing is for a puppy or adolescent, it accustoms him to the shape and strangeness of the feathers in his mouth.

A SELECTION OF WHISTLES FOR THE GUNDOG
24
A whistle and adjustable cord to hang round the handler's neck. Any type of whistle can be attached to it. This whistle is made of horn, it is the very best quality, a good shape to hold and the tone is neither too harsh nor too loud.
25
A cheaper version of the horn whistle, made in plastic and not so heavy.

26 & 27 STOP WHISTLES
These two whistles can be used as "stop" whistles. A good blast on one of these should halt and steady a trained dog if he is not heeding his handler. One is the referee-type whistle in plastic and the other a police-type whistle in metal, hard on the mouth and inclined to rust.

who has lost the use of his natural instincts is what you will have without correct exercise.

One of the top field trainers in America, Paul Sabo, considers the Vizsla to be generally more highly strung than other pointing breeds. Whether this is so or not, an owner can treat the Vizsla in such a way that the dog can become totally hysterical and out of hand. Nowhere can it be demonstrated more clearly than when being exercised. If he is encouraged to tear about, chasing sticks or leaping up and down for bouncing balls while the owner shrieks the dog's name, telling him to do this and that and never expecting him to obey for one moment, in no time the dog will become as witless as its owner. All hope of that Vizsla working would be lost.

A puppy needs gentle playing exercise until he is about three months old, to grow strong, sturdy and sound. After that he should have restricted exercise, plenty of play and short walks partly on the lead and partly off. This way he learns the discipline of walking to heel and has the freedom he needs when off the lead. At no time should he be allowed to tire or wear himself out. This will only take off weight and since his bones are still quite soft at this age, his whole bone structure can alter if too much physical strain is put upon him.

If your puppy plays in the garden with your children, try to teach all to play gently and calmly as they would have to with a toddler. Children's wild games will only cause him to become over-excited, teaching him habits that are difficult to cure such as non-stop barking, nipping and holding onto clothes. All this may seem fun at the time, but as he grows to adulthood he can become an anti-social nuisance and a problem. By that time he will find it very difficult to control himself. If he learns mental discipline when a puppy, this does not mean repression but exactly the opposite, I mean helping to train him to use his natural resources, respecting him as an animal instead of using him as a plaything for humans.

By four months any self respecting puppy if taught sensibly, should be able to walk to heel on the lead and, dare I say it, off the lead! He should sit on command, on and off the lead, should stay, not for any length of time perhaps but at least absolutely steady with you by him and at a short distance. If you are gentle and firm he will enjoy his lessons. All this can be done as you exercise him. Thus he will learn to behave when he is out You will find he is not difficult to teach to come to you when you call. The more you work with him, the more attached he will be. His responsiveness will improve every day, your walks bringing great enjoyment to you both as he develops and matures into a sensible dog. One of the joys of a Vizsla is that he will rarely let you out of his sight. Many times I have tried to hide from mine but never succeeded nor have I ever lost one, however far they range they always seem to have you in sight.

As your Vizsla matures, whatever you intend doing with him — showing, working or as a companion — basic exercise and training is very necessary and well worthwhile, he can take more and more exercise as he grows on and develops.

You can expect him to obey your commands without making allowances as you would when he was a young puppy. On the lead never allow your dog to cock his leg at every corner, nor should he sniff at every person or dog that he passes. Teach him to walk quietly by your side.

When he is off the lead let him range wide, giving him every opportunity to be independent and think for himself. It is especially important to allow him to do this if you wish to work your Vizsla. If he is over trained in obedience, particularly in heel work, when he has to stay close, the Vizsla can become too dependent on his owner, waiting for orders anxiously, becoming tense and over excited, not wishing to leave his owner's side. If you are aware of this and recognise it happening you can usually solve the problem by letting the pressure off. Allow him to walk quite loosely on the lead. Forget the sit and stay exercise close to you, try to do more distance work, but a little at a time. If that does not cure the problem forget any formal training for a week or two and encourage him to run freely. Do not call him if he begins to range far, it is rare that this one will go out of sight! A good tip I was given by a gundog trainer that particularly seems to apply to the Vizsla was, "Any fool can get a gundog to walk to heel, It's getting him out on a 'send-away', teaching him to be steady when he's at distance, that's the difficult one ". It is easy to train a Vizsla in basic obedience, he learns so quickly, sometimes too quickly for his own peace of mind. This is when he can come unstuck. Too much pressure too early will either make him very bored by the whole thing and dig his toes in or worse, he will become senseless and stupid.

If you are lucky enough to have water nearby, encourage your Vizsla to swim. Most love the water and take to it naturally. Allow a puppy to paddle about on the edge. If you throw something in and make it a game at first, he will soon learn to swim. The water retrieve is a lovely sight to see and should be one of the Vizsla's natural abilities and essential if you want to work him, for he has to retrieve in and out of the water. Some of my Vizslas plunge in and out of the water as a normal part of their exercise. They love the sea, leaping into the waves putting their heads beneath the water to search for seaweed. They will swim far out with any member of the family willing to swim with them. So whether you exercise your dog in the country or in your local park, it is possible to train him up to a point, if not providing a pheasant or two, at least he could acquit himself as an intelligent, well behaved dog that is a pleasure to be with.

If you show your dog or you have a puppy and wish to show him, it may be necessary to change your exercise routine at times, especially as the all important show looms ahead. I have discussed basic exercise and all it can entail. If you show, there is a specific type of exercise your Vizsla needs in order to have him in top condition.

This means his body must have achieved the highest possible muscle tone throughout. This allows him efficient muscle co-ordination under any condition, at work or at rest. If he has too little muscle tone, is too fat or too thin, or has too much muscle, his ability to function correctly will be limited. So the type of exercise he needs will be based on developing every muscle he has and the best way this can be achieved is to give him gentle, rhythmical, steady trotting or walking day after day on hard ground. It does not have to be as boring as it sounds. Choose a walk that has hard and soft ground. Give him half a mile trotting or walking on the lead with his head up — he cannot develop neck muscle if his head is down — when his head is held correctly the rest of the body will be properly balanced, allowing all the muscles to come into play. Trotting is the natural pace for the dog. If you jog at the same time you will both be as fit as a fiddle. If there is a bike handy there is nothing like making your dog do all the work while you sit back. Give your Vizsla three or four weeks of this form of exercise, allowing him to run freely for the other half of the walk and there will be a marked difference. It may also tighten up his loose elbows, feet and pasterns as well as creating a second thigh you never knew he had.

The judge Percy Whittaker once said to me, "I like your dog, but for goodness sake get on a bike". I had no idea what he meant and asked him to explain. "Look at his front. It needs to tighten up. His bones are good enough but he needs his muscles tightened." Three months I pedalled and my dog trotted. It did the trick. The dog became a show champion and gained thirteen championship certificates. The trotting treatment cannot improve incorrect bone structure, it can only improve the muscle tone. Never try it too early — one and a half years old is soon enough. Otherwise the strain on undeveloped limbs could cause problems and create deformities.

There is no reason why a Vizsla cannot be exercised in any weather, if he is taken out in snow, rain or heat he will adapt. Although his coat seems thin, if he is used to the cold he will not mind. A working Vizsla may be out in the wet all day with no ill effects at all. If the caring owner cossets him too much he will find the change from duvet to winter weather difficult to adjust to, but treated sensibly, he is delighted to accompany you at all times, encouraging you to roll in the snow, swim, walk, trot, jog or amble, whichever you wish as long as you are out together. He is not a dog for those who do not like to brave the elements, nor is he suitable for those who do a quick turn round the block and back to bed. He is a dog who must have exercise and should not be denied that for one day of his life.

Figure 4.3 (left) Start Training Early: the dog should look "free" (photo Diane Pearce)

Fig. 4.3 Mrs. B. Douglas-Redding "Elder Statesman of the Breed" shows how with Sh.Ch. *Wolfox Fabia*

Figure 4.4 Fitness should be the aim – a muscular dog of 14 months (bred by the author)

CHAPTER 5

GENERAL CARE OF THE VIZSLA

Routine grooming, nail clipping, care of the teeth, ears and eyes should be started from puppyhood, thus he will learn that they are part of his life just as he has to accept his collar and lead.

CARE OF THE NAILS

Click, click, click, click, I hear as we walk down the road. I know what that means — his nails are too long. I knew they were too long last week, why do I always put the job off? Because my Vizsla hates having his nails cut. Force, pleading, anger, even a stocking over the head (highly recommended) will not work. My own inexperience and an acquaintance's over-enthusiasm to help gave him a poor start. The first time my dog's nails were cut every single nail bled, the result being a Vizsla with an aversion to anyone touching his feet, let alone cutting the nails. To make matters worse, I persuaded a member of the family to hold him while I did the cutting but this was no answer, we struggled away while he panicked and we lost our tempers with him and each other. Another member of the family passing by this dreadful scene asked innocently, "Why does he need his nails cut anyway?'

Well, many years of experience later, the answer remains the same. Nails need to be cut. The nail grows in a curve and if it grows too long at worst it can curve back into the foot, but before it reaches that condition, it touches the ground. As the foot is placed on the ground, the pressure will force the toes and pads apart because the nails will touch the ground first. This will cause such discomfort that the dog will try to shift his weight off his forehand to his quarters, thus he will not be balanced correctly, creating a sort of strutting action in the front. If the nails are short, the pads will touch the ground first and if the foot is correct the muscles will keep the foot sufficiently tight to bear the weight correctly.

It is generally believed that a dog with a good front and correct movement will automatically wear his nails to the correct length if given enough road work. However, I have dogs with poor fronts who do not need their nails cut and dogs with good fronts who do.

A small puppy has sharp claws that can scratch his dam and his siblings, so it is important that they are cut when he is very young and of course it is a good opportunity to condition him to the practice of having his nails attended to regularly. To start with, when he is tiny use a pair of the smallest nail scissors, his nails will be too soft to cope with the guillotine type of cutters which I find the best type of the older Vizsla. Never be tempted to cut the nail too far back, even if your

Vizsla is behaving himself. Cutting a little and often and never to the point when he winces, avoids the trauma of giving the dog pain and a bleeding nail. Once he is hurt he will begin to fear the whole operation. It is very easy to cut too much off, because it is very difficult to identify the blood supply in order to avoid it.

Arterial blood is brought from the heart with each heartbeat to the entire body. As the arteries get smaller and smaller they are known as arterioles; and finally they narrow down to only allow the passage of one blood cell at a time. These very fine tubes are the capillaries, a fine network which allows the oxygen of the blood to pass freely into the tissues and carbon dioxide from the tissues to enter the capillaries and back to the heart through the veins. In the nails the same process occurs but the terminal arterioles are more exposed and are near the tip of the nail. Thus, when cutting the nail carefully, the pink you observe is the network of capillaries which will not bleed but obviously if you cut further back, the artery will be severed.

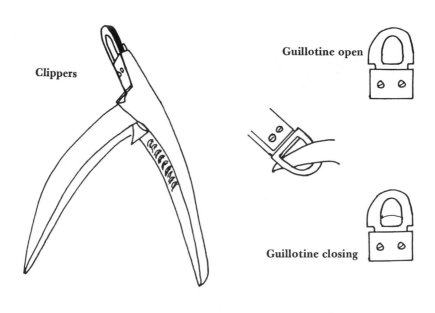

Figure 5.1 Guillotine Nail Clippers (suitable for the Vizsla's strong nails)

I have found a method of cutting nails which suits me and my Vizslas. I make the sitting arrangements as comfortable as possible. A large armchair, good light, and some biscuits are provided. I sit on the chair, my dog behind me or lounging on my knee. I have the bisucits to my right but these are only to be used as a reward. I gently pick up one paw, holding it loosely in my left hand. I cut one claw a little at a time and deftly reward him with a small piece of biscuit from my right hand and praise him. Part of the trick is to talk to him "non-stop" which will reassure him to the point of boredom. I insist that he remains sitting or lying and that he never gets off the chair. If you are determined enough in your own mind that you are going to remain gentle, calm and firm, the most difficult customers who have had years of non-co-operation, dare I say it, succumb in the end! It may take a few sessions, but each one will become shorter and the dog more confident that you are not going to hurt him.

If you do make a nail bleed and it has caused discomfort, without fuss take the other paw and token cut at least one or two nails in order that your Vizsla keeps his confidence in you (as a rider is advised to re-mount after a fall).If he settles, finish cutting the nails on the paw that was bleeding.

This method excludes severe chastisement or force, so nail cutting days are no longer a dreaded task but are taken in our stride. I have written at length on this subject because it is raised so often as a problem. Having tried so many methods myself, I understand why it should be so.

CARE OF THE EARS

If there is dirt clinging to the outside of the ear the Vizsla usually can shake it off when it dries. Because the inside of the Vizsla's ear is hairless, it should keep clean, but this is not necessarily the case. The Vizsla's coat is quite greasy and so is his ear, so the inside of the ear should be inspected periodically because it may need cleansing. Usually, the dank deposit you see in the inner ear is a mixture of wax and dirt. It is never advisable to poke about with a cotton wool bud or a piece of material twisted round a matchstick. It is dangerous to force anything into the tender regions and narrow passages of the inner ear.

The outer ear can be cleansed with cotton wool dipped into a mild solution of witch hazel or with a little olive oil. Witch hazel leaves them smelling sweeter. If the wax and dirt is difficult to remove from the inner ear an infallible remedy is the application of a few drops of Otodex. It softens and frees the secreted wax which the dog can then shake out. It is simple to apply. My vet recommended this treatment and on reading *The Dog's Medical Dictionary*, (first edition published in 1906) the author, A J Sewell MRVCUS, suggested using Otodex — And I always thought it was the latest remedy on the market! It can be bought at some chemists and of course at any good pet shop.

If your Vizsla shakes his head flapping his ears constantly, it is advisable to consult the vet. He may have ear mites or an ear infection that should be attended to professionally.

CARE OF THE EYES

The Vizslas's eyes need little attention, if they are neither deep nor prominent and the eyelids fit closely as the *standard* requires. If there is a slight accumulation of mucus in the corner of the eyes on waking, it can be removed by soaking a small piece of cotton wool dipped in salt solution — enough salt to cover a sixpence in half a cup of warm water! For those of you who are too young to remember what a sixpence looks like, one teaspoon of salt and one pint of warm water. Bathe each eye with a separate piece of cotton wool thus avoiding transmitting any possible infection from one eye to the other. Always wipe the eye from the inner corner to the outer corner. If there is any discharge of pus which persists, take advice from your vet.

Figure 5.2 The eyes should be free from mucus

CARE OF TEETH

The cleanliness and health of the gums are important. If the teeth are neither dis-coloured nor have deposits of tartar, there is no need to treat them. Up until the age of two years a good diet and plenty to chew is usually sufficient to keep them healthy. But as the Vizsla ages, tartar often forms at the gum margin. This is the name given to the brown, yellow and black matter which hardens into a claculus, spreading under the gum. If it is not treated, it can cause deterioration of the gum causing tenderness and bleeding and become infected, causing offensive breath. The teeth can be cleaned with a toothbrush and toothpaste, also the teeth and gums can be swabbed with cotton wool or gauze dipped in salt or bicarbonate of soda. I find hydrogen peroxide most beneficial, the bubbling action cleansing between the teeth as well as the gums. If the tartar persists to a degree, a dentist's scaling instrument can be very effective, otherwise it may have to be removed by the vet under anaesthetic.

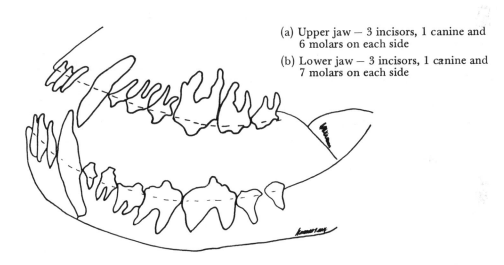

(a) Upper jaw — 3 incisors, 1 canine and 6 molars on each side

(b) Lower jaw — 3 incisors, 1 canine and 7 molars on each side

Figure 5.3 Permanent Teeth

Figure 5.4 Dentist's Scaling Instrument for removing tartar

89

CARE OF THE COAT

I appreciate the Vizsla's short coat having owned a long-coated breed. His smooth coat requires little routine grooming except when moulting and this he does moderately. I find a rubber glove the most effective. It can be bought at most shows from one of the many stands. This glove fits over the hand like a mitten. When used on a youngster go gently or he may find it too painful, but used on an adult a thorough rub-down stimulates the circulation and the secretion of the natural oils as well as toning up the muscles. Any loose hair or dirt will come away. Polish the coat with a velvet duster or a piece of silk and the Vizsla coat will shine with added lustre. It is not necessary to bath the Vizsla, even before a show. If his coat is really muddy give him a good swim. Shampooing his coat will remove the natural oiliness of his coat and tends to produce dandruff. If a Vizsla is pampered, he will behave as if he is. Keep him hardy, bathing him and allowing him to wear a coat will not help him if he has to stand in the rain for long which he may have to do if he works or shows. On the other hand, if he has had a pleasurable roll in some disgusting mess, you may be forced to bathe him!

If a Vizsla is kennelled, his coat may become dusty and scruffy. Try to give him a rub-down with one of the dry shampoos (there are many on the market) wiping it well into the coat rubbing it up the wrong way as well, then rub him down with a soft duster, and his coat will probably gleam if he is in good condition.

In America, it is the custom to trim the facial whiskers. In England, so far, the whiskers endearingly remain!

Finally, ears that smell, a breath that smells or a coat that smells can indicate that the dog is not well. When a dog has a temperature, his coat often has a musty smell, so the warning signal should not be ignored. It is best to call your vet.

CAR SICKNESS

Many young puppies are sick in the car, apart from the unpleasant task of clearing up, it does not need to be taken too seriously and generally the youngster grows out of it as he becomes habituated to the motion of the car. Rarely does it continue into adulthood. Most Vizslas love the car and are very good travellers, but there are exceptions which lead us to wonder what causes car and travel sickness.

The condition in animals is based in the main on some disfunction in the inner ear. In all mammals the inner ear is fundamentally concerned with the maintenance of balance. It consists of the labyrinth which is three semi-circular canals all structured at right angles to one another, each consisting of very fine cartilage and containing fluid called the endolymph. This fluid does not quite fill the canals. With whatever movement either slight or violent of the head in space there will be a shift in the levels of the endolymph in the semi-circular canals. This will immediately be transmitted to the higher centres in the brain where the movement is at once appreciated at the level of consciousness and so the animal makes immediate adjustments to its position in order to retain its balance.

Therefore when travelling along a road the car makes all manner of deviations in terms of its horizontal angle the animal will experience frequent shifts of his head and body angle, causing the fluid balance in the semi-circular canals to change. The dog's brain receives a message that imbalances are occurring and immediately the animal adjusts his head and body to rectify the movement. But if there is any impairment in the inner ear such as injury, infection, or inflammation the fluid levels may be affected therefore the nervous impulses to the brain will be impaired and the animal will not be able to adjust his head and body accordingly, therefore he will suffer from giddiness, nausea and vomiting.

A puppy of 7 weeks will travel more comfortably than an older puppy whose sense of awareness and fear is more developed in every way.

To try and avoid travel sickness in an animal never feed a puppy before he goes on a journey. He is less likely to be sick if he is in the front rather than the back of the car. Do not add to the puppy's problems by becoming apprehensive yourself because a dog will sense it and if his discomfort continues his own apprehension may be enhanced with the result that what began as a physical problem also becomes psychological. This may result in a dog developing fear of the car. He may become conditioned to fear travelling and this is the problem that eventually needs to be sorted out. Initially a visit to the vet is essential so that any infection, injury or inflammation can be dealt with. After that the dog must be re-conditioned — short car rides taken calmly and without fuss. These can be lengthened as he becomes re-assured and eventually he will gain confidence and with maturity the problem in most cases will be solved.

Occasionally the discomfort remains, either there is a deformity in the ear or the conditioning has been too efficient. I have an old bitch who still disappears if she anticipates a car ride. If I put her on the front seat where she is quite comfortable, she does not pant, she does not dribble, she just looks unhappy. She cannot forget.

GIVING YOUR VIZSLA MEDICATION

If your Vizsla's health on recovery from an illness depends on a form of medication, be it a pill or medicine, he is in a chancy situation if his owners hope that he is not bright enough to notice the goodies are wrapped up in his favourite piece of meat or crushed in a teaspoonful of raspberry jam placed in his tripe. If it is not eaten disguised or otherwise, it is no wonder his owners become agitated, they are counting on luck.

As in every other aspect of Vizsla ownership, if he is treated sensibly and firmly he will behave accordingly. A foolproof way of administering medication is to give it personally. Sit him between you and a kitchen unit, talk to him calmly and firmly, as you count out the pills place them on the surface of the unit, if he has to take medicine, have someone close by with it ready poured out on a teaspoon. Bend over your dog and with the left arm over the back of his neck (so he cannot move backwards easily) slip the first and second fingers of the left hand into the corner of his mouth on the off-side, placing the thumb into the corner of his mouth on the near-side as soon as his jaw relaxes, as you say "open" praising him, keep the 1st, 2nd and 3rd fingers in his mouth firmly and deftly put the pill into the back of his throat, pushing it as far as you can, quickly close his mouth and hold his mouth gently and he will swallow it down. Praise him but do not let him move until he has taken the prescribed amount.

If he has to take medicine, open his mouth as instructed, slip the teaspoon in from the side and tip the contents down his throat. It may be a messy job to begin with but with practice you will both become adept, and the medicine will go down in seconds! Praise your dog and he will feel pleased to have earned it.

THE VIZSLA BITCH IN SEASON

The first season can commence at nine months but could be as late as fifteen months. If the Vizsla bitch has not shown any sign of coming into season by then, perhaps it would be advisable to have your vet look at her. In general Vizslas seem to vary their season. The cycle should be every six months but many come in every eight or nine months.

The duration of the season or heat is from the first day to the twenty first. There are particular days in this cycle when a bitch ovulates. It is during this time that she will accept the male and if mated can conceive. It is generally understood that the tenth day to the fourteenth are the most likely day of oestrus. It is rare that if she were mated on the fifteenth day that she could conceive.

The pre-oestrus cycle commences when the vagina thickens, and the vulva swells, the skin colour changing from pink to grey. The early signs are not difficult to see because the Vizsla coat is so short. The second sign is the commencement of her discharge. This should be deep red. As the heat continues, the loss will usually lose colour becoming pink and even paler up to the day when she reaches oestrus.

Oestrus. This is the period when the ova are shed and the bitch "stands". This is the term used when she stands stock still with her tail twisted to one side, indicating that the male may mount her. Her discharge will be straw-coloured and almost negligible after the days of oestrus, then the discharge will disappear and the vulva will return to normal unless the bitch is in whelp when it may remain slightly enlarged.

These are some of the facts. It must be recognised that there are many variations at every step. It can be very bewildering. No two bitches behave alike. A bitch can vary her timing frome one season to another. Some bitches bleed profusely, others hardly at all. If there is little loss, it is difficult to follow the cycle, but fortunately it seems to have nothing to do with the bitch's fertility. I have a bitch who has borne 26 puppies in four litters in her time and she hardly bleeds at all. I also have a bitch who always has a pale pink discharge up until the twenty-first day whether she mates or not.

I have always found that a Vizsla in season is very meticulous; she cleans herself endlessly, her fastidiousness reaching the point of obsession!

Care of the Vizsla in Season

Take no risks; keep your bitch away from any chance encounter! From day one confine her. She may need to be kept away from dogs until the twenty-first day, whether she has been mated or not, although it is very unlikely that she could conceive after the fifteenth, but it could occur! Beware of your wish to take her out to give her a good run even though it may be before anyone stirs or late at night when the owls hoot. You may look around and to your surprise find two animals attached to your lead, one of them not a Vizsla! Better to confine her in an enclosed space and stay with her while she is outside — some dogs can climb over very high fences!

There are various anti-mate powders on the market. These can be useful towards the finish of the season, but such are nature's arrangements and so strong the Pheremones, if two animals want to mate and the time is right, no anti-mate is going to get in the way!

CHAPTER 6

WHETHER TO BREED OR NOT

If you have a Vizsla bitch, the inevitable question arises of whether to breed from her or not. Those who have been in the breed for any length of time will probably understand the market for Vizsla puppies, but for those who are new to the breed and have not had the opportunity to appreciate what breeding their bitch could entail, it would be as well to consider the pros and cons. It must be made quite clear that there is no profit in breeding Vizsla puppies. If they are well reared and cared for, costs may just be covered if the puppies are sold at seven or eight weeks old, but since the Vizsla is by no means a popular dog and is only for the specialist they are certainly not suitable for all homes. Anyone wishing to breed their bitch should consider where their responsibility lies.

There are some vital questions that need to be answered. Can you sell the puppies and if you cannot have you the facilities for keeping them as they grow?

If you sell a puppy to a home that turns out to be unsuitable are you prepared to take him back? Or will you care enough to spend many hours helping to rehouse him? If the answers are not in the affirmative, perhaps the next question should be how much is the breeder prepared to care for the puppies he has bred?

Is it good for a bitch to have a litter? It is debatable! Some vets agree that it is, many state that it is arbitrary. I feel the question is irrelevant now with so many dogs roaming the streets. Whether it is better for the bitch or not, what is the quality of life to be for the progeny? And if she produces say, five bitches are they also to be bred for their own good? In my experience, there has never been any significant change in a bitch's behaviour after producing a litter. A silly excitable type of animal does not transform into an intelligent sedate sensible matron. She usually reverts back to all that she ever was, showing no sign of maternal fulfillment, satisfaction, or happiness after the puppies have gone. Her figure may be a little fuller, but not necessarily so since ageing can have the same effect.

So what is in store for the young she bears? Some novice breeders discover too late — not much!

The potential purchaser may want a puppy for showing, for working or as a pet. If he wants a Vizsla for showing, he will, if he is sensible, go to a breeder who has had some success in this field and is knowledgeable about it. If he wants one for working, knowing that the best gundogs come from stock (trained to point, hunt and retrieve), he will go to a reputable breeder, known for that particular strain. So where does this leave the pet owner with ten puppies? It must be made clear that a litter reared in the warmth of the kitchen with plenty of loving care from all the family and every desire satisfied have received the start in life they need. But the only market is other pet owners, and how are they found? There are all those friends who so wanted a Vizsla puppy, but they tend to fade away when the puppy is a reality! Or there is the owner of the stud dog who can sometimes provide help. Advertising in the dog papers, or magazines such as *The Field* or *Shooting Times* can produce many customers or none, depending on the time of year and whether there are other Vizsla litters born at the same time. For example, a litter ready for homes in July or August is generally a difficult time of year for selling, as nobody wishes to take a young puppy on holiday. Neither does anyone want a puppy at their feet over the Christmas season (let us assume that no one would wish to sell a puppy for a child's Christmas stocking!).

The delightful little Vizsla puppies are no longer sucking. Their doe-eyed mother no longer cleans after, looks or gazes at her offspring, warm and contented, unable to use their tiny legs with their feet and nails so perfect and untried, eyes shut, tails still long, tiger stripes not yet dry. Imagine what will those few you cannot sell be like at twelve weeks? Even advertising has not relieved you of all of them, and some of the replies you refused because they did not seem suitable homes. But by now you are feeling desperate, and any home would do! You cannot accommodate or contain these sharp-toothed, chewing, lively puppies who escape from anything into anywhere, capable of such destruction and mess, let alone smell.

The conclusion is that proper facilities for puppies are vital. If these are provided, unsold puppies can be accommodated easily, thus relieving the necessity of making a quick and possibly unsuitable sale.

Choosing a home for a puppy under pressure can frequently result in a decision you might later come to regret. So far, we do not have a Rescue Service for Hungarian Vizslas, although it could become necessary in the future, if those who breed do not take care.

The Cost of Whelping (A Cautionary Tale)

This is a sample of the sort of problems that a Vizsla breeder may have to face if things do not go according to plan and the bitch has a difficult time whelping. It is as well to know what you may be in for in terms of time and cost:

> The bitch had started to whelp in the middle of the night, had four puppies and then stopped. She had no more whelps for two hours, so we called the vet. She attended to the bitch and more puppies followed. She promised to return if there were further problems, and indeed, there were. Two more anxious hours followed, with no sign of a puppy. The bitch was by now in great distress. Out came the vet again, and to our great relief, more puppies arrived safe and sound. There are now ten beautiful puppies and the vet leaves.

The bitch and whelps were, no doubt, saved by the prompt attention and skill of the vet. However, in many areas, vets cannot be called out at any time of the day or night. They insist on the animal being taken to the surgery. This could cost you not only the vet's fees, but also the life of the bitch and her pups. There follows a sample account for one litter of pups:

VETERINARY ACCOUNT FOR ONE WHELPING
(based on average veterinary fees)

First visit plus treatment
Second visit plus treatment   £40

If the bitch has not managed to whelp her puppies it would be necessary for her to have them by caesarean section or she could lose all her puppies.
Cost of operation — approx. £100

Normal post-whelping costs (for 10 pups)
Post whelping check by vet plus cost of injection or
treatment if necessary —   £14 +

Visit by vet to remove dew claws, dock tails and a general check-up
after whelping — £14 plus £1.50 per pup — Total =   £29

Usual protective injections at £12 per pup —   £120

Worming programme starting at 5 weeks, for example
1 bottle of Antipar —   £2.45

Total cost — approx £305

Provision Necessary for Puppies After Leaving the Whelping Box
It seems appropriate at this stage to discuss the provisions needed for puppies once they can climb out of their whelping box. The bitch has, by this time, decided that she is happy anywhere but with her demanding team of puppies. She will go to them to relieve the discomfort of her breasts filling with milk, but prefers to leave them before she is mauled and scratched by them. This takes place around the fourth or fifth week after whelping, and at this stage the puppies will have commenced weaning. They need to be removed to a place where they can run and play in an enclosed area — not the kitchen! Before they are born, one fondly imagines a few sweet puppies tottering about one's feet, never needing to urinate or defaecate. It is unbelievable how a litter of puppies can wreck a room in no time at all once they are running about. Ideally, the puppies need a place to sleep, a place to play in the warmth, free from draughts, and an outside area of concrete safely wired and puppy proof where they can play when the weather is fine. They need a place outside when the weather is good so they can feel the warmth of the sun on their backs, enjoy the fresh air, and feel the sense of freedom without coming to any harm.

Bedding
The indoor area needs some form of bedding, such as straw or shredded paper. I have never found that straw gives the puppies ticks or fleas, but they do sometimes smell of faeces and urine. Puppies kept on shredded newspaper are warmer, and they don't smell as the paper absorbs the mess immediately. The only disadvantage is that some shredded paper is grey and although harmless gives the puppies a grey, shop soiled appearance! However it is possible to find white shredded paper that does not do this. It is a very cheap form of bedding.

Space for Playing

This room or kennel should have plenty of space for the puppies to run freely. The pups can still sleep in their whelping box or a cosy, boarded in area off the ground at one end furthest from the door free from draughts. It should be made totally puppy-proof, so that they cannot escape; free from furniture of any use or value, a place for puppies rather than humans, the only furniture provided being their playthings! Of course, it must be heated, with plenty of natural light and a source of artificial lighting which is necessary for tending the puppies in the evening or at night.

Time for the puppies

I hope these few facts may help you to understand more clearly what breeding from your Vizsla bitch really entails. It is quite an undertaking. One item that has not been discussed at all so far is the amount of time it is necessary to spend on rearing a litter. This is infinite and I can only warn you that if done well, it is a non-stop job. It is impossible to have a full-time job and a litter of puppies as well. After weaning, they need to be fed four or five times a day so that by the time one meal is over and the dishes washed, it seems as if it is time for the next! Nevertheless, the unaccountable hours spent enjoying a litter, watching every move they make, many would say is the reason they like to breed. It is true that this period is only for a short while, if the puppies are sold at the right age. But everyone should be prepared for the certain disruption of the general household routine for an unknown length of time.

Undaunted, you may still feel you can manage a litter of puppies; you know you can find good homes, you are able to cover the costs, you have plenty of room for them, and you are satisfied that you have the time. Have you taken into account that enormous litter of eleven or twelve puppies who will need hand-rearing from the start because the dam has only seven nipples and not enough milk to go round? Supplementary feeding every two or three hours will be essential. It is impossible for a bitch to manage such a large litter on her own. Without intervention, you will have poor puppies and a very tired and exhausted mother.

If there are any deformed puppies in the litter, for example, one could have a cleft palate or a damaged limb, you will need to have them destroyed by the vet. A small, feeble whelp needs your constant attention, day and night, for he may be pushed out by the dam. Survival of the fittest is an instinct which is evident in a litter of pups. However we think of our Vizslas, they are still part of the animal world. Like all animals, they will deliberately push away the weakest.

Some breeders choose to keep only six or seven puppies in a litter, destroying the rest in order to leave the dam with the ideal number of whelps. She can then feed herself and they will not leave her drained. Culling comes easy to some, while others cannot countenance such a policy.

You will also need to decide what to do if you have a puppy with four white legs and a snow-white chest. Although a cosmetic fault, this is not allowed in the *standard* and is absolutely wrong for a Vizsla. In England to a pet owner, these faults may seem unimportant, but it may not be understood that if these Vizslas were bred from, the Vizslas could look like a different dog in no time at all. If this puppy is kept, he could go to a pet home, but must not be bred from — incorrect marking can easily be passed on. This should be the condition of the sale, but of course if homes are hard to come by, the breeder may not feel he can call the tune.

Do not feel that if you decide to keep a large litter, and are going to supplement feed by hand, that this in any way gives the puppies a bad start in life. It does not — on the contrary, it gives them a very good start. To feed from the mother and have such close contact with a human so early on will help the puppy thrive emotionally and physically, In fact, the process of imprinting by a human cannot start too early. The runt of the litter is often the best adjusted puppy of the lot, because he has been given special attention by the breeder.

To conclude, the bitch you own may have the home that gives her all she requires. Her puppies may not be so fortunate.

Your Bitch as a Brood Bitch

It is now necessary to consider the suitability of the bitch you own as a brood bitch. However fond you are of your Vizsla it is essential that you look at her from a breeder's point of view, so you have to be objective. Can she contribute to the breed? Can you appreciate her faults as well as her qualities? Read the breed *standard* so that you know it back to front, take a good look at as many other Vizslas as possible, and in this way you will learn more about your Vizsla by comparison. Be advised by others in the breed whom you respect.

A good brood bitch is invaluable as foundation stock for any kennel. She may not be the showy winner of all the prizes, or have the extra something that always catches the eye first, but a second look may reveal some of the essentials — a sound temperament, imperturbable outlook, composure, lack of nervousness, and a steadiness of character that you can trust. A good doer, she could work, make a good family companion or show with the best. This is the bitch who is most likely to care for her puppies and provide milk and security for them and hopefully contribute to the breed. The bitch to breed from should be strong, well built and fit. It is no good expecting her to produce good pups if she is not strong enough for the task. If she is not well muscled she will find it difficult to carry the weight of her whelps. If she has a saggy top-line, it will sag even further. If she has poor feet and weak pasterns she will tire easily and if her elbows are out they will 'go out' even further. If her quarters are weak, her unborn puppies will become a burden and what is more, she can pass all these unpleasant faults onto her offspring.

It is not advisable to breed from a Vizsla bitch before she is two years old or thereabouts. She does not mature fully, either mentally or physically, before this age. Therefore the strain of carrying pups too early could stunt her growth.

How many litters should she have? My vet always advises that as long as a bitch is fit and well, and still comes on heat be guided by her. It usually turns out that three litters are plenty, but there is no rule of thumb and one or two litters may be enough for a bitch to bear. It is not sensible to breed a bitch after five years of age. By that time she is more likely to have problems. You could be risking her life and her whelps by doing so. Do not go by what you wish, but be guided by the health, age and behaviour of your bitch.

It is not advisable to mate her "on the trot" (by which I mean mating her in successive seasons). It could take too much out of her. She should have at least one

97

Figure 6.1 Brood bitch who enjoyed feeding beyond the weaning age. (photo: Dr S Gottlieb)

season in between bearing puppies. She will not know or understand this, and will mate at every season if she has a liking for it.

Having considered the suitability of your Vizsla as a potential brood bitch, and satisfied yourself that she is able to fulfil at least some of the requirements, if not all, now is the time to consider which stud dog you wish to use. In order to make your task easier we should now consider the practical genetic management of breeding.

BREEDING OBJECTIVES

When adding up the pros and cons of which stud dog to use for your bitch, it is important to remember that mediocre stock breeds mediocre stock, and no wishful thinking can possibly change that fact. Let us start by asking the question, what sort of stock do you want to breed and what are the priorities?

It is essential to have a clear objective. Is the idea to breed one or two litters hoping to produce an outstanding puppy to show or to work, or to establish a kennel, laying down the foundations for future generations? The Vizsla breeders in England over the years have managed to maintain the characteristics as the *standard* states:

lively and intelligent, obedient, but sensitive, very affectionate and easily trained. It was bred for hunting for fur and feather, on open ground or in thick cover, pointing and retrieving from both land and water.

It will not be the Vizsla who is to blame if the characteristics are not maintained, but the present and future breeders. We should be proud indeed that there is no division between working and showing types as there is in some gundog breeds. I believe this is so because working stock is well to the fore in many of our pedigrees. Looking at the pedigrees of today it would be fair to state that the breed is well stocked with working blood lines. Many of our imports were brought over to work and certainly the early pioneers of the breed were dedicated to working their Vizslas. Few imports have been brought in as pure show dogs.

A decision must be made when considering any kind of breeding programme that the aim is "to breed a sound Vizsla of good temperament, capable of working and as good an appearance as possible". By sound I mean free from disease, defects, and all structural faults. To quote from David Layton's excellent book, *All Purpose Gundog*. (although he was writing about the German Short-Haired Pointer it is highly recommended to all Vizsla owners).

It is perhaps even harder to breed good German Short-Haired Pointers than some other breeds. One is not only concerned with handsome dogs fitting the *Standard* and being a credit to their breed, but also with producing dogs with inherent characteristics and suitable temperaments potentially fitting them to the task of being good all round gundogs.

The only way to establish that the stud dog you choose has at least some of these qualities and that he is likely to be dominant in any of them and that he could complement your bitch is to study the pedigrees, gathering as much information on these as you can, on the predecessors, on the sire and dam, grandparents and great grandparents. Better still try and see some of them. Look at the progeny that the dog has produced, remembering that however good he is, if mated to a mediocre bitch you cannot expect miracles! There is no easy way. I have thought, studied, talked about and looked at a particular dog over and over again, who on paper had all that I was looking for but somehow he and the dam did not click for me when I saw them together. When mated the litter was not especial either. Pat Lanz, breeder of Rottweilers, Komondors and Pulis, whom I have admired for years and who has bred top class stock consistently, her kennel *Borgvaale* is known throughout the world, has patiently answered my questions on breeding since I was first in Vizslas. She told me once, "Breeding comes down to instinct. If it feels right, it is right". But that remark was based on years of good, sound acquired experience and basic knowledge of dogs, and years of selection of good breeding stock, of selecting puppies for future breeding, thus building up a pool of desirable genes for typical stock. A breeding programme which is concerned with only one feature has much more chance of success. However the dog breeder is dealing with much more than this. Breeding presents a constant weighing up of good features and bad, based on knowledge of specific parts. Since the breeder cannot know for certain what characteristics are controlled by which gene combination — would that science and technology were so advanced as to enable the breeders to deal with separate genes — all he can do is to observe and acquire a grasp of genetic principles.

A feature that appears in one parent but not in the other but is inherited by all the puppies is probably the result of a dominant pair of genes in the parent who had the feature. If half the puppies have this feature probably the parent had a single gene for this trait. Genetic make-up can only be surmised over a period of time and each feature has its own genetic codes. So risks are being taken all the time in breeding. Like an ice-berg there is much more beneath that you cannot see than there is above the surface. Even so, there are obvious pitfalls that even the novice can learn to avoid. A breeder must remember never to mate two animals with the same defect. Also, remember to breed two animals who look similar — breeding two extremes only produces extremes.

In aiming to breed a sound animal, i.e. one which is free from disease, defects, and all structural faults, in principle, soundness should be sought for well before cosmetics. Do not misunderstand me — of course breeding for type is essential, but in establishing a breeding programme, a sound dog surely has to be the basis if you wish to continue to breed a dog who can work. It is incumbent on the breeder to strive to eliminate a disorder such as hip dysplasia before worrying about the tail set, which is a detail that rests entirely upon opinion and does not cripple the animal.

The practical genetic management may sound simple enough, but of course it is not. It consists of breeding from the best stock available, selecting those lines in which the defect appears infrequently which means learning to disregard rare cases of defects which may result from environmental causes, meanwhile, attempting to eliminate those lines which produce the defect repeatedly. For the practical breeder the widespread occurrence of inherited physical faults means that any breeding programme must be based on multiple criteria. For instance, you may find that you finally produce a Vizsla with the correct front but little behind or elsewhere to commend it.

So let us discuss in more detail the practice of breeding, always keeping in mind the sire and the dam that you wish to mate.

Each puppy inherits an equal number of genes from its parents. To illustrate this let us take the total value of the ancestors' influence as 100%, therefore each puppy inherits 50% from each parent. From its grandparents it gains 25% of its inheritance and from its great grandparents 12½%. So it is clear that a gene inherited further back is not likely to contribute very much. But if the gene for the same characteristic is received from both sides it will be doubled and therefore a stronger genetic characteristic. If closely related animals are bred they are likely to possess more genes in common than are those that are unrelated. We will consider three basic breeding programmes that are used:

1)   **In-Breeding**
2)   **Line Breeding**
3)   **Out-Crossing**

IN-BREEDING

This is the practice of breeding two very closely bred individuals such as father to daughter, mother to son, or brother to sister. It is not advisable for the novice to attempt this form of breeding because he cannot have had enough experience or knowledge of the "family tree". (For example, if two animals had entropion and they were bred together it is not going to improve the condition in the breed, especially if he has discovered too late that the condition was known to be found in both lines.) In the right hands, if both the dam and sire are outstanding, something really good could be produced but it cannot add new characteristics. The puppies could not be better genetically than either parent. Good qualities are fixed by in-breeding, but so are bad and they may be difficult to eliminate, so there is no chance of success if two inferior animals are used. The ever-optimistic breeder, having turned a blind eye will find the chances of success ever diminishing. Even though the breeder may decide to cull drastically, there are conditions such as hip dysplasia or epilepsy that often manifest themselves long after the puppies have gone to new homes.

Louise Petrie-Hay writes in one of her many articles in *The Shooting Times,*

> In-breeding, as far as I am concerned, is out. Good clean incest is always tricky. Look at what it does in humans — father and daughter, mother and son, sister and brother — that's in-breeding. If we knew everything there was to know about the dog and bitch and everything we knew was good, then by in-breeding everything would be accentuated and "tied" and we would have the perfect dog.

LINE-BREEDING

This is a modification of in-breeding. It is the practice of mating related stock but not so close as those used for in-breeding. Using grandmother to grandson, grandfather to granddaughter, uncle to niece or aunt to nephew, son or daughter to the mother's half sister or half brother, and half brother or half sister if the common parent is outstanding. This method may not produce such spectacular results and demands no less high standard in the choice of breeding stock, but can produce high quality progeny, taking longer to establish but much less risky than an ill-chosen in-breeding programme. In a carefully well-chosen breeding programme, if only desirable progeny are used from each litter, future generations will become uniform and of the best quality, reproducing itself, displaying the same characteristics, and an even litter will be seen. More significantly, they will look alike as adults, thus a particular line will be recognisable.

OUT-CROSSING

Out-crossing is not a specific breeding programme. It is a fundamental part of line-breeding and in-breeding programmes and is used to introduce "new blood" or a new characteristic into a closely bred line. It is the breeding of two totally unrelated animals. It is recommended that the sire be in-bred, thus probably fewer faults will be introduced than a widely line-bred sire. In this way, it is hoped to introduce different qualities needed in that line, but it is then advisable to breed the progeny back to the original line. The reason for this is that having introduced the quality the out-cross provided, the stud dog may also have introduced new faults which could be difficult to eliminate. But if at least one of the resulting progeny still retains a strong resemblance to the original "type" but has obviously inherited the new factor from the outcross, the constant characteristic of the line will continue. Be prepared to travel to use the stud dog who really suits, however easy it is to use the dog you have at home.

Breeding animals can be a heart-breaking business. Just as it seems that the slow process of improvement is coming right, all can be lost — a fine dog can prove impotent, a bitch barren, or some hereditary fault appears or a new characteristic never seen before can rear its ugly head. As a kennel becomes established and does well, the type known to that kennel may become over exaggerated without the breeder realising. It is very, very difficult to be objective. "Kennel blindness" is a fault that should be bred out, but it can be firmly established in breeders. It is very difficult to confirm failure when there are so many factors involved and even worse to have to abandon years of work. Trying to breed your dream Vizsla is like those games when you have to juggle five silver balls into five tiny holes. You may get one or two in and as the third finds its way home the others fall out. Sometimes, when it all comes right, it is a sheer fluke, but perhaps this analogy is not entirely right because there are specific rules that need to be adhered to and if they are followed there is much more positive chance of success sooner or later. It is imperative to have a good eye for a dog. If you have not one, borrow someone else's!

I do think that we are at a disadvantage in this breed because we have little stock to draw on. The rule, breed excellent to excellent, is correct in theory but impossible in practice. Any new stock that has been imported over the years has been absorbed into the breed and we have little to out-cross to.

I think it is true to say that there are few dogs who have repeatedly given the breed the same qualities of excellence. In all modesty, no breeder in Hungarian Vizslas could say there are many Vizslas of outstanding quality and excellence easily found in this breed. Serious breeders had an uphill task from the start since the first Hungarian Vizsla imports were brother and sister, *Ernest* and *Agnes*. They were the original stock that was bred from in England. Some of their progeny were also in-bred, so bad qualities as well as good were well and truly fixed. Although there is no longer any information available to prove otherwise, I doubt whether poor old *Ernest* and *Agnes* were "the perfect Vizslas in every respect".

It must be emphasised that for anyone wishing to breed seriously, a good strain must be established and this is rarely achieved unless the immediate forebears are of good quality. Each ancestor's genes become diluted in each generation. A particular animal cannot influence his descendants unless he carries dominant genes which pass on his virtues to his progeny down the line. Therefore one good dog amongst mediocrity is not likely to guarantee a desirable pool of genes. Therefore the relative values of the immediate forebears can be more rewarding if there appears to be con-sistency in sound typical stock.

MATING

Once you have selected the stud dog you wish to use and you have approached his owner and agreed on the arrangements, now it is the time to learn "the facts of life".

The Act of Mating

When a bitch is in season she produces the chemical known as pheromone in her urine and it is this scent that the mate receives, arousing him sexually. When the bitch is ready to be mated, the two animals will go through a preliminary courting stage which can last from two minutes to half an hour or more. The dog will nuzzle her, lick her ears, her face and her vulva especially, both displaying great excitement. They may run together, he may clasp her over the withers with his front legs attempting to manoeuvre her body beneath him. When both are fully aroused, the bitch will present and display her enlarged vulva, her tail twisted to one side. She will stand motionless ready to receive him. He will mount her, clasping her, his front legs holding her firmly round the flanks. He will search for the entrance of her vulva with his erect penis. If he is not successful, he may dismount and remounting, make another attempt. When he does find the entrance, his hind legs will make fast jerking, frantic movements. He will get a good purchase on the floor in order to make complete penetration. When he has succeeded and ejaculation has taken place, the prepuce of the foreskin of his penis will have been pushed back and the swollen bulbous glandis will be held in the restricting band of the vagina. This is known as the "tie". Neither dog can now be separated. The dog's semen has entered the bitch's vagina and "mating" has taken place.

The tie may last from five minutes to half an hour, or even to one hour. It is said that it is not essential for fertilisation that the "tie" takes place, but it is thought that it prevents the semen from leaking back.

While the animals are "tied" they may stand side by side, but usually the dog turns so that they are standing tail to tail with their heads facing outward, away from each other. It is thought that this position is adopted because in the wild, dogs are vulnerable whilst mating takes place. If they are standing in this manner, they are better placed to defend themselves.

As the mating pair are released, after the bulbous glandis has reduced to normal, a small amount of fluid will come away. Now the mating is over, the animals will take very little notice of each other. Sadly there seems little ecstasy, passion, or love in the act. Even the Hungarian Vizsla whom we cherish so is no different from any other breed. He, with all his need to give and receive love and affection from his humans, is totally promiscuous and fickle when it comes to loyalty either to his bitches or to his progeny. No nest-building for him or feeding the dam while she cares for his puppies, nor does he recognise his progeny when he sees them.

The Vizsla at Stud

The Hungarian Vizsla presents few problems as a stud dog if he is handled correctly as a youngster. He needs no particular preparation before mating as long as he is free from any infection, is fit and healthy and his diet is correct. Some owners will add extra protein to his diet but there is little need for this unless he has a lot of stud work. In this breed no stud dog is likely to have bitches coming to him every day! The Vizsla should not be large or heavily built compared to big breeds, thus he should have no trouble mounting a bitch as long as they are well suited in height and weight. His short coat presents no problems. There are no curtains of hair to keep out of the way!

The gentleness and sweetness of the Vizsla character is often demonstrated while courting in the preliminary stages. He seems to prefer to flirt and wrestle, enjoying the bitch's playfulness. He is not usually the aggressive type of stud dog who will dismiss the preliminaries, mounting the bitch before she knows it! Some seem to need encouragement and reassurance from the bitch that she will accept him. I think owners would agree that the Vizsla is considerate at stud, rarely wishing to force himself on a bitch if she rejects him. I have observed a Vizsla losing interest in the whole affair if the bitch appears to have no liking for him or if she lacks interest in the proceedings even though she is ready to "stand" and even though he is keen to start with.

The Vizsla temperament is such that he can be over conscious of the human element in the exercise, seeming almost shy at times. He sometimes mounts the bitch and then dismounts quickly again and again, regarding his owner. This is not unusual and entirely understandable if we realise that we are dealing with animals. We have arranged the mating, not they. In the wild there would be no human contact. Little wonder that the dog may be confused in this primitive act, if the observer is a dominating party in his domestic life. In order to mate successfully, the male needs to be dominant. This influences his behaviour on approaching the bitch sexually — an overbearing bitch may not allow a subordinate male to mate her. Thus the role the human plays should be as retiring and as quiet as possible. Handled with sympathy and understanding, the Vizsla will gain confidence at stud and become an expert on the job!

As in all aspects of owning a Vizsla, be there when he needs you but do not over-handle him or he becomes dependent and finds it difficult to assert himself except in totally subordinate fashion.

The Owner Handler

The owner of a dog will soon learn that he cannot request the use of a bitch, a mistake many new owners make until they realise that the apple of their eye may not be anyone else's. The owner of the breeding bitch makes the choice, choosing the male best suited to produce the best puppies by the bitch. The owner of the bitch has all the work of whelping and caring for the offspring and selling them, therefore it is he who will request the "use" of the dog. Once this has been arranged then the owner of the dog dictates the terms, such as stud fees and where and how the mating takes place. If the mating does not "take", it is necessary for the owners of the dogs to decide whether to allow a free mating when the bitch has her next season. It is generally accepted that this is the procedure.

It is important to decide whether one or two matings are necessary when the bitch comes to him. Every breeder will have his own opinions and methods based on his experience. Basically it is sensible to mate a maiden bitch two or three times. This will give her experience and as it is not quite so easy to know when a maiden bitch is absolutely ready because she may be so confused by the new circumstances she will not know whether to stand up or sit down! It is kinder to give her a chance to settle. For the same reasons the maiden dog should be given the chance to gain experience.

One mating is all that is necessary as long as it is certain that the bitch is in full oestrus and if both Vizslas are mature and both have proved themselves as a sire and dam.

I always prefer to mate Vizslas twice. The reason is that I am not very good at ascertaining exactly the moment the bitch is ready. I also find that if the Vizslas are from my kennel, they know and like each other. The bitches will accept the dog so easily they may be a couple of hours out! It is very rare but it has been known that a bitch accepted the dog kenneled with her at any time of the year!

The timing of the second mating varies again, depending on the owner of the dog, Some will mate them four hours later, some twelve, some 48 hours. After mating I count that as day one, leave them the following day and mate them on day three. Others may disagree but I have always found it successful. Obviously, it is difficult to do this if the bitch has travelled from a distance, but the stud dog owner should give those visiting an opportunity to choose. Whether it is convenient to either is another matter.

It is usually understood that if the dog has not been mated before, his first attempt at mating is free, the reason being that the dog needs to have a chance to "prove" him-self. Can he sire good puppies? So the first mating is a trial and just as important to the owner if he wishes to use his dog at stud as it is for the owner of the bitch. So it is courtesy not to ask for a fee. If this mating is successful as time goes on your dog proves himself a potent and worthy sire, depending on his merit and the demand for him, you can decide what you wish to charge. Any subsequent matings you may charge for, or you can ask for "pick of the litter".

The stud dog owner has every right to refuse a request to use his dog if it does not seem to be a suitable match. He has as much responsibility as the bitch's owner in spoiling or improving the breed.

A dog who proves to breed bad Vizslas can do great harm and actually changes the breed if used repeatedly. The dog's owner may feel that the puppies are not his responsibility, but they are if he really cares about the breed so it is helpful when your dog is in demand to acquaint yourself with a few facts. Does the bitch's owner have customers for the offspring? If not, what will happen to them?

As the dog's owner gains more experience he will learn that each mating is different, some easy, some difficult and complicated. He will discover whether his dog prefers to manage on his own or whether he needs his owner to help him "turn". He may like his owner to hold and comfort him during the "tie" or on the other hand he may hate being fussed over, preferring to be left entirely on his own. Whatever the procedure the owner should "be in charge". He will need to assess the bitch and her owner. If the owner is experienced in these matters, it will be helpful for him to remain and handle the bitch for you. On the other hand, if not, perhaps it would be simpler if you suggested that the bitch is left with you and return to collect her later. It is a very uncomfortable experience to mate two animals in the presence of someone who is shy, embarrassed, or squeamish. A noisy, impatient or talkative human will disturb the calm atmosphere necessary if the dogs are not to be "put off" or disturbed.

Where to Mate
The stud dog always "stands" on his own home ground. The bitch should always be brought to him. It is essential that the dog is settled and relaxed in surroundings that he knows well. He may be fearful and tense in a strange place, however good his temperament, he may fail to consummate. Therefore, always use the same place that is familiar to him. He will soon learn that it is where he mates. Choose a room that is warm, light, and airy, a place away from other dogs and normal household activities. Make sure that the family knows that you cannot be disturbed. You are not socially available for at least an hour or more!

The room should not be too large and there should be enough space for the dogs to run, but the area should be small enough for the handlers to reach their Vizslas quickly once the dog starts to mount the bitch after the pre-mating courtship. The floor must not be slippery because the dog has to get a good grip with his back legs. This rules out vinyl, lino, wood, even straw can be very slippery. The ideal is the best Wilton carpet! Failing that, a rough cement floor or grass will do. So, if a long, narrow, well-lit, warm room is available, well away from civilisation, carpeted with fresh green spring grass, cement, or an unwanted Indian rug, with facilities for making coffee or tea with one hand, these have the ideal conditions laid on!

Some owners may prefer to have their dogs mate outside. In this case, the bitch should be on a lead so that the handlers are close enough when the time comes to assist them. Weather conditions have to be taken into consideration. There may also inevitably be a row of faces peering over the garden fence unless those who are lucky live in the country!

The First and Last Mating

After the first mating and puppies have been produced it may be said that the male is a "stud dog". This first mating is obviously very important. Ideally it should take place at about 10 to 12 months, so that he learns the procedure when he is young. If he is fortunate enough to have his first mating with an experienced bitch who has a good sensible temperament, she will help him over his naivete without upsetting him. She should be a bitch who is keen to mate and who likes it, preferably one who knows him well. He will be bemused and shy at first and it is she who will chivvy and flirt with him endearingly, gentling the young dog into his first mating.

At what age is a stud dog too old to use? There seems to be no hard and fast rule, the owner will recognise the signs of old age creeping on and perhaps feel the dog cannot manage it any longer. This could be from nine years onward. In my experience, Vizslas of eleven and twelve can still be very potent sires, capable of siring good healthy puppies. The worry is that they could collapse on the job!

Handling

If the owner of the dog is a novice it is advisable to seek expert advice and help for the first few meetings. It is not just a matter of putting two Vizslas together in the garden or field and leaving them to get on with it. The maiden bitch could be badly frightened by a male. He could be bitten by her or he could be torn very painfully if he mated her and she pulled away or lay down. Both could decide that they would not like to go through that experience again! The male could be marred for life against stud work. So it is sensible not to learn by your mistakes in this case! Ask for assistance, do not be proud.

There are many different methods of handling any breed when mating. Every individual will work out his own method of helping his or her dog to succeed. Meanwhile, let us consider the handler's role in a simple uncomplicated mating with one person handling the bitch and the other the dog. Both Vizslas should be wearing a collar. Before introducing the Vizslas they should be allowed to relieve themselves, giving the bitch plenty of time to familiarise herself with the surroundings. Once they have met, leave them as much time as they wish to prance and play where they are to mate, the handlers remaining quiet and removed but alert to assist when the time is right. Eventually when the courting stage is over and the dog mounts the bitch, the bitch's handler should be close enough to gently hold her collar, placing the other hand beneath her belly, firmly supporting her weight. This will prevent the bitch from turning on the dog if she is so inclined and stops her from sitting down or twisting around. Some bitches will stand rigid to receive the dog but there are many exceptions and it is well to be prepared.

With this method, the dog is well protected. When they are mated and tied, the dog usually turns in order to stand back to back. Frequently the dog finds it difficult to effect this manoeuvre. His handler can gently raise the hind leg over the bitch's back and in this manner ensure little or no discomfort for either. At this stage both Vizslas may be happier with their handlers by them, needing to be steadied. The bitch may attempt to pull away from the dog so they need coaxing to relax. Both handlers can feel content the dogs have mated. Now they need to wait until the "tie" is over. Two low stools and a cup of tea will be welcome at this point. The dog will need little attention by now but the bitch will still need her handler to hold her head if she is restless. Both will have calmed down after the excitement and will appear passive. They may not seem particularly comfortable, their ears back, eyes red, panting and drooling. Little can be done for them at this stage. Eventually, when the dog's penis is finally released the handlers have little more to do than feed and water them and leave them to rest in separate rooms.

Handling matings is an art, there are some who never manage to achieve the right attitude. Their tension and unease for the welfare of the dog or bitch is quickly transmitted to each, causing confusion. It has to be accepted that if it hurts the bitch will cry and whine. If the dog does not manage to mate he will be uncomfortable, but not for long. Those who are expert at supervising matings are those who calmly accept the course of events giving the animals a sense of security.

Complications for the Stud Dog

It would seem ridiculous to discuss mating difficulties with the owner of a curly-tailed Don Juan of the neighbourhood — a strong force to be reckoned with for any unfortunate owner of a pedigree bitch. And I am sure those Vizsla owners who have always found the exercise runs smoothly will wonder that such a heading as "Complications" is necessary, but there are those, and I am one, who have needed advice at times, when usually through lack of experience, things have not gone according to the book.

Some Difficulties are Common to all Matings

1) Frequently the courting stage becomes protracted until both are exhausted and bored, neither Vizsla appearing excited enough to copulate. The most common reason for this is that the bitch is not in full oestrus or perhaps it is too late. If she repeatedly sits and snaps at the dog, especially if she has been mated before, then be guided by her and try some hours later or the following day. If it is after the fourteenth day, then probably it is too late. If the dog does not show much interest it could be for the same reason.

2) If the bitch is not ready to "stand" she will often sit down if a dog shows interest. She will also behave in this way after she has finished ovulating. If the dog does not get the message that she no longer accepts him, she may also snap, a sure sign that she may come out of "purdah".
Many young, experienced dogs will take time to comprehend which end is "the place for him" and in doing so will become exhausted and over-excited, frantically trying to mount the bitch from every angle. A short turn around the garden may calm him. If patiently handled, he will sort it out. In this case, it is necessary to take into account the Vizsla temperament. He can become over-anxious. He needs reassurance from his owner in case he feels he is causing displeasure, which will increase his bewilderment.

3) Occasionally, the dog may not be able to penetrate the bitch leaving him in a very uncomfortable predicament with his penis exposed and drying and the bulb partially enlarged. He may also have ejaculated outside the bitch. This can be due to his over-enthusiasm or difficulty in penetrating the bitch. She may have moved at the crucial moment or he could have misfired or he could have penetrated her but not completely. The wisest thing to do is to separate the two for ten minutes or so, allowing the dog to remain quietly by himself. I have found that usually he will be quite comfortable by then and ready to return and mate the bitch. But if he is still disinterested, separate them for a few hours, in order that he may forget the unpleasant experience. Some advise applying cold water to the exposed membranes but I have never felt it necessary, feeling the cure may be more painful than the temporary condition.

4) It has to be accepted that some dogs have their preference and do take a dislike to a bitch and vice versa. In some cases, it is best to recognise this and call it a day.

Type of Stud Dog

There are specific problems that can arise due to the type of dog that is being used. For instance, there is the **over-enthusiastic** Vizsla who could terrify a young maiden bitch. This one will not wait for any introductions or preliminaries but completely and accurately hurl himself onto her. He needs to be restrained for the bitch's sake, until she has had the chance to accept him. I would suggest that it is rare behaviour in a Vizsla.

The dog who shows **little enthusiasm** is difficult to deal with. He may not show any interest in the bitch, however keen she is. If she is a maiden it may not be a productive proposition at all. But have patience and do not despair, use some ingenuity. First try him on a mature bitch. She may behave in such a way that he finds her irresistible. You can help him to feel more confident by encouraging him to play, by jollying the two up, even throwing a tennis ball can get them into a playful mood. Sometimes this mood then changes to courting. Another trick that sometimes works is to remove the bitch for a few minutes and then return her with a flourish, hoping to change the atmosphere of boredom to ecstatic excitement.

But if this Vizsla's problems are deep seated, then we should look further and try and find out why he is behaving in this manner. Perhaps he has spent his entire life with humans, protected, petted and shielded from other nasty dogs? In that case, if he is young, this could be rearranged in some way. If he has lived with a dominating dog or bitch or played a very subordinate part in the pecking order in his kennel he may not have had the opportunity to mature sexually. In both these cases, the dog will manifest his lack of interest towards a bitch. The answer is that he should be placed for some time in an environment where he can establish his own identity. Probably an older dog would not respond, but I have known a case where a young dog living with his sire could not mate any bitch. The owner was advised to remove him and allow him to run with the other young stock. This was done and after a couple of months, the problem was solved. He no longer behaved as if he were suppressed. In fact, with a bit of practice and a lot of encouragement, he became a very competent stud dog.

I have been flummoxed by a young untried dog. On presenting him with a mature bitch who "stood" for him (proving the day was right) he sniffed her and that was that — showing no further interest. A few minutes later he climbed on and mated her! All theories flown to the wind. He lived with his top dog father and six bitches, one of whom was his dam, who dominated the whole kennel. He has displayed the same pattern every time he has mated a bitch even in his father's presence, disproving many a theory.

The **hesitant** Vizsla may appear to be interested and excited by the bitch but as he mounts her, he feebly gives up and slides off. Usually this problem can be solved. Often the reason for this behaviour can be attributed to his lack of experience. If it is the reason he will learn soon enough. Or he could be shy. He may find the proximity of his owner too embarrassing, especially if he has been chastised for his interest in bitches when it has been inconvenient. Or if the owner is over-dominating and interfering even in this situation. If the owner is sensible and allows someone else to handle the dog, someone who is not emotionally involved, but who the dog knows, all may go well. If not, then it may be one of the rare occasions when the humans have to remove themselves entirely, not advisable, but perhaps the only answer. I know a stud dog who has mated many times but will have nothing to do with the Vizsla bitch unless he is left alone with her and another who will only mate under a certain rose bush in the garden.

The dog may also hesitate to mate if he has been injured or hurt in any way during the previous matings. Given time and patience and much encouragement from a fond and flirty bitch, he may forget all about it unless he is a shy, nervy type. But in this case, perhaps it is unwise to consider putting him to stud in the first place.

I have seen two cases when the bitch has had a vaginal cyst. This causes an obstruction in the organ and of course it can cause great discomfort to the dog, complete penetration being impossible. His behaviour would seem unreasonable, dismounting the bitch at the very last minute, attempting to mate her time and time again, becoming more and more distressed until totally dejected he stands pathetically, his passion spent.

The Stud Dog Who Knows His Business

This is the Vizsla with the solid temperament, the one that works or could if given half the chance, the one that presents no problems when mating and if he does he can manage to overcome them pretty well on his own with a little help from his owner. His gentle, responsive nature is ideally suited to adapting to the temperament of the bitch if she is well disposed towards him. Expect him to take time. Expect him to have likes and dislikes. Do not expect him to be aggressive or forward or demanding in any way. Expect him to be as you have found the Vizsla to be, if he is well adjusted — romantic, affectionate, passionate, excitable and whimsical. He is totally reliable once he has confidence in himself and he knows what he is up to, learning by his own mistakes, but always needing his owners approval.

MATED JANUARY	DUE TO WHELP MARCH	MATED FEBRUARY	DUE TO WHELP APRIL	MATED MARCH	DUE TO WHELP MAY	MATED APRIL	DUE TO WHELP JUNE	MATED MAY	DUE TO WHELP JULY	MATED JUNE	DUE TO WHELP AUGUST	MATED JULY	DUE TO WHELP SEPTEMBER	MATED AUGUST	DUE TO WHELP OCTOBER	MATED SEPTEMBER	DUE TO WHELP NOVEMBER	MATED OCTOBER	DUE TO WHELP DECEMBER	MATED NOVEMBER	DUE TO WHELP JANUARY	MATED DECEMBER	DUE TO WHELP FEBRUARY
1	5	1	5	1	3	1	3	1	3	1	3	1	2	1	3	1	3	1	3	1	3	1	2
2	6	2	6	2	4	2	4	2	4	2	4	2	3	2	4	2	4	2	4	2	4	2	3
3	7	3	7	3	5	3	5	3	5	3	5	3	4	3	5	3	5	3	5	3	5	3	4
4	8	4	8	4	6	4	6	4	6	4	6	4	5	4	6	4	6	4	6	4	6	4	5
5	9	5	9	5	7	5	7	5	7	5	7	5	6	5	7	5	7	5	7	5	7	5	6
6	10	6	10	6	8	6	8	6	8	6	8	6	7	6	8	6	8	6	8	6	8	6	7
7	11	7	11	7	9	7	9	7	9	7	9	7	8	7	9	7	9	7	9	7	9	7	8
8	12	8	12	8	10	8	10	8	10	8	10	8	9	8	10	8	10	8	10	8	10	8	9
9	13	9	13	9	11	9	11	9	11	9	11	9	10	9	11	9	11	9	11	9	11	9	10
10	14	10	14	10	12	10	12	10	12	10	12	10	11	10	12	10	12	10	12	10	12	10	11
11	15	11	15	11	13	11	13	11	13	11	13	11	12	11	13	11	13	11	13	11	13	11	12
12	16	12	16	12	14	12	14	12	14	12	14	12	13	12	14	12	14	12	14	12	14	12	13
13	17	13	17	13	15	13	15	13	15	13	15	13	14	13	15	13	15	13	15	13	15	13	14
14	18	14	18	14	16	14	16	14	16	14	16	14	15	14	16	14	16	14	16	14	16	14	15
15	19	15	19	15	17	15	17	15	17	15	17	15	16	15	17	15	17	15	17	15	17	15	16
16	20	16	20	16	18	16	18	16	18	16	18	16	17	16	18	16	18	16	18	16	18	16	17
17	21	17	21	17	19	17	19	17	19	17	19	17	18	17	19	17	19	17	19	17	19	17	18
18	22	18	22	18	20	18	20	18	20	18	20	18	19	18	20	18	20	18	20	18	20	18	19
19	23	19	23	19	21	19	21	19	21	19	21	19	20	19	21	19	21	19	21	19	21	19	20
20	24	20	24	20	22	20	22	20	22	20	22	20	21	20	22	20	22	20	22	20	22	20	21
21	25	21	25	21	23	21	23	21	23	21	23	21	22	21	23	21	23	21	23	21	23	21	22
22	26	22	26	22	24	22	24	22	24	22	24	22	23	22	24	22	24	22	24	22	24	22	23
23	27	23	27	23	25	23	25	23	25	23	25	23	24	23	25	23	25	23	25	23	25	23	24
24	28	24	28	24	26	24	26	24	26	24	26	24	25	24	26	24	26	24	26	24	26	24	25
25	29	25	29	25	27	25	27	25	27	25	27	25	26	25	27	25	27	25	27	25	27	25	26
26	30	26	30	26	28	26	28	26	28	26	28	26	27	26	28	26	28	26	28	26	28	26	27
27	31	27	May 1	27	29	27	29	27	29	27	29	27	28	27	29	27	29	27	29	27	29	27	28
28	Apr 1	28	2	28	30	28	30	28	30	28	30	28	29	28	30	28	30	28	30	28	30	28	Mar 1
29	2	29	3	29	31	29	Jul 1	29	31	29	31	29	30	29	31	29	Dec 1	29	31	29	31	29	2
30	3	–	–	30	Jun 1	30	2	30	Aug 1	30	Sep 1	30	Oct 1	30	Nov 1	30	2	30	Jan 1	30	Feb 1	30	3
31	4	–	–	31	2	–	–	31	2	–	–	31	2	31	2	–	–	31	2	–	–	31	4

Gestation Table

I give an example of two instances when the experience of the dog allowed him to be in charge of the mating.   A mature bitch showing all the signs of her 'readiness' came to be mated, both behaved as if they had no idea why they were there, neither seemed to concentrate for long enough on each other for any length of time, preferring to trot about wagging their tails as if they were going for a walk. The bitch handler decided to hold her steady, this only encouraged her to sit by her handler, now at this stage if all concerned were novices this may have been a 'non event', but the bitch owner knew his bitch was 'ready', the dog was totally reliable and given the experience of the Vizsla temperament, both were encouraged to play, the handlers standing well away, the dog decided now was the time, pulled her toward him wrapping one leg round her thigh, holding her firmly by the other, and mated her.

The second mating to illustrate my point, was to be a maiden pet bitch. This mating proved to me the worth of a truly reliable confident dog, with a good sound temperament. The bitch also had a good temperament, for I am sure we could have been bitten if she had not. The dog was strange, the place was strange and she had no experience, she clung to her owner, who handled her well, he encouraged her to run with the dog and sensibly remained as kind but aloof as he could. She stood and was mounted by the dog and in a flash she turned on her back screaming, taking all by surprise. The dog was not deterred nor disturbed, he mounted her again, this time the handlers were prepared and both held her firmly, he mated and turned calmly on his own, meanwhile the bitch screamed and screamed, no amount of comforting pacified her. The dog remained quiet and the noise reduced to a whine. She was mated a second time and she behaved very differently, flirting and presenting herself as soon as he appeared, apparently unaffected by her traumatic experience — it could well have been painful to begin with, a bitch can have a spasm of the vaginal musculature (vaginismus) during mating. Now a young dog could well have been put off, from mating this bitch, experienced or not, nor is it the sort of mating a novice dog should be faced with for the first time. It is difficult for the humans to remain impassive on an occasion such as this, but it is necessary to leave interpreting to the animals, it is a mistake to try to equate their world with ours.

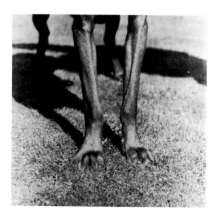

Fig. 6.2
HEREDITARY FAULTS IN THE BREED

'A Poor Front'
Loose Elbows, slack Pasterns and
flat Feet.
(photo: Diane Pearce)

CHAPTER 7

WHELPING

Pregnancy

One of the most fascinating and exciting aspects of Vizsla owning and breeding must be watching a bitch whelping. They are such natural mothers, they need little assistance while giving birth. They don't fuss or panic, they seem by instinct to understand what is required of them.

The construction of the Vizsla bitch is such that there is nothing to inhibit a normal birth. There is no reason why any bitch should not give birth quite naturally without complications and with minimum help from the owner. A visit from the veterinary surgeon afterwards would be wise to check that all is well.

The Pre-Whelping Weeks — The First 3–4 Weeks

The first three to four weeks after mating the Vizsla bitch should be treated exactly the same as usual, the same feeding routine, the same exercise, no extra tit-bits in your zeal and anticipation.

The Fifth Week

The first outward signs of pregnancy are the swelling and reddening of the nipples and those at the back will be the first to swell. This is not likely to occur before the fifth week. It is the first positive evidence that the owner will observe. If the bitch becomes fatter and broader across the back, but there is no physical change either in her nipples or in the fullness of her belly, then it is more likely she has been overfed and has a slight hormone change. Very easily done and a trap many of us fall into. Changes are imagined, the bitch is overfed and cossetted, our maternal and paternal instincts are coming to the fore.

Some bitches have an unnerving habit of producing similar pregnancy signs after their season. This is due to hormonal changes and seems more frequent in maiden bitches. It will be noticed that although the nipples redden and the bosoms at the back swell the belly does not enlarge. Usually this state of phantom pregnancy does not go to full term it is rare that a bitch produces milk, even if the bitch reaches the stage of nest building she will return to normal afterwards usually with no ill effect.

The Sixth to Ninth Weeks

After the fifth week the bitch should have her meals divided and the protein content increased. Her diet should be of the very highest quality and at this time it is advisable to give her extra vitamins. It is always sensible to be advised by your vet as to which vitamins he would recommend.

Exercise as usual until she is obviously in whelp and is carrying quite a burden, but care should be taken that she is not knocked or pushed if she is exercised with other dogs. She may behave as if she has no idea that she is in whelp. I feel this should be encouraged — if she is spoiled and petted, "poor little dog, be careful, don't do anything silly now, stay by me", your Vizsla will look at you and catch on very quickly. Your mood becomes her mood, your worrying her worrying. She will think there is something wrong.

She will not know that she should be knitting for nine! She will only know that you are in a state of anxiety and she had better be in one too. · So good food and sensible exercise (swimming is not advisable — one of mine, when I was not looking had a quick dip two days before her puppies were due. There was no harm done but this was taking my nonchalance a bit too far!)

Continue to increase the bitch's food as the weeks go by. It is not so much the amount she eats but the quality. She must have the very best. She deserves it since she is producing puppies and you will want them to be a credit to the breed. As her pregnancy continues, the extra demands of the whelps within the mother increase and it is the protein content in her diet that is the most important for her welfare as well as the whelps'.

On no account increase the fat or carbohydrate content in her diet such as biscuit or starchy food. She should not be overfed; a fat pregnant bitch is an unhealthy one. As the time goes on when the bitch lies on her side, the puppies can be seen moving, providing the final proof that she is definitely in whelp. Early on in their pregnancy some bitches will heave and sigh and look enormous, seeming thoroughly uncomfortable. Others will not be affected at all almost to the day of whelping, the size of the litter making no difference in either case.

About three weeks before the birth, it is sensible to introduce the future mother to her whelping box. If she will sleep in it happily, she will be more comfortable there than anywhere else, but unless it is in your bedroom, she will be happier near you and you can keep an eye on her.

The date of mating to the date of the birth is sixty-three days — that is the gestation period. Rarely are the puppies early or late.

The Whelping Box
It is as well to have all the necessary items for the birth prepared in advance. A whelping box is the major item.

Place the box somewhere secluded, well away from open doors or draughts. A room where the bitch can be left in peace without fear of being molested by other animals or children. The whelping box needs to be a solid long-lasting serviceable piece of equipment. It is possible for an amateur to make a sturdy box at the cost of about £25, taking from three to four hours. The method may shock the true carpenter, but as long as the local wood merchant is there to give advice and as long as he cuts the wood to exact specification the box can be put together by anyone who is practical and handy with a hammer and a screwdriver. The box must be large enough for the bitch to lie comfortably, and the sides must be the correct height so that the bitch and whelps can be tended easily and so that she can get in and out without effort, as well as affording enough protection to contain the puppies for the first few weeks. Some breeders do not use a "pig rail" or "shelf" fitted inside the box, but by experience I have found an "escape route" essential to ensure the puppy's safety should his dam lean on him. I prefer narrow shelving set at the correct height all the way round the inside of the box, because it prevents an errant puppy nearly strangling himself by poking his head between the pole and the box.

To Make a Whelping Box 3ft 6ins x 3ft 6ins

1. **Four pieces of wood — deal — 3ft 6" x 9"**
2. **Wood for base of box — plywood or block board**
3. **Oval nails — 1½"**
4. **Glue**
5. **Pencil**
6. **Hammer**
7. **Screwdriver**
8. **Gimlet**

For Shelving

1. **Two pieces of wood 3ft 4" x 3"**
2. **Two pieces of wood 2ft 11" x 3"**
3. **Twelve shelving brackets — 2½"**
4. **Screws to fit brackets**

Method

Glue and nail the four pieces of wood to the base, one by one, use the glue liberally along the edges before nailing. Remember to place the nail with the grain of the wood or the wood may split. Use about six nails to each side. Then with the pencil trace a line 3" from the base of the box all the way round, this will give the height at which the shelf must be fixed. Screw three of the brackets to one of the lengths of 3ft 4in wood. One in the centre and the two others 2" from the end. Transfer this to the box and screw the shelf into place along the pencilled line. Fix the remaining three lengths, applying the glue before fixing. Allow the glue to dry (approx. 12 hours) then sand the wood down. Finally paint the box with a polyurethane varnish, apply liberally over the brackets so that the edges are not sharp.

Adding Height to the Box

If the puppies are to remain in the box after they are agile enough to walk and climb, it is simple to add another panel to give it more height so that they cannot climb out. Requirements:

1. **Two pieces of light wood, measuring the length of one side — approx 9" or more**
2. **Eight pieces of wood approx 1ft x 2"**
3. **Two pieces of carpet measuring the length of each side and long enough to fold and nail over the top of the added panel.**

METHOD

Nail or screw the 'legs' of wood exactly opposite one another about 4" from each end. Then fix the carpet in place. Thus the whole panel should fit over the side of the whelping box, the soft carpet allows the bitch to jump in and out without hurting herself. At this stage the bitch may be more comfortable lying outside the box, if she has a comfortable bed nearby, she will stay near her puppies and tend to them when necessary.

FLOOR COVERING

Whilst the bitch is whelping, layers of newspaper are the most practical lining on the base of the box, they can be replaced as soon as they are soiled. After whelping a softer warmer covering of thick material can be fixed. There is a product on the market now, that can be bought in quantity, so that it can be cut to the size of the box. One in use and one in the wash. A square of this product can be fixed to the floor of the box by screwing a metal door sill on either side of the box. This can easily be taken up and replaced by a clean piece.

The Infra-Red Lamp

An infra-red heat lamp is a necessity. It is no use thinking the puppies will be fine in the kitchen where it is warm. It cools at night or when a door is opened. Unless there is constant heat the puppies will become cold and if they have to struggle to keep warm, inevitably it will give them less chance to "do well". At worst, they may not survive. The temperature required is about 75 degrees Farenheit. The puppies need this heat for about two to three weeks. If the lamp is suspended slightly to one side of the box it enables the puppies and the mother to move beneath it or away from it as they wish.

ITEMS NECESSARY FOR THE BIRTH

1)   A whelping box
2)   An infra-red lamp
3)   A low table — here you can put all the items necessary for the whelping
4)   Newspaper
5)   Waste paper basket
6)   Towel, bowl and soap for washing hands
7)   Sharp-ended scissors for cutting cord or bag
8)   Cotton wool for wiping whelps' eyes, nose and mouth
9)   Towel for drying whelps

10) Clock for noting the time between delivery of each whelp
11) Scales, pen and paper for weighing and recording birth weight
12) Drink prepared for the hard working mother while giving birth
13) Some sort of matting — this is to prevent housemaids knee while tending birth— you may be kneeling for hours and a comfortable chair for you when there is a lull in the proceedings!
14) Cardboard box with hot water bottle covered with a blanket — this is for the whelps. If necessary, the whelping box can become rather crowded if she has a large number of whelps.

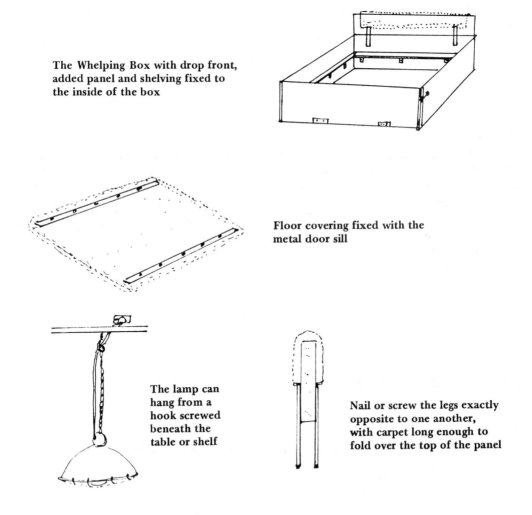

The Whelping Box with drop front, added panel and shelving fixed to the inside of the box

Floor covering fixed with the metal door sill

The lamp can hang from a hook screwed beneath the table or shelf

Nail or screw the legs exactly opposite to one another, with carpet long enough to fold over the top of the panel

Figure 7.1 Whelping Box and Infra-Red Lamp

The Pre-Birth Signs

There are two signs that the puppies' birth may be imminent, one being a sharp drop in the temperature —take this twice a day, a few days before the expected date of birth. This is easily done by inserting the thermometer gently into the anal passage about half an inch, leave it in for three minutes. When it is obvious that the bitch's temperature is several degrees below (the normal temperature of the dog varies from 100 degrees Farenheit to 101 degrees, depending on the time of day and the individual dog) then this coupled with loss of appetite — although not all bitches lose their appetite — is a good indication that the long-awaited puppies are due to arrive.

Some bitches make a great fuss nest building; attempting to scrape and dig up their bed. They will move about restlessly, unable to settle anywhere. Other bitches will seem unaware of the life moving within them, until the last moment.

The first puppy will not be long in coming when there are regular and strong contractions. There is nothing to do but remain calm at this point. A quiet voice and a gentle presence will help her over this stage, which can be bewildering for her, especially if she is a maiden. She may pant violently, her abdomen distending and retracting. She may cry in her discomfort, but after she has given birth to one or two puppies this stage seems far less painful to her.

The Birth

As the puppy is born head first it may shoot out at an alarming rate, bag broken, umbilical cord trailing along attached to the whelp, no sign of a placenta, another may arrive still in its bag encased in the finest membrane looking like a burglar with a stocking over his face! A maiden Vizsla bitch who is not an old hand at the job may not necessarily be able to cope, but one who has whelped before may break the bag, bite the umbilical cord and mop up the mess herself.

If the maiden bitch is bewildered by the whole procedure do not be alarmed if she is frightened by her first whelp, it will not take her long to learn, but meanwhile the bag will need to be carefully nicked with the scisssors and the umbilical cord cut — it should be cut ½inch from the puppy's abdomen. The remaining piece will dry up and eventually fall off. The afterbirth to which the umbilical cord has been attached within the mother will usually appear as a dark mass, sometimes there is so little of it you hardly realise it has come away. Most dams will eat the after birth but it is not advisable to let her eat too many or she may vomit or it could also be the cause of diarrhoea.

Draining the Fluid

The next job is to drain the fluid and its a crucial one. Turn the puppy upside down — he may not have shown any sign of life at this point — and literally drain the fluid that has collected in his mouth and lungs. Holding the puppy in your left hand let the body hang down head first, place the right hand under the throat running your hand up to the corners of the mouth. At this point the mouth will open — if it is not open already — and out will flow quantities of fluid, or so it will seem, the whelp will cry and to the relief of the dam you can return her newborn.

After the birth of the whelp, it is surprising to see that he is striped like a tiger. It can be quite a shock if you are not expecting it, but it is normal. The stripes disappear after a couple of days, looking very pretty while they last. The bitch will lick the newborn from top to toe, pushing him about quite roughly with her muzzle. Thus he is stimulated by her in the most natural way to urinate and defecate. Her instinct to do this is a wonder to observe. She will continue this stimulation and swallowing the contents until they are old enough to 'perform' on their own, but she continues to keep the box clean until the puppies are weaned. Her competence is remarkable to observe.

While the bitch is whelping she should be allowed as much to drink as she pleases, warm milk as well as water. If she is unused to cows milk, Lactol is less likely to up-set her. She could also have an egg or two added to the mixture. The general opinion is that this regime is continued for about twenty-four hours after the birth of the whelps, thus allowing her digestion to settle after eating the afterbirths and her general cleaning up. It is also recommended that for the following few days she is only allowed white meat such as chicken, fish or rabbit.

I have a Vizsla bitch who is now a great grandmother. She loves everybody's puppies, but puppies and people need cleaning. To sit next to her is fatal. She insists on washing you. Her poor puppies were always violently cleaned by her. Her last family — she gave birth to 12 — had such a hard time as they were born we had to restrain her, as her licking became furious; but she soon tired, her excitement and enthusiasm waning by the twelfth puppy's arrival, her obsessive cleaning becoming a brief wash and brush up before the next arrival.

It is amazing to watch the maternal feeling of the bitch manifest itself, her protective instinct already showing in her anxiety as she sees her young picked up.

Putting the Puppy on the Breast

The whelp may need a bit of help in feeding for the first time. Some feed easily from the start, others find it difficult to hold on to the nipple until he gets the feel of it in his mouth.

To help him, the easiest method is to hold the mothers nipple in the right hand, placing your left forefinger and thumb on either side of the puppy's mouth squeeze slightly and the mouth will open, put the nipple inside and away you go! It may be necessary to repeat this several times, the puppy does not always get the message seeming determined to starve! But when he does latch on and the dam is licking and nuzzling the puppy there is a sense of relief all round, the tiny whelp finding it unnecessary to suck now, holds on while the milk flows down his throat.

The Length of Birth Period

The next whelp may arrive soon after but if there is no sign of another whelp after two hours then you should seek the advice of your vet. But if all goes according to plan further contractions will announce the next whelp. There will be a sort of rhythm — a whelp arrives, he will learn to feed, then he can be placed under the lamp to dry off and will be out of the way. As further whelps are born and the numbers increase to a stage where it is difficult to manage and the box becomes overcrowded, place some of the whelps in the cardboard box which you have already prepared with a warm hot water bottle under the blanket. They will be safe until the mother has finished whelping, then they can join the others.

The ideal number for a Vizsla mother to cope with is six or seven whelps, more than that can cause problems if she has not enough nipples to go round! Also a larger litter does tire and bring the mother down. If you have seven puppies, preferably more bitches than dogs, then you should be well pleased.

It is not always clear when the last whelp is born, if you can no longer feel a lump or see any contractions and the abdomen looks empty and feels empty. If there has been a long lapse since the last whelp came, then usually these signs indicate no more puppies. But beware! Sometimes there is another tucked away so when you take the bitch outside to give her a change of scenery and to relieve herself, keep a good eye on her just in case another drops out — it has been known!

You may also leave her sleeping peacefully with ten puppies and come down in the morning to find eleven or twelve.

All the whelps have finally arrived. They are asleep, the dam sleeps also, content and exhausted. Her milk has come in and the puppies have fed. She left her puppies reluctantly to relieve herself and on her return she assured herself that each puppy was still in the nest — touching each with her nose. She had a good drink and lay down beside her newborn.

You must be exhausted, need a drink, a feed and a good sleep as well. But just for the moment relax and recall an experience you will never forget, watching and listening to the newly born litter of Vizsla puppies. The cleanliness and neatness, her fastidiousness and caring, the lack of fuss and the ease with which motherhood is accepted is impressive.

The Vizsla needs you to be close at this time. She will reward you by utter devotion to you and the puppies. The little help that she requires from you is nothing to the pleasure she and her puppies will give in return.

WEANING AND FEEDING

The Vizsla puppies will establish their routine of feeding and sleeping, providing the dam has adequate milk and the puppies have plenty of warmth. The litter will sleep closely together in a huddle a little away from their dam if they are contented. As one wakes, the others will too when it is time to feed. The dam will keep her puppies and whelping box spotlessly clean for the first few weeks. Although she may tolerate the humans she knows and who are close to her, do not expect her to accept strangers anywhere near her puppies. Her instinct is to protect her young against any predator as she would in the wild.

Early Feeding
You will notice as the puppies move towards their mother to feed they search for the nipple. When he has obtained a good suction, he kneads the mammary gland with his tiny feet, thus stimulating lactation. The puppy wraps his tongue round

the base of the nipple and once the milk is flowing, he will relax while he fills his tummy. If a puppy continues to fuss, sucking and slurping noisily, pushing the breast with his nose, it is a sign that the milk is not coming. Either someone else has been there first or the breast is so engorged with milk that he cannot get the whole nipple in his mouth. When all the whelps are settled and feeding side by side like sardines there is no more contented sound than their grunts while the bitch lies ever watchful but relaxed.

Ideally there should be a nipple for every puppy. If there are not enough nipples to go round, it is important to be watchful. The larger, stronger puppies can easily push a smaller aside. It may be necessary to give a supplementary feed to ensure that the puppies have adequate milk if the dam does not appear to have enough or if the litter is a large one.

If all is well, the puppies will grow rapidly and gain weight. It is advisable to weigh them at least once a week at this stage. By the third or fourth week depending on the size of the litter, it will be time to think about weaning the puppies. This is the process of introducing solid food so that by the time the puppy has reached six weeks he will not require his mother or her milk, although if he is still with his dam at eight or nine weeks, depending on her maternal instinct he may still feed from her as well as taking solid feeds. Contrary to many theories, the dam is usually happy to stay away from her puppies as they grow. They become demanding and tend to maul her. It is a pathetic sight to see a bitch stand to feed her puppies while they hang from her nipples. They try to cling on with their claws and can scratch her badly. The puppies' nails must be snipped with nail scissors as soon as they begin to grow or they become as sharp as pins.

WEANING

While the puppies are being weaned, they will not take so much milk from the dam thus a natural process will take place, as they require less so she will produce less, until her milk dries up completely. There is a period of a few days sometimes when she may still produce milk even though the puppies have gone. This will pass and looks more alarming than it is. Milk may drip from her nipples but do not be tempted to express her milk to relieve the engorged breasts, otherwise the cycle will be perpetuated. Give her plenty of exercise, restrict her fluids and if the weather is warm and she likes swimming it will help to relieve much of her discomfort. The vet can provide pills to aid drying up the milk but the condition will right itself after two or three days. The bitch usually gets her figure back after two and a half months to three. I had a bitch who won a CC three months after whelping! Obviously some bitches do take longer than others. Also much depends on how many litters they have had, and how soon she comes off her pups.

Weaning is a crucial time in the puppy's life. It needs the utmost care and attention on the breeder's part. A set back at this stage of development can severely affect their growth. Some breeders wean their puppies onto a semi-solid milk feed to start with. Others prefer to commence weaning by giving good quality cooked or raw minced meat, such as beef, lamb or chicken. The bitch will often indicate when she feels the puppies are ready to wean by regurgitating her food for them. The consistency and temperature allows the puppy to quickly learn the trick of eating. When offering meat to the puppy roll it into a ball (about 1oz) mixed with a little Bemax in the palm of the hand. Sit him on your knee, you will not need to force it down his throat, just allow him to sniff it and lick it, he will soon start to nibble. Always introduce one new food at a time, and only offer the puppies one extra feed a day at first.

When the time comes to start weaning, it will be necessary to organise the method in such a way that all goes calmly without confusion. If there is no routine puppies will be crying and whining in the most distressing way. For instance, if puppies are being hand fed individually to start with those who have fed should be separated from those who have not; otherwise there is no way of knowing which has eaten or which one has not.

As the puppies grow on and they feed from dishes it is much easier to feed them divided into two, for instance, four bitches in a penned off area and four dogs outside it. Thus the control over what seems like an army is greater and each puppy can be observed as he eats. When dividing the puppies up always put the large ones together to feed, thus the smaller are not pushed out.

If a supplementary milk feed is necessary after a week or two, one of the simplest methods is to feed them three hourly and then four hourly. For the first feed, for example, feed four bitches by hand leaving the four dogs to have a good feed from the dam. For the second feed, hand feed the dogs allowing the four bitches to have a good feed from the dam. After each feed those that have been hand fed should go back on the dam so that they can feed from whatever is left. Puppies normally lap towards the end of the second week. If supplementary feeding is necessary before that they will need to be bottle fed.

At seven weeks the puppies should be on four or five meals a day, two or three cereal meals a day and two meat meals. For example:

8.00 am	—	milk and cereal meal
		1 tablespoon powdered milk.
		1 tablespoon Farax
		7 oz of water —approx.
12.00 pm	—	meat and biscuit or complete food meal
		2—3 ozs of minced meat
		2—3 ozs of meal or biscuit

The food must be soaked to a palatable consistency

4.00 pm	—	as morning feed
8.00 pm	—	as lunchtime feed

The puppies must have the correct vitamins, they may also have eggs, fish or even Heinz baby foods. At this stage the bitch will need approximately two pounds of meat a day and one and a half pounds of biscuit or complete food, split into three or four meals a day as well as plenty of fluids — water and milk drinks.

By the time a puppy is three months old, his feeding routine and his capacity for accepting any new food should be fairly well established. If his digestion is upset, it will have far less long term affect than at five or six weeks.

The puppies may be fed individually each having his own bowl, or two or three to a dish. To begin with I prefer to feed them individually. In this way I know how much each one has eaten and whether he is taking sufficient nourishment at each meal or not. Some Vizslas are slower and more careful eaters than others. I can often trace this back to grandparents and great-grandparents. Sh Ch *Waidman Remus* was always a voracious eater and many of his progeny have the same habit. *Galfrid Leda of Russetmantle* on the other hand is a very slow, careful eater, never faddy, just slower, and many of her progeny are the same — Ch *Russetmantle Troy*, her son eats very slowly but is a good doer. Obviously in these cases it is not survival of the fittest. If they were all put together as puppies and given the same bowl to eat out of, it would be a matter of survival of the fastest eater — the others would starve! If each puppy has his own bowl it also educates him to eat alone. If he has been reared to fight for his food, he may find it difficult to adjust when life is less fraught with his new owners!

While the puppies are on a milk diet, they drink very little water, but it is as well to offer them a drink after a meal. It is not advisable to leave the bowl down all day as they will only paddle in it — alright in the summer but a bit cold in the winter.

WORMING PUPPIES

Even though the dam's worming programme was up to date before she whelped, and even though there is no sign of worms in the puppies' faeces, it is absolutely essential that the puppies have a strict worming routine recommended by the vet. All dogs have worms and all puppies have them also or rather the larvae of the worm is in their system.

The most common worms in the dog are the roundworm and the tapeworm. It is the roundworm that can infest the puppy. If the infestation is severe, he will lose condition and his growth will be stunted, because the worms feed off the puppies' tissues. The symptoms may be loss of appetite or a ravenous appetite, diarrhoea, potbelly, and lack of sparkle. If the condition has not been treated, worms like fine grey threads may be seen in the faeces and of course the older they get the larger they grow.

Generally, puppies receive their first worming dose at four or five weeks old. This is usually a syrup such as Antipar. After that he may be given a pill in the form of Coopane or whatever your vet recommends, at seven weeks, nine weeks and so on until the puppy is six months old. The pills are best given after a meal and popped down the puppy's throat. The method of putting any pill in food, hoping the dog may eat it without knowing is hit or miss. Much better to educate him to accept that you will open his mouth and place the pill on the back of his tongue from the start. One day he may need life-saving pills such as antibiotics. If he is trained to accept pills from you from the start, you will have no trouble. But if a puppy is wormy and the condition is not treated, this may have a long term effect on his condition.

Figure 7.2 Mr W Foster with the beautiful bitch Sh Ch *Kinford Zsuzsi*, the first show champion bitch in Britain.

CHAPTER 8

IMPRINTING

A puppy is born with certain functional patterns, enabling him to survive i.e. sucking and sleeping. As he grows from day to day, his behaviour will be influenced by his earliest experiences. Therefore they way in which he is imprinted is vital to his welfare if he is to reach his full potential. Emotional sensitivity is a necessary part of the socialisation process and this (automatically) makes the puppy susceptible to psychological damage if he is not treated well. I am suggesting that those of us who have known a shy Vizslas, an aggressive Vizsla, an excitable Vizsla, a fussy one, the clinging type or the one that could not work, should not always put the blame on the poor gene and the well-worn pedigree. I am proposing that some of this behaviour could be a result of ignoring a critical need in our puppy's rearing.

WHAT IS IMPRINTING

Imprinting is an irreversible process by which a puppy when exposed to repeated stimuli appropriate to his stage of development, can be programmed as a computer, thus an impression is established in the central nervous system. This "impression" is physical and is termed a nervous pathway.

It has been established by intensive research programmes, one of which was run at the Jackson Laboratory in America on dog behaviour for nearly twenty years, that there are particular periods in the very early life of the puppy when this process is at its most effective. John Paul Scott and John L Fuller have written the most authoritative volume, *Genetics and the Social Behaviour of the Dog*, based on their research at the Jackson Laboratory. Particularly important was the discovery of "critical periods" which exert a lasting influence upon adult behaviour and a dog's relationship with humans. I will discuss these "critical periods" in detail later but first let us establish how "imprinting" takes place having received the necessary stimuli. Unlike the learning process which requires some active participation from the subject, imprinting is an entirely passive process, the puppy has no choice in the

125

end result.

With the advances in scientific understanding of the structure and function of the nervous system we could talk of any dog's attributes in terms of the underlying "neuronal structure". A neurone is the elementary cell of the nervous system. There are billions of neurones making up the brain, spinal cord and all the nerves emanating from them to the entire body, also from all the body's structures, organs and specific senses back to the brain and spinal cord.

A neuronal pathway consists of a series of connected neurones along which an impulse must pass. Thus a puppy when exposed to artificial feeding from a human instead of its dam will have this repeated experience impressed or imprinted on a selected pathway. Conrad Lorenz in his original work with goslings, found that in the absence of the true geese parents, he was adopted by them as the parent. Thus the gosling's infant nervous system was exposed exclusively to the reception of stimuli from a human and so humans were imprinted instead of geese on the susceptible neurones. Thus environment can have a directional selective effect on a developing puppy and what can be observed at a very early age is the interaction between the environment and the definitive qualities of the animal. It will be found that a litter of Vizsla puppies, all raised under the same conditions, with identical dam and sire, identical feeding routine, will still react differently to their environment because their innate qualities will not be the same. Thus the moulding of a puppy's personality is affected by its inborn temperamental characteristics and shaped by the stimuli he receives from his environment.

I give an example of this in an incident affecting two puppies, brother and sister of twelve weeks old and reared together. We were standing at a zebra crossing and a lorry came hurtling past. Too late, I realised that both puppies were badly frightened. They were shaking and panting, their ears pinned back and their tails clamped between their legs. I reassured them both as best I could. The bitch responded immediately. From birth she had been adventurous, taking each unknown step without a backward glance, very bright and quick to learn, always full of confidence. She had had a fright and showed fear but handled it quite differently from her brother. He had always been slower to accept changes, would hesitate at each unknown step but once taken he would be full of confidence, a gentler puppy altogether. His reaction lasted much longer. He shivered and shook all the way home, wishing only to slink into his kennel. He sat there pathetically, his eyes darting round fearfully. It took days to reassure him, repeatedly taking him back to the same spot when there was little traffic about, until one day he was able to walk across glancing neither to the left nor to the right, nor behind him! As we stood on the same spot where the lorry had gone by, his tail would be up and no sign of worry. Now they had both received the same imprinting and socialisation from birth, both had received the same stimuli in experiencing this "fright" but had dealt with it differently.

It is not profitable to attempt to estimate what is the proportionate contribution of "nature and nurture" but it is profitable to stress the need for domestic dogs to be allowed to grow up in an environment in which correct imprinting by human beings comes about. It must be stated that the brain of any species be it dog or human in infancy does not distinguish between a good or useful trait or a bad or harmful trait, therefore it is up to the breeders and owners to assure themselves that they are doing all they can to socialise their puppies in the best possible manner i.e. any puppy which has not been handled by humans will never attach himself to humans in later life; he will appear shy and display a great lack of trust in people.

Goran Bergman states in his book *Why Does Your Dog Do That*, that the results of imprinting are in some respects different in different breeds. Some appear to be easily imprinted, others less so. Some become, through imprinting, extremely strongly tied to one single person while other breeds are always just as friendly towards all friendly people they meet. He also states that Setters, Springers, Spaniels and other game dogs related to them have a reputation for being friendly and rarely aggressive. The Vizsla is part of this group. I think most breeders would agree that he is not difficult to imprint. His capacity for loving and needing human affection and his need to serve — as with all gundogs — allows him to enjoy his working relationship with humans. His attachment to the human race is a delight. A Vizsla which has not had the advantages of good socialisation is a poor, shy cringing creature, longing to be friendly but terrified to put his trust in anyone or any other Vizsla or breed for that matter. The Vizsla is not necessarily a one-man dog. Obviously he will be more attached to the one who cares, feeds and exercises him, but he quite easily transfer his affections to others who will do the same for him. I have known instances where he has been expected to be a "one man dog" and this type of relationship has not succeeded. In one case, a newly acquired puppy had been expected to show total loyalty to one member of the family and it resulted in confusion, the puppy becoming fearful of the member who insisted on forcing his affection and firm discipline in order the make the Vizsla puppy "his" dog. The puppy finally refused to walk or accept food from his "owner" but would from any other member of the family. Thus not only was the puppy psychologically disturbed but the family was upset too!

THE CRITICAL PERIODS

Let us now consider these vital critical periods in a puppy's life when he is most susceptible to imprinting. It is important to remark that some experienced breeders may feel that the view that unless puppies are introduced to particular stimuli by a certain date, is too dogmatic and too rigid. Of course there are exceptions to every rule and I am sure in this case many exceptions. We are dealing with living beings, not inanimate objects but it is as well to know and understand the well researched data first and then to apply this to the experience.

In Michael Fox's book *Understanding Your Dog*, we are provided with well-researched information as to how the puppy's brain develops and how its maturing relates to what behaviour the puppy is capable of at different stages of growth.

Clarence Pfafferberger who wrote the fascinating book *The New Knowledge of Dog Behaviour* and also Scott and Fuller all agree (after extensive study), on the premise that if a puppy experiences proper socialisation from three weeks to sixteen weeks, it will reach a satisfactory level of behaviour. They submit that if this is not observed and the puppy has not been allowed the dignity of being an individual, it will have not ties with people. Scott writes:

> the evidence is that puppies have a short period early in life when positive social relationships are established with members of their kind, after which it becomes increasingly difficult or impossible to establish them. The same applies to their relationship with human companions.

Clarence Pfafferberger writes:

> a puppy who has no socialising before it is sixteen weeks has little chance of becoming the sort of dog that anyone of us would want. The time is so short, once it has gone it can never be retrieved. The implications of this in the development of the dog are so great that it behoves a puppy raiser to employ this time wisely. It can never be made up at an older age.

So when are the clearly recognisable critical stages that are characterised by certain behaviour patterns and emotional reactions? The first three weeks of a puppy's life are spent surviving. It needs food, warmth, maternal care, plenty of sleep and its litter mates. It makes enormous physical strides by the end of the third week. It can urinate and defaecate without being massaged by its dam. It's teeth begin to appear, it can hear, its eyes may have opened by the twelfth day or thereabouts. It has learned to crawl backwards and forwards and it may be able to totter.

Its brain, being inactive at birth, commences to develop a number of neuronal pathways but it is not until the puppy is three weeks of age that they are fully functioning and this is when the puppy reaches social awareness. His environment starts to shape his life, his intelligence and emotions begin to function, socialisation, as the Americans call it, or imprinting can begin. Thus, **from three weeks to the seventh week is the first critical stage.**

It is said that the brain and nervous system develops to the capacity of an adult at this time, but of course without the experience. This is the period when the puppy should ideally be imprinted by its own dog world i.e. its dam and litter mates and by a human being or human beings in order to form stabilised relationships with humans and dogs. In nature, most animals and birds are imprinted by their own species but since the dog needs to form attachments to the human world at this time, the more the humans have to do with the puppy, the stronger the imprint will be. This little being will start to feel sociable, he is aware of his litter Vizsla mates, his mother, or any other dogs or humans who come into his field of vision. He will wag his tail and totter towards his owners. If he is taken from the nest at this time and socialised alone with humans he can become over attached and will find it difficult to relate to other dogs. He will become "dog-shy". If he does not get sufficient human contact, he will grow up to be "people-shy". If he has too much human female contact, he will respectively be shy of men and vice-versa. Thus at this stage without close attention to these specific needs, the puppy:

will not reach a satisfactory level of behaviour

Pfafferberger states in his book:

> the period of twenty-one to twenty-eight days is so strange to the puppy that at no other time in a puppy's life can he become so emotionally upset, nor could such an upset have such a lasting effect upon his social attitudes . . . I believe, if there is a time when a puppy needs its dam more

than any other time, it is probably the fourth week, from the twenty-first day to the twenty-eighth day. This is the time of very rapid development emotionally, he should not be moved from his mother for any length of time during this week. To wean at this time may upset him so that he may never be able to compensate from the abrupt break. A week after at twenty-eight days he has already become so well adjusted that weaning will have much less effect.

So we can see that at this time the puppy's life in the nest becomes suddenly very active and interesting. He needs as much affection and fondling from humans as possible. He needs to have children visit him and play gently with him. He can be removed for much longer periods and by the sixth week the dam could be removed from her pups without any harm done. If he spends some time each day with humans, on his own, after the fourth week, he will form his attachments as a companion. It allows him to develop as an individual forming his character and gaining self confidence. If his life until now has been filled with loving care from his own and from humans he will be well on his way. **The second critical period is from seven weeks to twelve weeks**

This is the time to form a man-dog relationship. The puppy has been weaned by now. His dam is no longer interested in spending much time with her young. He can make the transition from his litter mates to his new home (if he is to be sold) without trauma as long as he has all that he requires — plenty of attention and caring. He needs this change. It is not desirable for him to stay with his dam or his siblings necessarily as could be supposed. If he is left with his siblings in an enclosed area without the chance of experiencing new people, new places, new territory, new noises, he will suffer from institutionalisation. An outgoing puppy may adjust later, having had the necessary treatment at the three to seven week period, but an innately more timid individual may find each new experience in his life becoming a dreadful trauma to face. If Vizsla puppies are not sold at this time, the breeder will need to spend a lot of his day socialising the puppies — no easy task. The Vizsla is such a lively, vital, intelligent dog and as a puppy cannot be left to his own devices for long.

He requires his very active brain to be put to full use. The sort of treatment he receives from humans during this period will affect his attitude to them. Because every dog inherits the "pack instinct" this is the time when he will be ready to accept human dominance. Never again will he be so prepared to yield or can the human leader so bind the puppy to him in order to shape his character traits as he can during the first and second critical stages. Training can only be in the form of games, but with affection, gentleness and firmness, the puppy learns who he must respect.

The Third critical period is from twelve to sixteen weeks. This is also the start of the juvenile period which continues until the puppy reaches full sexual maturity. Serious training can and should commence and the transition from play training to disciplined training should be affected. I am not necessarily including training for work. Many trainers differ in their views as to when a Vizsla puppy should be trained for the gun. I mean elementary obedience and manners.

At this time, although a puppy may have accepted his human pack leader, and had all the advantages of maturing as an individual, he will be feeling his feet, asserting himself and trying out everyone and every dog in his world. If he is living with other Vizslas, it can be a disturbing time for them for he will challenge each one in turn playfully and if he is not "put in his place" in the hierarchy he can be very disruptive

129

as he can be in the human world. At this stage, a Vizsla puppy's boisterousness and energy seems to be at its height. He is no longer a cuddly little puppy, but lithe and strong.   At this age he is too big to carry and he will find every chance he can to wilfully flout authority. This sense of fun and need for activity seems boundless. It is a difficult time for his owner, but it can also be a very enjoyable time, for a Vizsla can enchant you if you have a sense of humour, because he has learned to clown.

One of my puppies amused us for hours at this stage. She would sit on a chair with a tennis ball, gently pushing it to the edge. She would hesitate and look up, regard her audience and deliberately push it over the edge with her nose, wait until one of us picked it up for her and repeat the performance all over again. She had us all retrieving her ball beautifully and dutifully, but trying to teach her to retrieve anything to us was quite a different matter.

It is absolutely crucial by now that the Vizsla puppy respects his owner and the human world. If there is any sign of challenging in an aggressive way, then he must be reprimanded. It it is not fixed at this stage, then it could become a serious problem as he grows older. A sense of territorial rights will be developing as well, so it behoves the owner to prepare himself. If the reason for this probable behaviour is understood and it is dealt with firmly and explicitly, the puppy will learn that there are certain modes of behaviour that are totally unacceptable and he will obey.

For example, if a puppy is sitting on a chair and the owner requires him to move and the puppy growls, the owner has the opportunity to confront the situation and settle it once and for all. If it is shelved, the puppy will learn in no time that growling is very effective and biting too if the end result is that he gets his own way every time. So we go back to the repeated stimuli of what we want in order that he behaves in a particular way. But here, we have an example of conditioning wherein the puppy by now is playing an assertive role. The puppy growls, he is removed forcibly off the chair with appropriate verbal remonstrance such as "No!". The puppy may respect this and learn his lesson, but if he jumps back and growls again, then he is deliberately challenging authority, so he needs to be taught that:

a) he can only sit on the chair when allowed

b) he must never growl at you (this is most important)

So it must be demonstrated clearly by the owner that this behaviour is not acceptable and the remonstration must be repeated over and over again until his challenging ceases. He has to respond now, not tomorrow or next week, but now. I believe that Vizslas rarely show challenging aggression if they are sensibly handled when they are puppies. Even the adoring possessiveness they have for their owners need never reach the stage of guarding them if they are taught to acknowledge that their place is on the hearth rug and not necessarily on the knee or the duvet, unless invited.

A puppy from three to four months can develop phobias, demonstrating a sudden fear of strangers, unfamiliar places and loud sounds. This can be very worrying if he has been or appeared to be perfectly well adjusted before this. Providing that he has had all the necessary rearing up to this time and is well adjusted, he will grow out of this anxiety period. He needs reassurance and repeated stimuli of the same experience that caused the anxiety, understanding of course that there are some unpleasant experiences, such as fire or the dog next door who would fight to the death, that no dog would ever be expected to accept without fear and if he did he would be foolish. But the puppy will be reassured if he is given the opportunity to meet many strangers, taken to unfamiliar places, has car rides, train rides, even boat rides. Widen his horizons, do not cosset him, but help him to learn that his fears are unfounded. Sheltering him in the kitchen or kennel will only aggravate his anxiety. What he needs is experience. If it is taken too seriously by the owner, the Vizsla's tension can increase. I find that he can be laughed out of this mood, jollying him along by playing with him can help him to forget.

Even though it is very difficult to believe that the difference of a week or two could have such long term effects and many would dispute these findings, having the knowledge that there are such important stages in the life of a puppy must inevitably increase the breeder's awareness of his needs. In my opinion, the Hungarian Vizsla with his particular high sense of awareness and intelligence, his gentle temperament and need for giving and receiving much physical affection, his contrariness and strength of will makes for such a complex, emotional creature that incorrect socialisation makes him a very insecure, fearful, unstable dog who goes to pieces with little provocation and is absolutely useless for work, nor would he make a trustworthy pet.

But given all the rearing he needs, no one could deny that he can be the most constant companion anyone could wish for.

BOOKS USED AS REFERENCE ON IMPRINTING

1. *Genetics and the Social Behaviour of the Dog*
   by John Paul Scott and John L Fuller

   This book is an authoritative information on the behaviour of the dog based on nearly 20 years of reasearch at the Jackson Laboratory where both authors were senior staff scientists at Bar Harbor, Maine, J P Scott is a graduate of the University of Wyoming and Oxford University and obtained his PhD from the University of Chicago. He was Chairman of the Department of Zoology at Wabash College and is presently Research Professor of Psychology at the State University of Ohio. He has also written *Animal Behaviour* and *Aggression*.

   John L Fuller received his PhD from Massachusetts Institute of Technology. He has had various treaching positions at universities. He is senior author of *Genetics and the Social Behaviour of the Dog* and is currently Associate Director of the Jackson Laboratory.

2. *Understanding Your Dog*
   by Dr Michael Fox

Dr Fox is a qualified vet with a Doctorate in Psychology from London University. He is currently the Associate Professor of Psychology at Washington University and Associate Director for Research at St Louis Zoo. He is a recognised authority on canids and several scholarly studies on animal behaviour have won him wide acclaim in the scientific community. He owns a rare Telomian dog, several wolves, foxes, jackals, and coyotes.

3. *The New Knowledge of Dog Behaviour*
   by Clarence Pfafferberger

Clarence Pfaffenberger is a Member of the Board of Directors of Guide Dogs for the Blind. He was assigned the task of finding the ideal puppy which would become the ideal guide dog. Many years of collaborating with those working at the Behaviour Research Laboratory at Hamilton Station, keeping valuable scientific records. Contributed to the work at the pioneer institutions at Fortune Fields and the Seeing Eye.

Figure 8.1 Sh Ch *Calversam Braeville* (Mr & Mrs J K Dickinson) — handled by Mrs S Cox
(Photo: McFarlane)

CHAPTER 9

PICKING PUPPIES FOR PEOPLE

A PUPPY'S CHARACTERISTICS

The litter is ready to leave the nest and each puppy ready to make his own way. From a breeder's point of view this is a crucial time. All the previous planning and arranging has come to fruition. Is there the Vizsla of all time in this litter? A future dual champion? Such are the questions and the excitement, intensity and anticipation these little scraps of russet gold engender.

"How can you bear to let them go?" puppy purchasers ask. I can bear to let them go, if I feel the quality of life provided is just what he needs. I love the hours spent deciding which puppy will suit which home best. After pairing them up, I am thrilled when I hear that the new owners are pleased and enchanted by the little Vizsla who will share the next 10 to 14 years as part of their lives. Any breeder has a great responsibility in this respect. After all, if you sell someone a coat and it does not suit, it probably ends up in a jumble sale. What happens to a puppy if it does not suit?

The breeder needs to assess which puppy will best suit the customer's requirements. The more time spent watching, handling, petting and understanding the puppy, the more familiar each puppy's characteristics will become. One puppy tries to scramble up, another pushes him aside already asserting himself. Another sits and gazes, patiently watching, while the others vie for every attention. Meanwhile, who is that sniffing and snorting around on his own with an independent air? He's using his nose and seems to be onto something, his tail wagging furiously. Perhaps he would suit a customer who wants a Vizsla for working? The quiet one who gazes at you so persistently and loves to be petted may suit the loving family who have owned dogs all their lives, perhaps he may be too gentle and doesn't have enough "umph" to work. Now there is one who really takes your eye. Trotting about bossing all the others, getting into mischief. Good topline already, chest well down, plenty of skin to grow into. As he sits you laugh as his skin falls in folds over his tail. He looks at you and wags his tail. His front is already acceptable at 7 weeks so perhaps he has good show and work potential? And so the gazing and choosing continues. Meanwhile their relationship with you and with each other flourishes. You will soon learn who accepts your authority more readily than others. You have noticed one more reluctant and less outgoing than all the others. If you put your hand out he does not approach you as the others do. He is the one who is always last, he does not seem to heed you. This is the puppy who needs special care and attention. As likely as not if he is given individual loving and socialising, gentle children can help a puppy of this type learn to communicate. Once he has gained confidence away from his litter mates, a few days of this "treatment" and although he may never be the bouncing extrovert of the litter, he will be a perfectly happy, well adjusted puppy. If there is a very shy, nervous, overly sensitive puppy who flinches at any noise, beware. Also watch out for the overly aggressive one, the one who at a few weeks old growls or snarls if you pick him up, then you are in trouble. You cannot blame your breeding programme, for even puppies from the same litter cannot have the same genetic construction and every now and again extremes can occur. Even so, it is the breeder's responsibility. Puppies like this should not be sold to unsuspecting customers. It could cause heartbreak.

Although the breeder may take great care counselling future owners, it is always advisable to encourage them to see as many adult Vizslas as possible if they do not know the breed well. A photograph can be very deceptive. The reality could be quite a shock! This muscled, lively dog may not be what they require after all. So three visits may be necessary;

1) Firstly to see the adult Vizslas, the dam and sire if possible, before booking a puppy.

2) Secondly to visit the puppies in the nest at 5 or 6 weeks old.

3) Thirdly to pick the puppy up to take home at 7 or 8 weeks old.

By this time it will be much easier to match the puppy's temperament with the needs and lifestyle of the future owners. A couple who like an active life with their pet, the husband doing a bit of shooting, or the retired couple or a family with noisy children, or the show home or the gamekeeper who kennels his dogs all provide different environments suiting some Vizslas better than others. It is vital that the breeder be prepared to refuse a customer if he feels the home would not be suitable.

On the sale of the puppy, the new owner will require:

1) A diet sheet

2) Details of worming and injections

3) The Kennel Club registration papers (if available) signed by the Breeder for transfer

4) The pedigree

5) Any information available on the breed

Unfortunately, some new puppy owners do not follow feeding instructions in spite of painstaking advice from the breeder. It can be very disappointing for the breeder and of course disturbing for the puppy because as likely as not he will have a bad tummyache.

In spite of the hazards of selling puppies, there is nothing so satisfying or so pleasing when doting owners return proudly, presenting their adolescent Vizsla, strong and healthy and obviously doting on *his* family.

BUYING A VIZSLA PUPPY

Whatever your purpose is in selecting the Hungarian Vizsla as your breed, you may find you have to wait some time if you wish to buy your puppy from a reputable breeder. It is clearly sensible to do as much research as you can into every aspect of the breed before embarking on buying your new puppy. Seek out a breeder who will willingly answer your questions, understands and indeed encourages your wish to have as much information as possible and your request to visit the kennels. As in all breeds, there are various types of Vizslas and it is only when the purchaser has seen a good many that he can discover which he prefers. Never allow yourself to be pushed into a sale. Any caring breeder will be pleased to spend time with a customer who is offering a good home. It is never wise to buy a puppy if partners do not agree. It can cause grounds for separation! Meanwhile the puppy suffers unbearably in the ensuing arguments, however good his temperament. No Vizsla of 7 or 8 weeks old can tolerate stress and tension. He is extremely susceptible to physical and psychological trauma at this age. He is entirely dependent on the humans in his life to supply his needs and does not have the comforting support of his dam or litter mates any longer. If he is the centre of arguments and shouting matches, it will not take long before he displays signs of deprivation. He will become disturbed himself, may be restless and incontinent, may develop diarrhoea, go off his food and become very clinging, whining incessantly. He may show signs of aggression or fear or destructiveness. His sensitive hearing can be affected by the constant rumpus. To escape from it all he may creep away and hide. All these signs indicate his desperate loneliness, isolation and unhappiness.

I do not feel a puppy should be left alone all day. If all members of a family are out, he could tolerate two or three hours alone, but the kitchen could be demolished on the family's return! Neither do I feel a puppy is happy kenneled by itself all day. In both cases it would be strongly recommended that he has a companion. This should be discussed with the breeder before acquiring a puppy.

If you are offered a puppy much older than 8 weeks, you will need to make certain that he is a happy, outgoing little Vizsla. For instance, if he is as old as 3 or 4 months, it would be very risky to buy him unless you knew the circumstances in which he had been reared. You would need to be quite satisfied that he had been socialised adequately. If he is still in a pen with other unsold litter mates, he is not likely to have had the chance of leading any sort of independent life away from them. Although he may appear a forward, friendly puppy when with his brothers and sisters, when on his own he could show signs of shyness, hesitation and stress, having lost all the support and security of his pack that he has known and lived with from birth. I would suggest that you have him on trial for a week so that you are able to see how he behaves away from his environment. A breeder should be satisfied with this arrangement and may suggest it himself, if he cares for the welfare of the puppy.

Do not be taken in by a breeder who guarantees a perfect pet, show or gundog. There must be few dog people with years of experience behind them in this breed who would ever commit themselves. It would be misleading a customer. At best, he could say, "In my opinion, this puppy has the essentials at the moment".

The most successful show or working dogs do not necessarily produce the best puppies. So do not be blinded by all the winning rosettes and cups on the sideboard. It does not always follow that all the progeny will be excellent, although the likelihood of getting a good dog from good stock with working and showing lines in the pedigree of course increases the chances — but many a bad workman blames his tools.

WHAT TO LOOK FOR IN A VIZSLA PUPPY

Temperament

A bold, lively, exuberant, playful puppy is how he should appear. An aloof, reserved manner is not the true Vizsla temperament. One who is interested in everything and everyone, whose nose seeks out every interesting smell, indicates the outgoing nature required. As he walks towards you with his tail wagging, showing pleasure and confidence, you can be assured that he is a puppy who wants your affection and will give you as much. When you pick him up he may freeze for a moment but relaxes as he licks or gnaws you, whatever the case may be! He should feel settled in the warmth and comfort of your arms enjoying his contact with you even for a brief moment. It is important that you feel his confidence and sureness of you. He may struggle to get down but you have felt that moment of contact and contentment. That puppy will be the one who has the true Vizsla temperament, regardless of his potential. The puppy who wriggles incessantly neither allowing you to cuddle nor stroke him can turn out ot be a livewire, a fidgety, restless Vizsla, one you will find difficult to relax with in your sitting room. Clearly, the hesitant, shy puppy will need much reassurance, love and support. The bold puppy who shakes when you pick him up could be the type who may develop into the aggressive, fearful Vizsla who may bite. Although many Vizsla puppies are hesitant and shake at strange new experiences, they regain their confidence in a matter of seconds. Whereas the former type remains shaking and takes much longer to recover. Thus the purchaser needs to spend time with the puppy he is offered and if he does not like what he sees, he has every right to change his mind, just as the breeder can change his mind if he feels the customer is not right for the puppy.

Some Physical Points to Look For

A Vizsla puppy should be sturdy and strong, at 7 or 8 weeks he does not have the elegance and grace of the adult. But at this stage he should look in proportion, his conformation can have a balance that is not exaggerated. Look at him after ten or eleven weeks and the length of his body or a length of leg would not form the compactness that it should and can at 8 weeks. By that time his legs will have grown too long and as likely as not every part of him will be out of proportion,

Figure 9.1 Look for a healthy bright-eyed puppy with a steady gaze

(because frequently the bone structure develops at a different rate) but as he matures his good outline will reappear. His chest should look broad and deep. Never expect a puppy to develop a deep chest if it is not so to start with. His chest must be well down to his elbow as he stands sideways. A straight back is essential at this age and again for a while this may be lost before the muscles develop. He needs to have rather strong, thick legs with good feet. A puppy with enormous flat, flabby feet with toes splayed apart standing easterly and westerly is not going to have good feet when he reaches adulthood. The foot should not be out of proportion, although soft and un-used. When the puppy stands alert his foot should look compact and the leg straight. A fiddle front at this stage does not grow into a good front. Do not worry about the knobbly knees. The knee is one of the growing points. Rather beware a smooth, flat knee, because the puppy may remain small. At this stage the quarters should have strength and a good, almost exaggerated turn of stifle. The second thigh should also be well developed. A straight back leg will not grow into that strong, powerful leg that drives of from the hock. A straight leg is required for the dog that needs strength for pulling, the Vizsla needs to move his body forward, powering his body into action as he moves.

If a puppy constantly holds his tail "gay" (perpendicular instead of horizontal) or if he has a sickle tail (a "gay" tail with a bend towards the forehand) he will probably continue to do so into adulthood. As likely as not, he will pass the condition on to his progeny and it has probably been passed down from his ancestors. Thus, it is important to look for a pup with a straight tail.

The head should be in proportion to the body, neither appearing too large and heavy nor too small and narrow. In profile, the muzzle should not look tapered nor the lip too tight. The eye should be fairly tight, covering the whites. Beware of a loose lower rim, even at this stage the shape of the eye should be correct. The colour of the eye will be difficult to assess at 8 weeks. It will still be in the transitional stage. If the sire and dam and the grandparents have the correct eye colour, it is practical to suppose that the eye will eventually become a shade darker in colour than the coat. The coat will probably be paler than in adulthood, but as the puppy matures the coat starts to darken down the centre of the back and the ears and the legs. The last to darken are the shoulders so at this stage the Vizsla can have a rather mottled appearance. Again when attempting to assess a puppy's future coat colour it is better to rely on the knowledge of the breeder and the pedigree. For example, if the line is known to have light coats or ginger coats or very dark coats, it is likely that the progeny will inherit the same colour.

Unless the purchaser has no preference for the type of Vizsla he owns and does not plan to breed, it is well to know that the small light boned little specimen will not develop good strong bones, nor will an enormous one reduce to the correct size when he reaches adulthood. Most breeders would agree I am sure, that a Vizsla puppy is surprisingly heavy. His legs are certainly not on the spindly side if he is a "good un". If he looks a model of an adult he will have little to grow into. The coat should be loose and the head should have wrinkled skin, not as exaggerated as the Bloodhound or the Sher Pei, but at this stage it must not be tight. If there are any signs of physical abnormalities such as lameness, skin problems, or diarrhoea, it is risky to take the puppy home unless you are perfectly satisfied that the condition has been dealt with by the breeder or the vet.

Preparing for Your Puppy's Homecoming

Be prepared to have your time consumed by the newcomer. Hours will be spent enjoying him if he is right for you. The naughtiness of the Vizsla puppy is incalculable. He will drive you to distraction with his rowdiness and sharp teeth, but his intelligence, charm, and familiarity will capture you and his trainability will amaze you. Even at 8 weeks he will make you respect him. That little golden dog has a quality of knowingness that can only be understood once you have acquired a Vizsla puppy.

Ask the breeder what food the puppy will require about a week before you fetch him. This will give you plenty of time to obtain all that is necessary in advance. Do follow the feeding routine as closely as possible to start with, whatever ideas you have on feeding. For the first few weeks it is important to follow exactly the same routine as the breeder recommends. Your puppy will need his own basket or base, his own blanket and a bowl for water and one for food, a small leather collar and lead or a slip lead—I recommend the leather collar. Unless you really know what you are doing, the slip lead can tighten and choke him if he is the type of puppy who is stubborn at first. Do allow your puppy to have his box somewhere where he knows he will be left alone in peace when he feels like it. He needs a place of safety. It follows that if he is constantly disturbed when he is tired, he will become bad-tempered, so the household should understand and respect his need for privacy. If a puppy starts to snap at children who constantly tease or pick him up when he is trying to sleep, it is not the temperament of the puppy that is at fault, it is the temperament of the children that should be questioned.

It is advisable to decide who is going to do all the "dirty work" before the puppy arrives. His life should follow a set routine at first; meals on time, toilet training consistent, times for sleeping and times for playing. He will soon settle into the pattern of the household. If he has one person responsible for organising him he will feel more secure, learning in a matter of hours who he can refer to if there are any complaints!

INJECTIONS

Your new puppy is at risk until he has had all the necessary injections. Whatever treatment he has had while with the breeder it is well to consult your vet on this matter. He is the professional and it is he who has all the up-to-date literature on the research programmes that have been initiated recently, especially on the disease Parvo Virus, which has caused such anxiety over the last few years. This fated disease mainly affects very young puppies and the older dog. When it first manifested itself, there was no antidote except that which was given to cats for this disease and of course, little or no research had been done on dogs. At last, we have a vaccine well tested and researched specifically for the dog. The early symptoms are vomiting and diarrhoea which will be blood-stained due to internal bleeding. In a very short space of time the dog is listless and dehydrated and complications result in a weak heart. The vet should be called without delay since it is better to be safe than sorry in this case.

So the basic essential injections necessary are the vaccines for protection against:

1) Parvo Virus
2) Distemper
3) Hepatitis
4) Hardpad
5) Leptospirosis

Distemper. This is a contagious disease. The symptoms are loss of appetite, loss of condition, rise in temperature, a cough, eyes weak and running, offensive breath and furred tongue. Possible vomiting and diarrhoea. The worst complication is the effect on the nervous system. The membranes which envelop the brain are invaded by the infection. This may lead to epileptiform convulsions.

Hardpad. Clinically, this disease may not be easily distinguishable from distemper until the characteristic hardening of the pad occurs. The symptoms may have an insidious onset and the disease may be well advanced before advice is sought. Early symptoms may be lethargy, loss of appetite, high temperature, a discharge from the nose which could be blood-stained and the nose may harden and crack.

Hepatitis. This is the term given to inflammation of the liver, the symptoms being loss of appetite, listlessness, vomiting and diarrhoea. In applying pressure over the region of the liver, pain may be felt. The dog may be jaundiced. This can be seen in the white of the eye which becomes yellow.

Leptospirosis. This disease is an infection with a micro-organism known as spirochaete. It is a serious and sometimes fatal disease. No time should be lost in calling the vet. The symptoms can be listlessnes, loss of appetite, loss of condition, high temperature, dehydration, external haemorrhaging and uraemia due to kidney infection. Uraemia is a failure of the kidney to excrete waste products into the urine and these therefore increase in their concentration in the blood causing severe nausea and vomiting and retention of fluid.

This disease can be caught from rats urine so it is vital that a puppy is protected from any place where rats may inhabit. A rat will urinate in a drinking bowl therefore it is advisable policy to always renew the water each day, especially if the Vizsla puppies or adults are kenneled.

It can be seen that there is little to distinguish one disease from another as many of the same symptoms occur at the onset. Nonetheless, the owner will know that his dog is ill enough to ask for the services of his vet.

Even though it may be very disappointing that your new Vizsla puppy cannot be aired for all to see, don't allow him anywhere he may be able to catch these diseases until he is fully inoculated. He should not meet strange dogs nor go any place where he may pick up an infection, which means in practical terms, that he should be kept within the confines of his own home, unless he is carried or taken by car.

By the time your puppy has had his last injection, which could be up to 14 or 16 weeks, you will have grown accustomed to his face. The chaotic early days, disrupting the family routine, will have settled into some sort of pattern. Who could imagine this little golden puppy could cause such concern? Or jealousies for that matter between humans or other canines, imposing a re-arrangement of the pecking order? But ruffled feathers usually settle so that all can enjoy the new addition. So quickly will the new puppy settle into his "niche", that it would be difficult to imagine life without him!

HOUSE TRAINING

The Hungarian Vizsla puppy should not be difficult to house train. I am always delighted to hear from new puppy owners that they have trained their puppy in a matter of days. It means that the new owner had a plan of action and it worked, meanwhile establishing a good relationship with the puppy. A seven or eight week old puppy cannot be house trained if there is a hint of punishment in the air.

The bladder is controlled by the sphincter muscle. As the bladder fills with urine it reaches a certain point when the nerve supply to the muscle enables it to relax and the bladder will empty. A different set of muscles in the sphincter will enable it to close. The nerve tracts in the frontal lobes of the brain which control the functions of elimination are poorly developed until the puppy is 5 or 6 weeks old. He can then learn how to consciously control by conditioned reflex the opening and closing of his bladder and how to eliminate in a particular place.

The owner must decide where and when he is to "go" and who is to train him to "go" there. If it is made clear to him, he will not be confused. He can be trained to use the newspaper method indoors or he can be trained to "go" outside straightaway. Obviously, if it is winter there is not much choice. The advantage of the newspaper method is that neither owner nor puppy has to brave the weather! The disadvantage is that sooner or later the puppy has to learn to go outside and he may become confused. If he does not get the message, he will continue going to the same spot in the house while the owner stands outside with the paper. I am not very good at the paper method. I traipse from one room to another with the puppy stopping to "pee" on the way. I know I should stay in one room with the puppy and his heap of newspaper so that he will know exactly where it is but I find it difficult to gear my life to one room. The puppy should not be allowed the run of the house or he may find his own particular spot that suits him. I have a bitch aged nine and she still remembers a very comfortable bedroom carpet that she selected for her exclusive use when she was eight weeks old!

Training the puppy to go outside from the start seems a much simpler exercise although perhaps needs more concentration on the trainer's part. It means picking him up when he needs to "go" and putting him down on the spot that has been chosen for him. A large patch of soil or grass or sand would suit him well and once he has urinated or defecated there two or three times he will know that that is where he eliminates when he is put outside. The trick for success in this method is timing. A pup cannot ask to go out, but the owner can observe his pattern of behaviour. For instance he will need to eliminate after every meal so this is a good opportunity to condition him. He will learn to associate the door with going outside and soon enough

141

he will start to go towards the door when he feels the need to go outside. A puppy generally needs to urinate every two hours — often it seems like every five minutes! If the owner learns to anticipate, there will be accidents at first but a Vizsla puppy gets the message sooner than most. The golden rules are:

1) Decide to have your puppy with you every minute of the day for the first few days and concentrate on housetraining him.

2) Always take him to one spot to "go".

3) Praise him when he succeeds every time.

4) Never punish him, but be firm. If he makes a mistake, it has happened because he has not "got the message". Since it is you that is "giving the message" maybe it is the teacher and not the pupil who is to blame.

I overheard a puppy owner relating the terrible misdemeanors his puppy had perpetrated. "I'll get the better of the little bugger. He's not going to get the better of me. I shut him outside in the rain for ten minutes. I said to myself, 'that'll teach him'." Asked by the listener what had transpired, he droned on, "So you know, the bugger wouldn't go. He stood there shivering in the rain, defying me!"

The puppy was all of eight weeks old! The sequal was that at a year old, the "much loved puppy" would do all he needed to do outside for anyone else in the large family but not for him.

I recommend that a new puppy sleeps by the new owners bed in a comfortable basket or box for the first few nights after his arrival. He will sleep all night in the warmth and security and knowing he is not alone. He will be contented. It conditions him to wait to relieve himself until the morning. When he does stir and is taken outside straightaway, he does not get into the habit of waking and "messing" all over the kitchen floor. After a few days he will sleep downstairs with much less trauma, and providing the owner is there at the right time, he learns to wait until he is let out. Thus he will learn control. If a puppy passes water frequently, he may have cystitis. This is inflammation of the bladder which can be caused by an infection or a chill. A puppy can easily catch a cold by sitting on cold concrete or wet grass, especially if he is kenneled. He should be kept very warm and given plenty to drink but if the condition persists it is wise to call a vet. Usually it can be dealt with easily.

If your puppy has a loose stool most likely it can be cleared by a slight change in feeding and of course if his diet has been changed, it may have upset him. If he has frequent diarrhoea but seems fit enough, it could be due to an infestation of worms. If he suddenly appears to be ill and has diarrhoea keep him warm and keep calm for a couple of hours. You may find he is himself again in no time. I have never found the real cause for this but I suspect that the puppy has chewed some object i.e. a pebble, and it is passing through. If at any time there is any sign of a high temperature, or blood in the urine or faeces call a vet immediately.

CHAPTER 10

SHOWING

Watching a top show dog winning can be an exciting experience, perhaps never to be forgotten by the handler and the spectator. Exhilarating and moving for those who are addicts to see an animal in absolute peak condition displaying all the qualities for which he has been bred. No dog is perfect, but he must be as near to perfection as can be as we watch him go round the ring in unison with his handler — standing and gaiting together, moving as one it seems. All eyes are on the dog and his character and temperament oozing with confidence and happiness — he could not and would not be in this company however good his conformation if he did not enjoy the job in hand.

THE IDEAL VIZSLA

Who can use the term "just a beauty contest" when the dog before him in the group is so superbly constructed. Beauty is in the eye of the beholder; here the beholder may find beauty if he wishes but he must and cannot deny the facts; the more experienced will like the pretty head, the attractive coat, the lovely colour, but he will know that that is not all by any means. The framework beneath the flowing coat or the short thick fur has to be correct and that has nothing to do with beauty but the parts of the dog put together correctly, functioning without fault.

Each breed has its own *standard*, laying down guidelines to which each must conform. This is in order that that particular breed shall preserve its own particular type and function. Whether the dog we are watching in the ring actually performs the task it was originally bred for he must be bred so that he has the conformation and temperament making him capable of pulling a sledge, baiting a bull, rounding up cattle or sheep, going down a hole or retrieving a pheasant, running across the desert or racing. It is only by showing and competing with stock bred that safeguards the different breeds looking and behaving the way they should.

There are few people who come into a breed, hoping maybe, but not expecting to go right to the top. The hardcore of show goers are those who go from show to show meeting their friends enjoying the fancy with others. Thrilled to win when they do, and in the main appreciating those dogs who beat theirs if they are better.

It is they who give the atmosphere to the showing days, who are cheerful and still keen after hours of travelling, who will talk dogs all day and part of the night and help any newcomer who needs a hand, giving away willingly whatever dog know-how they have.

Everyone showing dogs, top breeders, top handlers, top judges have come into the fancy as amateurs at some time or other. There is no 'O' or 'A' level, no degree, no university. If someone is interested and wants to learn, if he takes part, he will. Knowledge of dogs has little to do with money or class, an enthusiast need only watch, ask and listen and a wealth of knowledge is at his feet.

If a newcomer finds he does not like showing, then he should give it up and leave it for others who do. Some people love to show, some love to work a dog, some love a dog as a companion and pet and some may have the pleasure of all three, but to discriminate and condemn those who may not have the fortune or wish to combine all these is presumptuous and foolish.

So, where does the Hungarian Vizsla stand in the winning stakes in the company of other breeds? — Not too high. It is still a relatively new breed. The first recorded registration in the Kennel Club was in 1953, but there are other breeds that have been imported since then which have been established more rapidly than the Vizsla in every way.

It is an invaluable lesson to sit by the ringside of the gundog group at a show. Compare the Best of Breed Vizsla's structure with the Best of Breed Labrador or Pointer for instance — the top winners of the established breeds are so sound and well made, the Vizsla cannot yet compare. Sh Ch *Swanside Miklos*, now dead, bred by Roger Simkin (by *Bingo vom Wurmbrandpark,* out of Sh Ch *Swanside Czarina*, owned by Minecke Mills de Hoog) was placed Res. Best in Show at the National Gundog Championship Show in 1975. An elegant dog and always beautifully handled, never put a foot wrong in the show ring. Others have been pulled out in the last six or four of the gundog group and some have done well at smaller shows.

Those who have tried to establish the breed on a footing with other gun dog breeds in the show ring and in the field have had an uphill struggle. Much of the recent imported stock have made a worthwhile contribution, but although there has been a gradual improvement in temperament and some physical aspects, the main fault in the breed 'a bad front', has never been firmly corrected. The result of this is that there are Vizslas who may not appear to have that particular fault but they may carry it genetically so the fault will and does recur again and again in the progeny. If the progeny are bred from the merry-go-round starts again.

The only way to learn about good dogs is to watch good dogs. Question why one dog wins and another doesn't, why the judge looks at certain points of a dog, why he ranks the exhibits in a particular order, etc. The more you study and question other participants, the more you learn about your breed.

If your intention is to show and breed seriously, while learning and enjoying showing, you will be gaining more and more knowledge. You will find that you have a good idea of your ideal Vizsla, your dream Vizsla! One day, it may be you and your Vizsla in the big ring winning best in the show or one of your breed standing on the red carpet. Arthur Westlake, who is now dead, said to me one day, "One of the most rewarding experiences was to be at the ringside watching a dog that I had bred taking top honours!" Most breeders would agree with these sentiments.

THE IDEAL SHOW CAREER

Let us suppose that you are a complete novice. You own your first Vizsla and you are really pleased with him. You have no idea whether he is good enough to show except that the breeder said he was a good one. If the breeder had said he will make a good show dog and you bought him at seven to eight weeks old, that breeder must have knowledge that no other has, because at that age it is impossible to be positive since a Vizsla goes through many stages. At 7 or 8 weeks old you think you have a world beater, but at 10 weeks he can look as if he has every fault in the book.

It is a sensible idea to visit a local show or two, just to observe and glean information. Find out what is expected of you and your dog, talk to the show goers. There are a wealth of facts you will need to know so here are a few to start with.

A puppy cannot be shown before he is six months old. For his first entry choose a small show, an Exemption or local Open show. You will find it easier and more relaxing, the competition not nearly as formidable as at a Championship show. Novices frequently enter their puppy in every class available. This is not sensible. It is tempting but a young puppy can tire quickly and become bored, so only enter him in one or two classes if you want him to enjoy his day. Aim to arrive early, giving yourself plenty of time to familiarise yourself and your puppy with the atmosphere and the place. For your Vizsla's debut, you will need to equip yourself with:

1) Your admittance card and schedule.

2) Safety pin or metal tag for pinning on chest to hold class number.

3) Money handy for buying a catalogue at show (This is vital because it tells your bench number, ring number and all essential information).

4) Bag for carrying the following:
Show Lead
Rubber Glove
Velvet Duster
Benching Collar and Lead
Blanket (for dog)
Water and Water Bowl
Food for dog (and something for you too!)
Clothing for snowstorms, pelting rain or a tropical heatwave!

So you have been to your first show, and you enjoyed it. Whether you won a prize or not it seems you have acquired a taste for this side of the dog game. You then try to gain as much experience as you can, entering your puppy in small shows with a Championship show in mind in a couple of months time. Remember that some Championship show entry applications must be received two months before the show date.

Depending on the classification for Vizslas there may be a puppy and a junior class. If not you will have to enter him in the first one or two classes that are offered. If you have found that your Vizsla is a natural, loves every minute of showing and is an extrovert you could enter the puppy stakes, but if he is likely to weary and become bored do not risk it.

When you have reached Championship show stage your puppy will have had some good wins in the smaller shows that you have been to, so although nervous, you will probably have gained confidence and a certain aplomb. You know that your Vizsla is not shy, he may stand and trot if in the right mood! Even so, neither of you could have been prepared for the noise and tension or the magnitude of the place nor the thousands of dogs and people — you will see more Vizslas than ever before. You will have the opportunity to compare different types and lines that you have heard and read about. You will meet the breeders and enthusiasts and some of your puppy's relatives too, perhaps.

We will suppose that your puppy wins both his classes. Now you can feel that you may have something good! You will then have to compete with all the Vizsla dogs who have won their classes. That means you are up against the winner of the open dog class who as likely as not is a Sh Ch or a Champion so you would not expect to beat him at this stage. But as you come out of the ring, you should be feeling very pleased. Stay and watch the other Vizslas being judged. Find out who does win the open bitch class. Then the best bitch, having won her challenge certificate, competes with the best dog who won his challenge certificate. Find out which of the two will get best of breed and go on to compete in the gundog group against all the best of breed gundogs.

At this stage the tension mounts round the ringside — everyone playing at judging and trying to guess which one will be put up. The two Vizslas are standing perfectly in the middle of the ring, the strain telling as you see the hands of the handlers shaking, their faces serious, not a muscle moving. The judge asks them to move their dogs again — he is finding it a difficult decision. They both stand again, the judge goes over to the table, collects the best of breed card and rosette and gives it to the dog's handler. Everyone relaxes, both the dogs and their owners and the crowd claps. The winner is kissed by the loser, a kind gesture and nice to see. The judge has a brief chat with the owner then the winners do a lap of honour and come out of the ring amid congratulations. When that happens to you for the first time, you will never forget it.

Suppose that it does happen to you a year or so later and it is you holding the precious prize, your dog's first championship certificate. You have gained your Junior Warrant and qualified for Crufts. You have worked your way up from puppy classes to junior, maiden, novice, to post graduate and limit and finally if your Vizsla gains his 3rd challenge certificate his title will be show champion. He can only enter the open dog class after this. Generally the competition in this group is really hot because he will be competing against the other champions and show champions in the breed. By this time you have done a lot of winning and losing too, so you know what it feels like to go cardless. You have managed to smile even so and to be gracious to those who beat you even if you felt it was not justified. But more important, you have asked questions, been modest and sensible enough to take good advice and recognised virtues and faults in your dog. Your handling has improved and you feel that it is a good partnership between you and your maturing Vizsla. Perhaps he has been through a stage of listlessness and boredom when you had to lay him off showing for a time, having no training and no show lead. Good walks and a bit of fun tend to cure this problem and the dog should come back as if he had been on holiday and start to show again with a liveliness and energy for the job.

Some of your friends and competitors will have experienced similar difficulties with their bitches. Invariably they "go off the boil" when they have been in season and during what would be the gestation period of nine weeks if they were in whelp, their minds are on nests rather than show rings!

You need to gain two more challenge certificates before you can call your dog a Show Champion. You will find it difficult not to take everything too seriously, your showing days are not the naive win or lose days that you felt in the beginning. Now they are tinged with not a little cynicism and wariness as well as a deeper understanding of people and dogs. To recognise that you are ambitious and need to win is important, if it goes hand in hand with the ambition to gain more knowledge of the Vizsla and a wish to see him find a place with the best in the ring and in the field, not just your dog but the VIZSLA as a breed, then whether you go home cardless or not, it will not be such a blow. You may have discovered a new dimension in yourself where your pleasure in seeing a really good Vizsla win transcends your losses.

When you do gain your 3 challenge certificates, you may have had it easy. For some exhibitors it takes a long time. Sh Ch *Chantilly Jester*, owned and bred by Heather McCabe, waited until *Jester* was over 2 years old. From then on he never stopped winning, taking on every newcomer until he was retired. (He died in 1984).

We have many Vizslas in the breed who never achieved the final championship certificate. They may win well in early classes as youngsters and seem to have a promising future, but eventually never quite make the grade. It is difficult to cut your losses, but you may have to. It is difficult to retire a top winning Vizsla too, since the best in breed needs to be seen. There is no point in retiring a good Vizsla to make way for mediocre stock. One thing to remember is that our breed can mature late.

So with your third championship certificate in your hand and best of breed rosette pinned to your chest for all to see, the rest of the day will be spent in a pleasant haze. If you have really worked hard for it you can spare a moment congratulating yourself. If you have won it easily, then you have been very lucky.

Now you have to go into the big ring. If you go into that ring expecting it to be a piece of cake, you will not have learnt a thing on your way up! If you know that it is very, very unlikely that you will even be pulled out in the last 6 or 8 then you have learnt a lot. If you understand what your chances are you have come a long way from the day when you first showed your puppy. You have assessed your Vizsla as a judge should, not as a novice.

WHAT THE JUDGE WANTS TO SEE

The judge assesses the conformation of the dog to the specification of the *standard*, he can best achieve his final decision, by examining the dog standing in a show ring posture and when the dog is gaited, so that he can see how the structure of the dog functions in action. Therefore to allow the judge to see your Vizsla at its best advant-

Free Standing

"Topping and Tailing"

Incorrect Handling

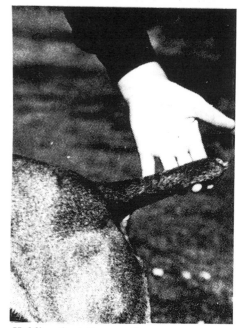

Holding the tail correctly

Fig.10.1 Bringing out the best in your dog

(Photo: Diane Pearce)

age you need to understand how to place him and move him correctly. So firstly we will discuss the different ways of handling and then how to set him up.

Setting the Dog Up

With your dog standing on your left hand side, hold his muzzle with your left hand, place his right foot then change over placing his left foot parallel to the other, check that the feet are in line with the tip of the elbow and the top point of the shoulders, this will immediately demonstrate the angulation of the shoulder and forequarters. Holding his head firstly, either by the muzzle or with his lead up behind his ears run your left hand over his back in order to place his back legs so that they too are parallel to one another, bend down and reach for one leg and then the other. They should be so positioned so that when viewed from behind they are straight and when viewed from the side, the dog presents a balanced picture, covering the ground adequately, demonstrating the correct angulation, the hocks being perpendicular to the floor. Check the balance again, by stretching the head and neck, slightly, thus he will adjust his weight so that it is distributed correctly. Finally position yourself   so that you have control of his head and forequarters with your right hand and hold his tail (horizontal) with your left hand, this is best done by placing the palm of the hand under the centre of the tail allowing it to lie there — **never hang on to your dog's tail to control him.** Thus your Vizsla should feel relaxed and comfortable because his whole body is being correctly supported. Smooth his back every now and then, and talk to him, so that he knows that he is pleasing you.

Practice opening your dog's mouth. This is necessary because the judge should always look at his teeth. Once the dog becomes accustomed to your handling him he should not mind a judge going over him.

How to Gait Your Vizsla

*Your Vizsla has to learn to trot b*y your side, this is the pace that demonstrates the dog's structure functioning at its most effective. The judge will instruct the handler to trot his dog in a triangle and in a straight line so that he can assess the dog's movement from different angles, his stride, topline and ground covering ability. When practising, place the lead up the neck, the head must stay at the same level throughout, the lead should be neither too tight nor too slack, thus he remains 'collected'. The pace should be a 'moderate but lively trot' and the handler can best do this by synchronizing his pace and the dog's in order to move as one. Keep him 'going forward' at all times when he is gaiting, do not allow him to pull away from you, otherwise he will not be balanced and he will start to crab, creating problems in his movement that he would not naturally have. Always keep the dog between you and the judge. Be attentive to the judge's wish if he requires a triangle, use as much of the ring as possible and trot your dog into the corners. When going straight, make sure it is not a diagonal! Never allow your dog to 'run into the judge', stop a few feet away from him, keeping your dog standing as alert as you can on a loose lead — this is when all the faults show up because you do not have a chance to pose him. If your dog can do all this with his tail wagging it will indicate his happy temperament and he will be a pleasure to watch.

How to Spoil your dog's chances

1) Stringing him up too tight on the lead, he will have to compensate by standing on tiptoe which will cause him to knuckle over and his elbows to come out. Some handlers prefer to place the forequarters by standing in front of the dog and lifting the feet off the ground together and lowering them into place, this can cause the hindquarters to be over-stretched, the forelegs being too far forward, it can also create a gap between the elbow and the brisket when viewed from the side.

2) Placing the back legs too far beneath the dog or too far back will distort his frame, he will hunch his back to try and compensate for the discomfort, also if the legs are placed too far back it will appear as if he has little turn of stifle.

3) Holding the tail too high spoils his topline, too low has the same effect, giving the dog a lifeless look.

Timing

Timing is an important factor if the dog is to be seen at his best. Never have your dog at a disadvantage whilst in the ring. Don't relax yourself nor allow him to forget that he is in the show ring, and that you expect a lot of him. When you first come into the ring set him up, so that he knows why he is there, and it steadies him as well as you. If you have to wait too long for the judge to walk down the line, let your dog relax by walking round you and set him up again.

As you are waiting your turn to be gone over make sure your dog is ready to go when the judge calls you up. Take your time setting your Vizsla up correctly and do not fuss him.

A good judge will give you time to set your dog up so that at his best points may be seen. A golden rule of showing is never take your eye off the judge.

HANDLING

Your ideal show career depends on how good a specimen your puppy develops into, but whatever happens you will need to learn how to show and handle him to the best advantage. There are very few dogs who cannot be taught to behave as they should, anyone who does obedience training will have learnt very quickly that it is always the handler who has not learnt to teach the dog correctly, rather than a dog's inability to learn. So with this in mind and that however good or bad a dog's conformation, a dog well handled is always a treat to see.

A Vizsla should not be difficult to train. He is a gundog so it should be his nature to want to please and work for you. He is usually very easy to train in basic obedience. Naturally as a youngster of three months you would not expect him to stand for long or tolerate much formal teaching for that matter, but as he matures, with patience and firmness you can expect a high degree of showing ability if you teach him right. He should be perfectly capable of standing and moving in the show ring to a very high standard.

The handler's personality, feelings and skills will directly affect the way the dog behaves at a show. If you feel your dog cannot learn to stand still or move correctly he is certainly not going to learn by himself. Give yourself confidence and some knowledge by watching good handlers, then try it. It is important to be patient with yourself and your dog. Of course you will make mistakes but as long as you admit to them instead of blaming your dog, no harm is done. When you show him, have the attitude that he is your pride and ever-hopeful joy. It is difficult when he does not show as well as you know he can. But as you both become more and more accustomed to the performance you and he can enjoy the experience together. If you are able to keep your sense of humour at the same time, everyone will enjoy watching you. Never believe that you are the only one who has difficulties or that you are the only one who is nervous and tense as you stand in the ring — some are cleverer than others at covering up their feelings. Of course your dog will feel the tension but this can be put to good use combined with the excitement and sense of occasion he can rise to it. Many if not all brilliant performers in other fields can only give their best when they are really keyed up. You can liken the day of the show to a performance in the theatre — months of hard grind with rehearsing until the day arrives. The tension mounts, tempers quicken, come the moment, it can either be a complete flop or a resounding success. Whatever the outcome, if there is talent there, it will come out sooner or later.

Teaching a puppy how to stand and move correctly and learning ring manners is quite a task. You will need to be guided by his temperament and stage of maturity as to how much you can expect of him. But from very early on, each day give him a few minutes of some sort of training. You can do this in your kitchen, hallway, or in the middle of the garden, park or field, in fact anywhere with a bit of space. Kneel down and stand him in front of you. It does not matter how he stands at first, just get him used to covering the ground, so that his legs are taking his weight equally. You can help him by holding his muzzle from underneath with your right hand or if he does not like that, steady him by holding his neck. Try running your left hand over and over his back to relax him. Talk to him and praise him so that he enjoys it. Then either place each back leg separately or by putting your hand between his back legs and lifting his quarters off the ground. Replace them gently down again so that he is standing squarely on his four legs then place your left hand under his tail and lift it so that it is horizontal. Of course it will not work at first — one end will go up, the other down, but it will come in time. You may get a surprise. He may do it perfectly well if you are firm. The golden rule is, always finish any lesson at any age, on a note of success. If a lesson does not go well, take him back to an exercise you know he can do, so ending on a good note. If lessons always end in failure and tension and your displeasure is obvious, your Vizsla is not going to want to repeat that lesson, so you will have a stubborn dog on your hands. If you feel you are losing your cool, leave your Vizsla in peace, do something with him that you can both enjoy and leave the lesson for another day. He needs to get used to being touched all over, so get into the habit of looking at his teeth regularly, inspecting his ears, picking his feet up, running your hands underneath and over his back, inside his back legs, and in the case of a male, his scrotum. Get him used to every move you know the judge will need to make. Once your puppy is used to his collar and lead you can introduce him to his show lead. There are many different makes and types on the market. Personally, I like a narrow leather slip lead that is not too long, the reason being that leather is easy on the hands and it is strong enough to check a Vizsla if necessary. I also like the colour of leather against the Vizsla coat, but it is important that you find something that suits you and that you find comfortable. Keep the show lead just for show training him and for shows, because a dog soon picks up the idea that his every day lead means walks and the other means using his brain as well as fun with you.

You need to teach your puppy to trot correctly as you would in the show ring. At first he will be all over the place, but if you trot gently, encouraging him, talking to him, keeping his attention and teaching him to keep his head up which he will do if you keep up an incessant chatter, he will be keen to hear what you are saying. When he does it right, take the lead off, let him leap and play, knowing he has pleased you. Then stop, put the lead back on again and trot, saying "trot" so that he learns the word. Soon he learns that when the lead goes on, you mean business. As soon as you take it off, he knows it means fun and games. This way, he really does enjoy the job in hand. The Vizsla loves working and pleasing and he loves to play. This will stand you in good stead throughout his life. In every aspect of owning a Vizsla, this is how you will get the very best out of him. You must never forget to praise him.

There are many different methods of showing the various breeds and it is an art to handle dogs well. The professional handler is there to display the dog to its full advantage. He will do this with such skill that it looks simple, but anyone who handles well knows it is not easy at all and takes much practice, time, patience and insight. It is said that a good handler can make a poor dog look good, or a bad handler a good one look poor. Maybe that is so, but if a dog is handled badly, no judge can see enough to make his own mind up.

So the time will come when your Vizsla is old enough for you to decide what method you will use, which manner of handling suits him best, taking into consideration that the freer and less cluttered up any dog looks, the more the judge likes it. Also, the Vizsla does not like being overhandled. He is best left alone and independent. He is also a natural fawner and if encouraged in any way will do so, so the less you touch him the better.

In the Vizsla breed it can be said there are three main methods of handling. We will not talk about idiosyncratic methods, but accepted forms of showing in the gundog world!

The Free Standing Method
This must be the ideal style. It can be seen in the Labrador ring to perfection. The dog stands alone with the handler in front of him holding the lead loosely, with a tit-bit at the ready. The dog stands stock still with its tail slowly swinging from side to side. A lovely sight, accentuating its excellent temperament and conformation.

If your Vizsla has a calm, placid temperament, is extrovert and enjoys standing freely, it is well worth giving it a try. There is no doubt that it is very effective when it works.

To train your Vizsla to show this way takes time. Tit-bits, firmness and praise must be used as always. To start with, try standing in front of him with the lead loose, and tit-bits in your hand. Concentrate on his eyes and say "stand" (it does not matter how at this stage). If he sits, put the tit-bits away, go back to him, stand him, using the word, run your hand along his back so that he begins to associate the hand movement with the word. When he feels steady enough, stand in front of him again and repeat the performance. If he stays for two seconds praise him and give him the food, but do not over-excite him. Stay calm, then try again and again and again. You can stand him correctly if you find he is getting the message and he seems really steady. Then the fun begins. Each day practice and you will find that he will stand longer and longer enjoying his sense of balance, and eventually you may find that you can count up to 100 (under your breath) without his moving. By that time I am sure you will have found that this method suits you both.

The drawbacks to this way of showing are numerous. Firstly, it is difficult to achieve with a Vizsla. His lively, vivacious temperament does not lend itself too well to having the handler stand so far away. Secondly, there is nothing like it for showing up faults, such as bad feet, elbows and all, and you cannot keep nipping back to put them right. Nor are there many Vizslas who will hold their tails horizontal on their own, so the correct outline cannot be achieved. If your Vizsla is the fussy type, he will keep smiling and wagging his tail at you for food. On the other hand, some Vizslas are not tempted by any tit-bit, or even curious once they are in the show ring. I have used this method and I found that if I put the tit-bits in my pocket, it seemed to be more effective. My Vizsla did not get quite so excited, but he knew they were there and his eyes would be riveted at just the right level. All I needed to do was to keep my hands waist high.

Topping and Tailing

This way of showing a dog has exactly the opposite effect of the Free Standing Method. The advantages are that the Vizsla is close to his owner which he likes. If he moves his feet or head they can be quickly corrected without the handler moving. The tail is held horizontal and it does not take so long to set him up.

To train your Vizsla to show this way takes less time and patience than the free standing method but you need all your skill to prevent him from turning his head towards you, since you are practically eye to eye!

Stand your Vizsla as you have taught him, holding his muzzle, you kneel down on one knee or two if you like, support his tail in the usual manner, allowing the lead to drop loosely round his neck.

The disadvantages are, firstly, the outline can be marred by the handler looking over the dog. If your Vizsla does not like being held by the muzzle, he will lean back away from your hand which will shorten his neck or he will lift his muzzle in the air too high causing his back to hunch in protest. Thus he will not be correctly balanced. If you are over a certain age, struggling up and down on your knees will not do your lumbago any good! I do not think this method is for a gundog breed, at least, not the larger ones since they should have an independent aspect and should be allowed to stand as naturally as possible.

Free Standing/Topping and Tailing

This is a compromise between the free-standing and topping and tailing methods. The handler stands, holding or supporting the muzzle or neck, or he can hold the lead up behind the ears, leaving the head entirely free. Meanwhile the tail is held in the correct position. The advantage in this method is that you are not restricted in any way, either by standing in front of the dog, or kneeling down. You are free to shift your weight either toward the head or to the dog's rear. You can stand close or at arms length. If your dog is really showing well that day, full of confidence and as steady as a rock, you can stand back, with the minimum of handling from you or on the other hand, if your dog has the fidgets you can be close enough to put him right.

Many handlers like to use tit-bits—a bit of biscuit, meat or whatever the dog fancies best. The Vizsla does not usually respond all that well. It can over-excite him and in many cases instead of relaxing him, makes him fuss. If tit-bits are used, better to have them in your pocket out of the way so that he can smell them. If you hold them out, the dog either leaps for them or just manages to be chewing a piece as the judge approaches to look at his teeth!

As far as I am concerned, I cannot handle the tit-bit. Either it gets stuck in my pocket and I cannot reach it or I drop it so that me and my Vizsla are both searching in the grass for it. Better not to confuse the issue with food unless you are very skillful.

Some handlers are assisted by a relative or friend, the plan being that the dogs attention will be attracted by waving or calling or coughing or whatever from outside the ring. This can work very well if they always place themselves somewhere in front of the dog. This exercise is not permissable by the Kennel Club regulations. No-one else either inside or outside the ring is allowed to assist the dog other than the actual handler.

Whichever method is chosen, and I suspect we all use a bit of each, what is essential is that we are decisive so that the Vizsla can understand what we are asking of him. Some dogs have more grey matter than others, but they cannot learn to show by themselves.

When practising with your Vizsla, try standing him before a full length mirror sideways and frontways (this is what the judge sees). It can be quite a shock. You think your Vizsla is set up just right, but you look in the mirror and everything is wrong! A friend is just as useful as a mirror if not more so for you can discuss, criticise, take it in turns to look at each other's dogs. The work and anticipation is almost more fun than the day itself.

Even though your Vizsla is your beloved pet and show gundog, the purpose of the showing is to perpetuate the breed, as it should be. A Hungarian Vizsla is a gundog which hunts, points, and retrieves. He should look like a Vizsla and be able to fulfill his function as one. All who show should be jealous of his unique qualities.

TYPES OF DOG SHOWS

Exemption Shows
Most people's introduction to showing comes from attending the small dog shows which are often held in conjunction with local fetes and agricultural shows. These shows are held under the jurisdiction of the Kennel Club and are known as *Exemption Shows.* Only four pedigree classes are allowed. These usually come under class headings such as sporting, non-sporting, working and utility. Other classes are the

novelty classes such as best short-haired dog, dog with the 'waggiest tail', dog with the prettiest face and so on. After all the novelty classes have been judged, the class winners compete for the best in show title. Wins at exemption shows do not count towards any titles, i.e. Junior Warrant.

Matches
Matches are often held by 'Ringcraft' clubs. They involve pedigree dogs only. Once again they are held under Kennel Club rules, although they do not need to obtain permission. An outsider is often called in to judge. Matches are really just a social affair which gives good grounding in ring behaviour.

Sanction Shows
These are licenced by the Kennel Club and are subject to more rules and regulations. A schedule has to be issued and the number of classes is limited.

Limit Shows
These are slightly more advanced than sanction shows. There must be a minimum of twenty-one classes if more than one breed is scheduled or if just one breed, a minimum of thirteen classes. Any dog which has won a Challenge Certificate is not eligible to be shown at the foregoing types of show.

Open Shows
These can have any number of classes and are open to all types of pedigree dogs which are registered with the Kennel Club.

Championship Shows
These are the shows at which the much sought after challenge certificates are awarded. These shows cater for nearly every type of pedigree dogs which are found in Britain. They are held all over the country, winning a class at a championship show means that one can enter for Crufts.

Crufts
To enter Crufts — this world famous show — one first must qualify a dog at a championship show. A show champion or champion dog can be shown at Crufts without having to qualify as it has already proved its quality.

Definition of Classes

Minor Puppy   For dogs of six and not exceeding nine calendar months of age on the day of the show.

Puppy   For dogs of six and not exceeding twelve calendar months of age on the day of the show.

Junior   For dogs of six and not exceeding eighteen calendar months of age of the day of the show.

Special Yearling For dogs of six months and not exceeding two years of age on the day of the show.

Maiden For dogs which have not won a challenge certificate or a first prize at an open or championship show (puppy, special puppy, minor and special minor puppy classes excepted).

Novice For dogs which have not won a challenge certificate or three or more first prizes at open or championship shows (puppy, special puppy, minor and special minor puppy classes excepted).

Undergraduate For dogs which have not won a challenge certificate or three or more first prizes at championship shows (puppy, special puppy, minor and special minor puppy classes excepted).

Graduate For dogs which have not won a challenge certificate or four or more first prizes at championship shows in graduate, post graduate, minor limit, mid limit and open classes whether restricted or not.

Post Graduate For dogs which have not won a challenge certificate or five or more first prizes at championship shows in post graduate, minor limit, mid limit, limit and open classes whether restricted or not.

Limit For dogs which have not won three challenge certificates under three different judges or seven or more first prizes in all at championship shows in limit and open classes, confined to the breed, whether restricted or not, at shows where challenge certificates were offered in the breed.

Special Open For open classes except that it is restricted as to weight, height, colour or to members of an association.

Field Trial For dogs which have won prizes, awards of honour, diplomas of merit or certificates of merit in actual competition at a field trial held under Kennel Club or Irish Kennel Club field trial rules and regulations.

Special Beginners For dogs and bitches shown by an exhibitor whose dogs have never won a challenge certificate in the breed. (**Note:** it is the exhibitor who has to qualify NOT the dog.)

Brace For two exhibits (either sex or mixed) of one breed belonging to the same exhibitor, each exhibit having been entered in some class other than brace or team.

Team	For three exhibits (either sex or mixed) of one breed belonging to the same exhibitor, each exhibit having been entered in some class other than brace or team.
Veteran	For dogs of seven years of age and over on the day of the show.

Special Regulations

When a dog is not fully registered at the British Kennel Club there are certain letters which must be placed after the dog's name on the entry form to indicate that permission has been applied for, but that the owner has not yet received confirmation from the Kennel Club. These are as follows:

N A F — Name Applied For

T A F — Transfer Applied For

ARAF — Active Register Applied For

FORM OF CLAIM FOR JUNIOR WARRANT

On application by the owner a Junior Warrant will be issued for a dog that has obtained 25 points while eligible to compete as a Junior (i.e. under 18 months of age) at shows.

The scale of points is as follows:

1. For each 1st prize in a breed class at a championship show where the challenge certificates were offered for the breed, 3 points.

2. For each 1st prize in a breed class at a championship show where the challenge certificates were not offered for the breed, or at an open show, 1 point.

    NOTES: (a) A class open to more than one variety of a breed is not a breed class

    (b) Only registered owner(s) at time of qualification may apply.

PARTICULARS OF CLAIM

SHOW:

DATE:

CLASS No.:

POINTS CLAIMED:

Figure 10.3 Claim for Junior Warrant

Junior Warrant

How do you gain a Junior Warrant? If your puppy turns out to be a good one and you discover that every time you show him you come out of the ring with a red card in your hand, it may be worthwhile trying to gain a Junior Warrant. This is a special award offered by the Kennel Club for puppies who have gained 25 points from the age of six months up to eighteen months. Three points can be acquired by any first prize won in a breed class at a championship show. At a championship show without challenge certificate for the breed or Open Shows, a first prize counts as one point. It is difficult for a Hungarian Vizsla to gain a junior warrant because we have so few classes at open shows or at many championship shows, it does mean chasing to shows far and wide. On the other hand, there will be fewer Vizslas competing for this award than in the breeds that draw enormous entries.

On attaining the 25 points the certificate has to be applied for. The Kennel Club does not automatically send it, as it does the challenge certificate. Unfortunately there is no way of recognising a dog who has won his junior warrant either. There are no letters before his name indicating this award. Even so, it is well worth noting up those wins. It will be a strong indication that the puppy will gain show champion status later on, although it is not always so.

THE WORKING VIZSLA
IN BRITAIN

CONTRIBUTED BY
Mrs. L. PETRIE-HAY

Figure 11.1 Two Champions — Top: *Galfrid Tara* (Mr Richard Houghton)
Bottom: *Russetmantle Troy* (the Author) (photo Diane Pearce)

CHAPTER 11

THE WORKING VIZSLA IN BRITAIN

A VERSATILE SHOOTING DOG

Originally the Vizsla was bred as a hunting dog, to find food for his master. Then he had to find game for hunters working with falcons or nets. Finally, with the advent of the gun, the Vizsla became a gundog. He must not be thought of purely as a bird dog (as in USA) since if properly trained he must hunt fur or feather on command. In Hungary 'Madar' tells him to run high headed in search of birds and 'Nyul' warns him that it is rabbits and other ground game that he must hunt. As an all-purpose gundog the Vizsla is rapidly gaining popularity in this country and in fact many are being exported to the Continent, America, Australia, Africa and New Zealand to people who wish to use them as gundogs.

Two pups were sent to Greece and their owner tells me that the bitch pup has grown into a splendid animal who performs particularly well when pointing birds. Sometimes she even seizes the quail from the air! The dog, he says, is with him day and night, very obedient, his performance as a hunter and pointer is excellent. He is also a good watch dog. He does not interfere with the domestic animals, rabbits, pigeons, hens etc., and if one wanders away he will shepherd it back. He is such a master of his trade that one forgets to shoot, one is so lost in admiration at his performance! Surely the Vizsla is the aristocrat of dogs, writes this owner. Similar letters of praise have come from many countries from people who have bought Vizslas as shooting companions. From Denmark I am told that the pup that was sent over is very aggressive in the way he dares to go into any bush to see if there should be some game! From Scotland I received a letter saying that their dog was not used for shooting but had adapted so well to the conditions of the hill farm he made a wonderful sheepdog and it would not be possible to work the hill without him particularly during the tupping season.

And another tells me that he has yet to find a breed of dog that can match the Vizsla for hunting and dogwork. He tells me that he has owned many different breeds but the Vizsla as far as he was concerned outshines all others.

Mr Gillan, who was the headkeeper at Balmoral, had considerable experience of training these dogs and considers them superior to German Shorthaired Pointers and

Weimaraners. Lord Londonderry's keeper was so impressed with one that he saw running in a trial that he bought a couple of pups the following season. One report I had about a bitch said that she had never been known to be sulky or do anything underhand, that although she was very feminine she was as tough as any dog when it came to facing cover whilst hunting, quite fearless, with an outstanding doggedness and determination of character. She had a first class nose and was a tireless worker. Another bitch, who died two days before her seventeenth birthday, had worked all her life not only as a gundog but also with falcons. All this is a testament to their adaptability and proficiency as gundogs, but they are also used by many falconers and also for deer stalking. In a copy of *Shooting Times and Country Life Magazine* in 1966 there is a report of the Welsh Hawking Club and a photo of Mr Jackson and Mr Lorant de Bastyai with their Vizslas. Laurent says of his dog *Pacal* that there was great harmony between *Pacal* and *Durak* his goshawk. The bird would watch and follow the dog, both were quite free, and he felt completely unnecessary in their company. John Gassman, well known as an experienced shooting and stalking man, wrote "One thing I am sure, having been with Pointer/Retrievers all my life, that the Vizsla will compare favourably with any of these breeds".

THE VARIOUS COMPETITIONS IN THE FIELD

In order to foster and protect the interests of the breed in this country there are two organisations, the Hungarian Vizsla Society and the Hungarian Vizsla Club. Both have run field trials over the years. The Vizsla Society has organised regular get-togethers which include trainings sessions also training days, field days and working tests, and they provide annual trophies which are awarded to the dogs which accumulate the highest points not only for working ability but also for conformation. Both the societies are represented on the Kennel Club field trial council. There are two representatives on the Kennel Club field trial committee who look after the interests of all the hunt, point, retrieve breeds.

In 1982 the Kennel Club authorised a Hunt, Point, Retrieve Field Trial Association on which both the Society and Club have two representatives. This Association runs an annual Field Trial Judges' seminar which is attended by all the panel A and B judges, learner judges, field trial secretaries and field trial stewards.

The Association will also have the task of organising a field trial Championship Stake when the Kennel Club sees fit to authorise one for the Hunt, Point, Retrieve group.

The *Shooting Times and Country Life Magazine* award annually a silver salver to the dog who has run in not less than 3 field trials and gained the highest marks, this covers all the hunt, point and retrieve breeds. It was first awarded at the game fair in 1977 for the 1976 season and has been won every year since by a German Shorthaired Pointer. Until 1982 Vizslas, although featuring in the awards and qualifying by running in 3 or more trials were never placed in the final line up, but in 1982 this was broken and Mrs Sylvia Cox's *Viszony of Vallota* came second having run in 9 trials and gained 50 marks, only two marks below the winning dog who ran in ten trials and gained 52 marks.

BHPR are the initials for a Kennel Club gundog classification — Breeds which Hunt, Point, and Retrieve. In February 1979 there was an opportunity to alter this from BHPR to P/R or Pointer/Retriever. The two words instead of six seemed a good idea, in saving of wind and paper. BHPR may sound attractive to some, to others it could be a drug or a trade union. So battle commenced on the pros and cons of an alternative umbrella title for such gundogs.

The title describes the variety of mid-European Pointers which, unlike English Pointers and Setters, are expected to retrieve from land and water, and also hunt in cover as well as in the open. Examples of such dogs other than Vizslas are the German Shorthaired Pointer, German Wirehaired Pointer, Weimaraner and Large Munsterlander. The Drentse Partridge Dog, the Italian Spinone, the Brittany Spaniel, also the Wire-haired Vizsla, would be included but are barely existent in this country. The only breed in this list which gives any indication as to its work is the German Pointer. In some ways this is to its detriment as many German Pointer breeders will agree.

The most common question one has to answer is "Do they retrieve?". **Yes**, all these breeds retrieve, and if they wish to run in field trials, then the Kennel Club stipulates that in order to win an award, this group of gundogs must not only hunt for game, point game, retrieve fur and feather, but also complete a water retrieve either of a bird from the water with a shot fired in the novice stake, or of a bird from land across

Figure 11.2 Mrs L Petrie-Hay with *Waidman Crumpet* and
Waidman Brok

a stretch of water as a blind retrieve with no shot fired in the open and all-aged stakes.

Eliminating faults are hardmouth, whining or barking, running in and chasing, out of control, failing to enter water. Credits are game-finding ability, style on point, drive, good marking, speed and efficiency in gathering game, good water work and quiet handling. This is expected from all the breeds, and all these breeds are capable of completing such a schedule although the style of work differs slightly. The Weimaraner, which is a larger, heavier dog, is slower and possibly more methodical than the more lightly built Hungarian Vizsla. The hairy Munsterlander is more inclined to forge through thickets, whilst the German Shorthaired Pointer air-scents on approach, and if no scent of game is available, wastes no time in working through the scrub. They all vary in their styles of pointing as do all Pointers. Much depends on the pointing situation — a classic point is produced by classic conditions, where scent of game ahead is carried high on the wind. Where little wind or scent is available, a tiny snatch of scent will spin a dog round producing an inelegant U-shaped point. When game is very close, the head will be low, the further the game, the higher the head, and more attractive the point. Style of retrieving varies more with the individuals than the breeds, and this also applies to their entry into water and style of swimming.

This is what the dogs described as breeds which hunt, point and retrieve, must be capable of doing in the field. The argument for altering this title was basically a dislike of the unnecessary amount of words which encouraged the use of initials. The alternative suggestion was Pointer/Retrievers which adequately described this type of gundog and is brief and simple. Those against the alteration argued that the word **hunt** was all-important since it emphasised the necessity for the dogs to search all types of terrain for the game they had to point, and they held that the use of initials was very popular in this modern age. Against this it was pointed out that all dogs must hunt before finding game. You would never expect to add the word 'hunt' to Pointers Setters or Spaniels. Why should it then be necessary for the Continental breeds? A good reason is that to the Englishman Pointers, Setters and Spaniels are self-explanatory, and the most ignorant amongst us understands the work of these dogs. But a Vizsla or Weimaraner gives no clue whatsoever until explained vividly and graphically as a breed which hunts, points and retrieves. By using the word 'hunt' it takes them out of the category of the Pointer/Setter group whose work is primarily on open stubble or moorland, and indicates the true use of BHPR's which is to hunt all types of ground, open, scrub, woodland, roots and marshes, anywhere in fact where game scent is available.

These were the pros and cons of the debate, and the final decision was that there should be no change. So whether you like it or not, BHPR is the official classification for breeds which hunt, point and retrieve.

VIZSLAS — MY PROBLEM
(An article first published in the *Shooting Times and Country Magazine*)

When God created the Vizsla he did so with his tongue in his cheek. He made a noble beautiful, agile, lithe, affectionate and intelligent dog. He gave him the eyes of a hawk, the nose of a Bloodhound, the speed of the wind and a mouth of velvet. He instilled an immense and urgent ability to work.   And then for fun he threw in a pinch of wilfulness as if to challenge man with the perfect shooting companion providing he had the patience and character to be master. He gave the Vizsla three commandments:

1. Thou shalt love thy master better than thyself
2. Thou shalt work hard and joyfully
3. Thou shalt bite neither man nor dog without just cause

But on the Vizslas family coat of arms the devil added the motto: "My will not thine be done".

It is said that if you have a Hungarian for a friend you have no need of an enemy. I can quote this in good conscience as it was told me by a Hungarian friend and perhaps it is the answer to this anomaly — the Vizsla. How can black be white? And is it not strange that with the years black and white fade into varying shades of grey?

This may seem an odd introduction to a breed which, once owned and understood, can be replaced by none other. To many these enigmatic qualities would be distasteful and unattractive, but to the Vizsla lover they are a glorious challenge which, if treated with kindness, patience, firmness and understanding, can bring rewards not often enjoyed by other dog owners.

Behind this eulogy there is a note of seriousness and a message which was sparked off by a letter from a worried Vizsla owner and by quoting and answering it maybe I can help to give a deeper understanding of this versatile and loving breed. If you read and heed what follows bear in mind that I never blame the dog — the chances are that I bred it! He writes: "He is well grown, fit and basically obedient. He quarters well in the open, faces any cover, and points steadily. But as soon as the quarry flushes the chase begins. If I use a check cord I have no trouble, and he is perfectly steady in a rabbit pen, but as soon as he is free in the field I lose control". How's that for contradiction? Not from the dog, but from his owner/trainer/handler. What does he mean "basically obedient"? Of course it is obvious, but what he should have said was that the dog has been basically trained i.e. the training a youngster gets when it is explained to him the manner in which he must behave.

This should always be done without distraction or temptation. Once perfection is achieved by willing obedience to certain commands then distraction and temptation are introduced gradually, but this should never be done before the result of the basic training has become **automatic**.

There are two training rules for Vizslas:

1. No chasing of anything at any time
2. Willing and complete obedience at all times

These rules must be implanted and, as laws, implemented from the age at which the puppy leaves the nest for all time. No relaxation of either should ever be permitted. With other dogs, very often if given an inch they will take a mile — with a Vizsla if given a millimetre he will take two miles.

Once basic training is achieved successfully there are three more rules to observe when live game is introduced:

1. During his first season he should never be allowed to flush the game he is pointing, this should always be done by the trainer with the dog dropping on command as the game flushes

2. If that game is shot the dog must remain dropped and *not* sent to retrieve. The dead game may be used as a retrieve but only after association of the point has been forgotten.

3. No retrieving of wounded game should be permitted during his first season. Only in this way can steadiness in pointing and retrieving be achieved.

It would be true to say that this training could apply to the other pointer/retriever breeds, or for that matter, to other gundogs. It is the application that differs. Remember that you are dealing with a loving, gentle, bloody-minded character, and that being firm is not as simple as it should be. An illustration of this can be shown by *Vlada*, a bitch who was given to me when 18 months old — thrown out by her trainer and unwanted by her owner, (naturally enough as he needed a gundog).

The history that came with her was that she had gone to a professional trainer at eight months. After the first month a good report was given, after the second difficulties were reported, six months later the trainer asked her owner to collect her as she was useless. She refused to retrieve. I found this hard to believe as, although in this case I did not breed her, I knew her breeding well. It was admirable. She joined my family and fitted in well and happily. During the summer I put her through her paces gradually. She hunted and pointed well, was steady to flush and shot and was obedient. We did no retrieving.

When the season started I took her out with an older dog and let her work but the retrieves were only asked of the other dog. At the end of the day I sent her for a bird dropped in sight but in long grass. She galloped out eagerly for it, found it and then looked straight at me and returned without it. No amount of persuasion or jealousy would make her pick it up. I repeated this three or four times during the following weeks with varying game but always with the same result. It was puzzling because she went so gaily for the bird. I had of course tried turning my back to her but to no avail. The answer came unexpectedly.

Yet again I had sent her for a bird; this time it fell on the far side of the hedge and for the first time I was unable to observe her. Luckily, unknown to her, there was a gun standing in the gateway. He told me that she went to the bird, picked it up and carried it through the hedge. She then stopped, looked in my direction, put the bird down and galloped in. Somewhere along the line she had been overpunished, either for running in or possibly for pegging a bird, but that punishment had never been forgotten nor was I ever able to overcome the effect.

So, returning to our problem trainer — his problems would never have existed if he had followed the rules. That is why perhaps, although in this case we are shutting the stable door after the horse has gone, this advice may be useful to those who have puppies now. It is also given as a serious warning to those who covet a Vizsla, having enjoyed seeing a well trained one working. Don't rush into buying one lightheartedly but only if you have a gentle, patient character that can return love and loyalty which will be thrust upon you and are prepared to give the time necessary to achieve control of the boundless energy and enthusiasm which a Vizsla possesses for the work he was

Figure 11.3 Bingo Vom Wurmbrandpark C.C. Winner as well as a working dog (photo: C.M. Cooke & Son)

bred to perform."

In due course the *Shooting Times* received the following letter:

Sir, — I am bemused by the article by Louise Petrie-Hay. I am Dutch and have shot over this breed on the Continent. Mrs Petrie-Hay writes that the Vizsla was given "the eyes of a hawk, the nose of a bloodhound . . . " This is an unfortunate choice of words. One of the FCI disqualifications is Hawk/windhover eyes and it is accepted that the bloodhound was introduced to the breed in the late 19th century, so developing the heavy forehead that our breeders now strive to obliterate. Why must the English make lap-dogs from a tough and proven dog like the 'Magyar Vizsla'
J A Bosch van Drakenstyn. Holland

The editor's comment ran as follows:

In defence of Louise Petrie-Hay we must make it clear that in referring to "eyes of a hawk, nose of a bloodhound" she was extolling the keen-sightedness and power of scent owned by the Vizsla and not commenting on its physical appearance. As for lap-dogs! We suggest that Mr Bosch van Drakenstyn pays a visit to the *Waidman* Kennels. He will be hard put to find any lap-dogs amongst the working retriever-pointers owned by Mrs Petrie-Hay. Ed.

THE VIZSLA AS A MULTI PURPOSE DOG
(a letter from a friend in Scotland)

"When my two Labradors met untimely ends within a short time of each other a few years ago, I decided not to replace them with the same breed, about which I was concerned with the results of breeding for show and inbreeding. I decided to pick a breed which I considered to offer both a high percentage of working dogs and a greater degree of 'dual purpose'. My Labradors were both excellent 'bird dogs' (as our friends over the Atlantic might say) and first class for roe stalking. Since I consider it to be imperative that any woodland deer stalker has a dog available, I felt absolutely naked without a dog for a short period, during which my roe stalking was very restricted. Having been to Hungary a short time before and seen Vizslas for the first time, my wife and I decided that despite their light coloured eyes, this was the breed for us. That this choice was, in our opinion, correct, we have confirmed by acquiring a puppy to understudy our 4½ year old dog. I find it invidious singling out dogs that I have had in the past, all of which have been great pals and good workers, but I do feel that our older Vizsla has fulfilled my requirements better than most, and happy as I was to be told by a friend that my dog has the best nose of the dogs on our shoot, an even higher compliment was to overhear on a friend's shoot my host saying to another gun "That's a bloody good dog of Ian's". I hasten to point out that I really never trained the Vizsla — it wasn't necessary. Indeed he never had to be house-trained and really neither did the puppy (now 8 months old), because the situation never arose.

Although my dog's principal role now is grouse, partridge and pheasant shooting, originally it was primarily roe stalking. This entailed, and entails, either being on hand in vehicle or house whilst I am sitting in a 'high seat', or, more often, accompanying me on a stalk. His first buck, when he was perhaps 8 months old, I remember well. My wife and I sat up a yew tree high seat and when the buck emerged I shot him, the bullet passing about one inch in front of his heart as it subsequently transpired. He turned and ran off, as one would expect with a heart shot, but a subsequent search failed to find him lying a few yards into the wood as expected. I went and fetched the Vizsla pup, and he immediately took me down the side of the little valley and started up the other side. I called him off as he had gone too far and was clearly on the wrong track.

To cut a long story short, my wife and I spent a restless night and were up at dawn next day and searched for 2 hours in vain. As we gave up I decided to follow the line taken by the Vizsla pup, and there, of course, 20 yards further on from where I had called him back lay the roe buck — or what was left of it, for clearly a vixen and cubs had welcomed such a windfall in the night.

Since that time my Vizsla must have been involved in stalking well over 100 deer, and has been invaluable to myself and friends. I rely heavily on his judgement, senses and reactions both with regard to warning me of the presence of deer that he has seen or smelled and of which I was unaware, or with finding dead deer. He has been a regular companion on red deer stalks on the hill too, and whilst he is generally left behind for the final approach, he has accompanied me on a crawl, stealthily creeping low to the ground by my side. On frequent occasions he has warned me of the presence of deer ahead, and he indicates this by pointing red deer with his tail down (as a result of being whacked for starting to chase them when young). He points roe with a slightly higher tail. Similarly one can tell from his reactions whether he is pointing a pheasant, partridge or grouse, or whether he is pointing a rabbit or just a warm recently vacated spot.

I have not taught him to "bay dead", i.e. give tongue over a dead deer, as expected in Hungary, because I don't know how to do so. However, he is able to convey the message to me in his own way without noise. Similarly, he is useful in my every day work in finding calves on the hill, or sheep in thick bracken etc. I am always amazed at how he seems to know when we are after deer, rabbits, pheasants or whatever, concentrating on the species being sought and largely ignoring the others. He accompanies me when I go to work in the fields on the tractor, staying close by the tractor, within 200—300 yards anyway, whilst I am ploughing or whatever. Occasionally he picks a vantage point where he can watch me, and lies down, and rarely he gets fed up or cold or wet and goes home, but mostly he goes up and down the field parallel to me. Another useful feature of our Vizsla is his message carrying, varying from taking notes from my wife or myself to the other from the bedroom to elsewhere in the house, to bearing a note telling me that tea is ready from my wife in the house to where I am working at the far end of the farm yard, as he did yesterday.

I have never subscribed to the view that working dogs cannot be pets. Our sheepdog prefers to sleep out in the byre at night, but otherwise shares the house in daytime, but the Vizslas live in all the time and appreciate warmth and comfort. The older dog always comes up to the bedroom when the alarm goes off, or when it should have gone off, and judging my wakefulness and receptiveness, either lies beside the bed or says good morning. He is then invited up to lie beside me for a while before I get up, with his head buried under my arm. The puppy has, in the last few days, started to be allowed on the bed in the morning, though is as yet rather a fidget! He shares my wife's side of the bed, until she rises to milk the cow, leaving me to enjoy a few idle moments with a Vizsla on either side! In my opinion this 'softness' in no way spoils the Vizsla's working ability and indeed I feel that it enhances our relationship with each other. The Vizslas are good house dogs too, and whilst always friendly to authorized visitors, I feel that unauthorized ones might well have a less friendly reception.

Whilst always delighted at the prospect of a walk or a trip in the car, it is the sight, smell or even sound of the getting out of a gun or rifle which really makes the dog happy. To my mind the Vizsla is the ideal all round rough shooter's dog. Though he will sit quietly at heel during a driven shoot, he prefers to work, hunt and point as well as retrieve.

I believe that in Hungary the field trial for Vizslas includes blood trailing a deer and retrieving a fox. My Vizsla would doubtless score badly in a strict Hungarian trial, since he probably lacks the style required in such things, largely because I am not interested in such perfection from him, but he can trail a deer and retrieve a fox and has done both. I should be sorry if British Vizslas were to lose their ability to perform as a really all round sporting/hunting dog as a result of field trials concentrating on the 'bird' or small game hunting side of their ability."

FALCONRY — THE CASE FOR USING A VIZSLA
(an article by Martin Jones, the falconer)
Published in H.V.S. Newsletter

"The falconer's choice of dog tends to be a little confused at the best of times, and depends a great deal on the terrain and type of bird he flies. This I shall endeavour to explain:

Basically, the types of bird flown may be split into two main categories — falcons and hawks (with eagles and buzzards generally flown in the manner of a hawk).

Falcons are birds of open country, possessing long pointed wings and a short tail; they generally kill by stooping at their quarry. Whereas hawks are more direct in their approach, possessing a far longer tail and a more rounded wing, enabling them to manoeuvre after their quarry in enclosed country.

Hawks may be flown with a modicum of success without the aid of a dog, but a good dog will increase the number of flights and help bring more game to book. A great many dogs can be pressed into service for the purpose of working out hedgerows and rough ground. I have seen Spaniels, Labradors, Terriers and an assortment of mongrels used with varying degrees of success, but my own preference has been the pointer/retriever breeds (though no retrieving is required) — I exclude pointers and setters for use in enclosed ground with a true hawk.

In all branches of falconry where a dog is used, there is an inestimable value in the time a pointer gives one to move into a suitable position prior to the flight; a tremendous advantage when flying a hawk and a 'sine qua non' when flying falcons at game.

As the whole object of flying a falcon is to witness the stoop at quarry, there is no point in walking-up game and slipping a falcon as they flush. Indeed, the falcon is normally hooded to prevent her being tempted should this occur accidentally.

Very few falconers are able to afford the luxury of a separate dog handler, therefore, steadiness and complete 'handability' is essential as the falconer will tend to concentrate on his bird.

The ground for flying falcons must be as open as possible with a minimum amount of cover for the quarry to seek refuge in and thwart the relatively unmanoeuvrable falcon. Density of game need not be very high — a good point every twenty minutes is considered ample.

On obtaining a point the falconer unhoods and casts his bird off; whereupon the experienced falcon, seeing the dog on point and appraising the situation, will start to mount. In level flight, falcons have little edge in speed over grouse or partridge, so an experienced falcon will mount as high as she thinks fit to ensure a good stoop. Game will often spring wide of a low-mounting badly positioned falcon, without any attempt

Figure 11.4 John Powell with his Goshawk and *Galfrid Milo*

171

being made to flush, as they know instinctively that in this way they are unlikely to be caught.

Whilst the falcon is mounting, the falconer walks round in a semi-circle, to head the point from an upwind direction. When the falcon reaches her pitch (as high as she is likely to go) then the falconer and dog combine to flush the game. Frequently, the falcon will drift out of position and it is essential to be able to arrest the dog immediately and continue when the falcon is back in position. Eventually, one hopes, the game is flushed, the falcon stoops, there is a puff of feathers, and a grouse or partridge is dramatically brought to book.

The use of a dog for flying with the true hawks is generally simpler and is rather like using a dog for pot-hunting with a shotgun — get reasonably close and you're in with a chance.

So far no reference has been made to the Vizsla, as I thought it better to give a resume of the sport and involvement of dogs in it.

My preference for the pointer/retriever breeds as allrounders in the hawking field has already been stated, and a great deal of my hawking has been done with the aid of German Shorthaired Pointers. However, the last dog (or rather bitch) I obtained for falconry was a Vizsla, and I shall attempt to give my thoroughly biased reasons for this choice.

The need was a for a dog that was gentle, co-operative, will to please, not headstrong and yet not too much of a 'potterer'. I considered German Pointers but had been rather disheartened in recent years by the number of headstrong ones I had seen, that had ruined rather than enhanced several days hawking (was it dog or handler?). Wire-haired Pointers I knew nothing about at all, which together with their relative rarity precluded them from my reckoning.

Weimaraners I had little experience of, but had seen one with foot problems (inherent?) and had heard reports of their unsociability towards other dogs. Also, Munsterlanders were rather an unknown quantity, though I knew a couple of falconers who used them primarily with Goshawks; besides which I have always been rather anti-long-haired dogs (idleness on my part as I dislike the attendant grooming and dog hairs all over the place).

Although I had not seen many Vizslas, the breed had impressed me. They did not appear too headstrong and did not seem to have been affected by an general popularity and consequent attendant evils, and appeared to fit my requirement for a general hawking/shooting dog.

That decision was taken two and a half years ago, somewhat hastened by the fact that Jock Shelley had a smart litter of pups close by, one of which (the smallest bitch) had really taken my fancy. Since when the bitch has performed well up to expectations both in the hawking and shooting field, including two seasons when I have been flying at grouse professionally, with frequent compliments.

If there is a complaint to be made, it is that she does tend to be puppyish if worked with another dog for a while, suddenly deciding it is playtime — to exasperated shouts of "for heaven's sake grow up'!"

CHAPTER 12

PROGRESS IN THE FIELD

There follows a year by year account of the field events for the Vizsla held between 1973 and 1984.

Until 1973 the activities of the Hungarian Vizsla Society were confined to newsletters and information about the breed, but in this year the first field trial was organised and from then on a number of other stimuli were introduced to encourage the non-shooting Vizsla owner to learn more about the working ability of his dog and how to train and control this ability.

Reports taken from The Hungarian Vizsla Society's Newsletters

THE FIRST FIELD TRIAL HELD BY THE HUNGARIAN VIZSLA SOCIETY

The following is the report and results of that first Novice Stake.

Report and Results *by Eric Greig*

The 3rd November 1973 was quite literally a field day for those members who visited Margaret and Bill Sanderson's delightful home at Thorphill, Morpeth. On that day, the Society ran its first Field Trial, and if this first attempt may be used as a guide, the future of subsequent meets looks to be bright.

Eight dogs were entered and that number ran, although Louise Petrie-Hay's *Bella* was sportingly substituted with *Sipa*, as the former was in season. The dogs came from as far apart as Worcestershire and Perthshire, and the distance travelled did not appear to have had any adverse affect on their fitness. Some handlers travelled to Morpeth the previous day staying overnight locally in a pub, or, as one enthusiast did, slept out under the stars with his dog ensconced on her bed in the vehicle; whilst others had an early start from their homes, trusting that fog and ice would not be too severe.

The day was without rain, mild and humid with a very light variable breeze which changed its direction often. This made for difficult scenting, and game seemed to realise it, as they either sat tight, or, as we suspect, moved low leaving the dogs with a problem. Only one entrant, the winner, had a warm retrieve; in fact he had two in very quick succession on pheasant; the others had to be content with cold retrieves at the water test on pigeon. The judges, Margaret Sanderson and Roger Phillips were most patient, giving the dogs and handlers every chance to come onto game, but it was, with a couple of exceptions, not to be; and they were confined to judging mainly the quartering, facing cover and handling, before the break in proceedings for lunch.

Whilst in the morning, the work had been on the north side of the farm, the afternoon's work took the southerly direction which had more cover, and eventually ended at the river where the water test took place, just before dusk. After the test, the whole party were taken by tractor and trailer back to Thorphill Farm, where the judges and steward did their sums to place the dogs in their order of ability on the day.

The judge's notes and comments give the technicalities of the meet, and they are shown below; but it should be noted and remarked upon that the handlers of the first, second and third prize winners had never previously taken part in a field trial. On the strength of this, the Society hopes that all those members who thought they would like to run a dog, but did not have sufficient experience will take heart and enter the next event. One cannot thank Margaret and Bill Sanderson too much for allowing us the privilege of using their ground, which in itself is a major concession, but also to shoot for us, judge and feed us as well, places their hospitality in the highest possible bracket.

Judge's Notes *M Sanderson*

The Hungarian Vizsla Society held their first field trial at Thorphill on November 3rd, by kind permission of Mr W S Sanderson. This was not an easy trial to judge as scent was very poor, with little or no wind; apart from this I personally enjoyed judging the Vizsla's work, placing as follows:

1ST Mr E W Berry's *Windover Ripp* who worked well on open ground, and in hedgerow; had a very good point, was very steady to flush and shot. He did a quick retrieve and a very good water test. He was well handled by his owner.

2ND Mr G E S Greig's *Saline Caroline*, this bitch worked well on open ground; had a good point; was steady to shot; did a very neat water test and retrieve. Well handled by Sorley Greig.

3RD Major G Maitland-Smith's *Starleypoint Ulles*. This dog worked his open ground well; was very steady to shot. He did a good water test and retrieve. Well handled by Mrs Maitland-Smith.

Two Certificates of Merit were awarded to Mrs Auchterlonie's *Saline Achilles* handled by Mr A MacRae, and Mr R Anthony's *Capeland Cascade* handled by her owner. Both these dogs worked well and did good water tests; they just did not have the luck of the first three dogs.

Report and Results

Field Trial in Suffolk (1974)

The Society's second field trial was held in Suffolk. The following is the report:

Report and Results

A Novice Stake for Vizslas only was held on Saturday October 26th at the Marshland Estate, Sudbourne, Suffolk by kind permission of Mr A Heyman, QC. Fourteen entries were received, four withdrew owing to the ill-health of the owners, and one failed to attend — so in fact nine dogs competed. The weather was unbelievably good considering the storms on the previous day and the rain on the following. Scenting conditions varied considerably as the sun warmed and dried out the wet cold ground. Stubbles, cut seed kale and sugar beet was worked also a small area of potatoes. Game was plentiful, consisting of a plethora of hares, some partridges and a quantity of pheasants. The two guns performed their task admirably and the dogs had ample opportunities of retrieves on feather — no fur was shot over novices. The water retrieve was held on the Iken Estate and the dogs were tested with a swim of about thirty yards, which all were allowed to partake in as there was a special award for the best water retrieve, kindly presented by the secretary, Mrs K Auchterlonie, who very sadly was one of those unable to attend.

The outstanding winner was Mr Heyman's bitch *Matai Vica* who put up an excellent performance showing style, speed, nose and exceptional retrieving ability both on seen and blind retrieves. She was steady both to flush, shot and fall of game and had a staunch point on a myxy rabbit right under her nose which she made no attempt to move in on. She also won the water award by a very bold entry and a quick return but only by one mark above Mrs Phillip's dog *Waidman Buda*. Mr Greig's *Saline Caroline* came 2nd. This bitch worked well and sensibly showing her experience over the younger dogs. She found game and pointed staunchly — was steady and made a good retrieve. 3rd Prize went to *Mintalla* owned by Mr Van Helvoort and handled by Mrs Petrie-Hay — this 20 month old dog did all that was asked of him, he was steady to a number of hares, pointed in the roots and retrieved to hand. He completed the water retrieve but his inexperience was obvious. Two dogs were eliminated for falling into the temptation of the numerous hares, one for hardmouth, one of them failed on a retrieve, another who had completed the card finally refused the water, and another inexperienced bitch failed to find and point the game available owing to poor ground treatment.

In the judges final assessment at the end of the day they agreed that apart from the winner the obvious potential working ability of all the dogs was hampered by the lack of competent handling. More experience by the handlers will go far to improve the performance of the dogs. The judges expressed their enjoyment and interest and thanked all those who competed under them.

The prizes which were kindly given by Major W Petrie-Hay went to:—

1ST Mr Heyman's *Matai Vica*   1st Prize
                                    Kinford Trophy
                                    (Prize for best Water Retrieve)

2ND Mr Greig's *Saline Caroline* 2nd Prize
                                    Provanston Cailleach Challenge Trophy

3RD Mr Van Helvoort's *Mintalla* 3rd Prize

GSP ASSOCIATION FIELD TRIAL (1975)

In 1975 on January 11th the German Shorthaired Pointer Association held a field trial in Hampshire:

It was a Novice Stake — 12 dogs ran — 8 German Shorthaired Pointers 3 Weimaraners and one Vizsla (*Waidman Brok*). The dog with the highest marks was *Brok* — so a little bit of Vizsla history was made in that this was the first time that a Vizsla had competed in this country against German Shorthaired Pointers and Weimaraners and beaten them. BUT, and here is the rub — no 1st or 2nd prizes were awarded, *Brok* got 3rd prize and one Certificate of Merit was awarded to a German Pointer.

According to the judges after the first round, the standard of work was exceptionally high. After the second round only 6 dogs qualified for the water retrieve, two refused to enter the water and of the four remaining dogs (1 Weimar, 2 German Pointers and *Brok*) *Brok* was awarded 3rd prize as his total marks were not high enough to warrant better. He made two mistakes and both of them were avoidable by better training on my part.

His ground treatment, game finding and pointing marks were above average. The retrieve he had in the second round was a pricked hen pheasant dropped about 100 yards in high marshland grass. He marked it well, went straight to the fall, found the bird, picked it up and started to come in. He stopped once, put it down to get a better hold (this is not penalised by the judges) and came on — when about 15 yards from me he fell into a cross dyke, he recovered, came out still with the bird but then he put it down, shook and said "that's enough" — this was only about five yards in front of me so I went forward and collected the bird — but he should have brought it to hand and as a result got a low mark. At the water the bird was thrown into a fairly fast running narrow river, it drifted almost to the far bank, so that when *Brok* retrieved he went up onto the far bank — having climbed up with the bird he was reluctant to return, but after considerable persuasion on my part he did bring it back. But of course this again lost valuable marks. In both these instances more attention in training would have made all the difference between a 1st and 3rd prize. That is why I say although I am delighted with the success it is not good enough. A Vizsla must get a 1st prize next season when competing against the other pointer/retriever breeds — I shall do my damndest to see that it is *Brok*, but this surely should give an incentive to other Vizsla owners to take just that extra bit more time and trouble in training during the summer months so that we can prove the true working ability of our dogs.

THREE FIELD TRIALS HELD BY THE VIZSLA SOCIETY

Later in the year the Society organised three field trials:

Mr J Brockbank and Mr E Young very kindly invited us to their moors at Dufftown and Tintohill and once again Mr A Heyman offered us the Marshland Estate in Suffolk. These trials were a "qualified" success, not owing to any lack of game, entries or enthusiasm but entirely to the element which is out of our control — the weather. All three were novice stakes.

Report (*by Lord Joicey*)

Dufftown, Banffshire. Saturday August 16th 1975. There were 12 entries and one reserve—

10 runners consisting of 5 Vizslas, 4 German Pointers and one Weimaraner. Conditions were made difficult by continuous rain and although the whole morning was spent advancing into a steady breeze the dogs found conditions too difficult for them and only one point on grouse and two points on hares were recorded during the whole of the first round. In these conditions the judges had inadequate information to express their views on individual dogs. Coveys took wing several hundred yards ahead of the line but a few single birds sat tight, enough for nine points to have been registered had the dogs covered their beat more thoroughly and had they worked closer in front of the guns.   There is room for much improvement in quartering and in ensuring that the dog's nose covers the whole of the beat with the minimum waste of time. After lunch the handlers asked that the stake should be abandoned and the judges agreed to do so and to go straight to the water retrieve where all dogs entered water and retrieved their pigeon.

****

On September 6th we foregathered again, this time on Tintohill and Evan Young was our host. Tony Jackson and Sandy Levanton from *The Shooting Times* were with us to shoot and take photographs. The report and pictures were published on September 18th and 25th. Our judges this time were Mr Rankin Waddell and Mr Eric Greig. George Richmond very kindly acted as a gun and Mr G Sterne, the president of the German Shorthaired Pointer Club was with us on the hill for much of the day. There were 12 entries and 4 reserves — 13 dogs ran — 6 Vizslas and 7 German Pointers. Yet again the weather was unkind — intermittent light rain and no wind at all. There appeared to be no scent whatsoever. Grouse were seen in plenty and within shot, but the dogs ran into them indicating lack of scent. The points obtained were all on the few hares who decided to sit it out instead of tempting the dogs with a mad dash. After lunch the judges decided that all game must be shot regardless of whether it had been pointed or not, and in this way retrieves were available and a result obtainable. This time the water test was carried out in a reservoir.

The Results were:

1ST — Mr I Sladden's *Inchmarlo Jasmine*
2ND — Mrs Layton's *Midlander Oriental Ranee*
3RD — Mr I Sladden's Sh Ch *Inchmarlo Raphoe*
(All German Shorthaired Pointers.)
Reserve and Certificate of Merit — Mr A Heyman's Vizsla *Matai Vica*
Certificate of Merit — Mrs K Auchterlonie's Vizsla *Saline Achilles* who was awarded the
    Provanston Caileach Challenge Trophy.
The *Shooting Times* kindly gave a box of cartridges to the Guns' Choice. This was Mr Elliott's German Pointer *Inchmarlo Solas*.
    Again it was a very enjoyable day only marred by the lack of scent.

****

On October 11th we all met at the Marshland Estate by kind permission of Alan Heyman. Last year we had an excellent day on this ideal ground and this time we were lucky again. 12 entries and one reserve. 11 dogs ran, Vizslas only this time. Lord Joicey and Mr G Sherring judged.

Judge's Report

Results: 1ST Mr J Parke's *Matai Pirok*, 79%
2ND — Mr A Heyman's *Matai Vica*, 68%
3RD — Mr T West's *Galfrid Gelert*, 64%
    A few heavy showers later in the day did nothing to spoil this excellent novice trial, run on the lovely wide stubble fields and sugar beet of the Marshland Estate. Most of the eleven runners obviously lacked much experience of the shooting field, but nevertheless displayed great keenness and potential ability, quartering of the ground was for the most part free and unrestricted, and on a rather difficult scenting day nearly all the dogs reacted to the scent left by the plentiful head of pheasants, partridges and hares seen. The majority of dogs did not have the experience to interpret the meaning of the scents they were picking up and in some cases the handlers did not understand the messages, which the dogs in turn were trying to convey to them.
    The three eventual prize winners, however, showed themselves to be no strangers to the shooting field. Mr Parke's bitch, *Matai Pirok*, was beautifully handled, she ranged freely, but under complete control, and all the time was working to find game. She indicated clearly the near presence of game in the roots, tracked with caution a pheasant running on ahead, and then held it on a steady point. When this was flushed and shot, she made a good job of the retrieve. Mr Heyman's bitch *Matai Vica*, also quartered beautifully, having a stylish point on some partridges in the open, which rose

176

wild, she too gave an excellent performance in the roots, but overshot her mark for the retrieve, and for a brief moment became over-excited. The third dog, Mr West's *Galfrid Gelert,* did not quarter with quite the same fluency as the other two, but showed himself a reliable game-finder both in the open and the roots. This was an excellent performance for a first appearance in field trials. The ground placed at our disposal was superb for pointers to work on, and also for the spectators to see what was happening at all times. Mr Heyman and his keeper gave the judges every help in advising how best to work it to show game to the best advantage of the dogs. The water test caused 2 eliminations, but otherwise was well performed. An excellent lunch at the Orford Oysterage completed a thoroughly enjoyable day for which much gratitude is due to our hosts, Mr and Mrs Alan Heyman.

John Parke is to be doubly congratulated as the day before he won the Weimaraner Club novice stake, running against German Shorthaired Pointers, Weimars and a Munsterlander. This is the first time a Vizsla has been placed first in a stake for all breeds which hunt, point and retrieve. Well done John!

FIELD TRIAL (1976)

In 1976 a field trial was arranged at Biggar in Lanarkshire but owing to lack of sufficient entries this had to be cancelled.

The First Open Stake Field Trial

The first open stake field trial was held this year and the judges were Sir Michael Leighton and Mr. Howard Fisher.

Judges' Report

The Hungarian Vizsla Society held an open stake field trial on October 30th 1976 at Marshland Estate, Woodbridge Suffolk, by kind permission of Mr A Heyman.

The day was warm and misty with occasional outbreaks of drizzle. Wind conditions varied from nil wind to a strong wind and scenting conditions were generally not too good. The ground worked was open stubble and roots taking in hedges and a rough pit. Game was pheasant, partridge and hare, rabbits were also seen.

The standard of work was not very high and we were unable to award a first prize. One or two dogs were going very well and showing a good standard of work but committed cardinal sins, so putting themselves out of the stake. In this category fell Mr K Stammer's German Pointer *Maylock Maree,* who impressed in the first run very greatly. Also, Louise Petrie-Hay's *Waidman Zimba* who worked nicely in the roots but spoiled himself after finding game well.

No first prize was awarded. Second was Mrs M Layton's German Pointer bitch *Midlander Oriental Ranee* handled by Dr D Layton. This bitch was disappointing on her first run by being unwilling to get out and quarter freely. She was steady to a shot hare but rather spoilt her retrieve by not delivering to hand. On her second run she went much better finding game in the roots and being steady. Again a sloppy delivery spoiled an otherwise very good retrieve.

No other placings were possible but Certificate of Merit went to the Vizsla of Mr T West *Galfrid Gelert.* This dog ran nicely on the stubble, scenting well and indicating good game finding ability. He also went well in the roots finding birds, being steady to flush and shot and retrieving well. His water test was very poor which removed him from contention for a placing. His handler should, however, take encouragement from the dog's general working.

MEETING AT INKBERROW (1977)

1977 saw the first Vizsla get-together; it was held in August at Inkberrow

PROGRAMME

11.00 am   Welcome by the President and chat-about.
11.30 am   Basic obedience in two groups for dogs under and over one year old.
                  Walk to heel on and off the lead.
                  Sit on command. Sit and stay, return to dog.

Sit and stay and recall. Sit, stay, recall and drop half way.
Walk to heel, shot fired, dog to sit.
Walk to heel, shot fired, dummy launched, dog to sit.
Retrieving: Simple seen retrieve
                Blind retrieve
                Memory retrieve
                Double retrieve
                Retrieve over jump.
Running rabbit on elastic for steadiness test.

12.30 am	Instruction by Sheila Gray and practice in dog show technique and requirements.
12.45 am	Pointing caged rabbit and pigeon either on scent or sight. No flushing or retrieving. Initial quartering up wind.
1.00 pm	Dog Race (The Vizsla Derby!)
1.15 pm	Demonstration on dizzying pigeons and the advantage in training of their use in pointing and flushing. Simulated field trial demonstration given by Sheila Gray and Virginia Phillips. Quartering allotted beat, point on pigeon, steady to flush and shot, continue quartering, dummy launched across line of work, steady to shot and fall retrieve on command.
2.00 pm	Break for lunch.
3.00 pm	Convoy to water. General swim about for all dogs, competitive retrieving to encourage the less bold to swim.

Retrieving: Simple, thrown dummy, dog allowed to run in.
                Lunched dummy, dog to retrieve on command.
                Unseen retrieve from water with no shot fired.
                Unseen retrieve across water with no shot fired.

4.30 pm   Dogs dried off and carriages called.

It was with great pleasure that the President, Mrs Virginia Phillips opened the day with a speech of welcome to exactly 50 people and their dogs. They had come from as far afield as Kent, Dorset, Essex Wales and Derby.

The enthusiasm and appreciation of so many Vizsla owners was most satisfying for the organisers. The class was split into two groups, with the dogs going through the exercises according to their ability. The object was not to train the dogs on the day but to demonstrate to the handlers what to aim for and how to achieve it. The programme attempted to go through the whole schedule of basic training up to field trial standard.

The training session was divided into three periods — basic obedience and retrieving, pointing and flushing and water work, and it was stressed that the training of a pointer/retriever should follow this pattern until all three facets were perfected for steadiness and ability. Only then should hunting, pointing, flushing and retrieving be combined. Basic obedience and retrieving of all sorts were tackled first with a wide variety of standards and results. Generally speaking basic obedience was good and the speed and delivery of seen retrieves was good. Steadiness seemed to cause no problems but much work will have to be done by those present on handling their dogs onto a blind retrieve.

This can be made easier if, for every seen retrieve, two blind retrieves are also given. There were no failures when the dogs were asked to retrieve over a jump.

The class was then instructed by Sheila Gray on the art of dog showing, and I think that this was probably the largest single class that any judge has yet seen in this country! It was a glorious sight to see so many Vizslas parading round, with not as much variation in conformation as one might have expected.

We then moved into the small field where the dogs were encouraged to point the caged game. No easy task as many dogs will not point as the game seldom gives off a fear scent. However, with perseverance and the example of the dogs who did point, most of the dogs were seen to be pointing and were being encouraged to hold their point. Finally the dogs were lined up at the top of the track with their 'slippers' while their owners went to the lower gate. On 'go' a cloud of russet gold was seen blowing at gale force across the hay field in TWO directions — one towards the calling owners and the other in the direction of the caged game! There had to be two winners of that race!

Dogs and owners re-united, we moved across the lane to the big field where the general requirements for, and behaviour at, a field trial were explained. Virginia and Sheila then put their dogs through simulated conditions to demonstrate the importance and purpose of the exercises previously done. Other dogs would have liked to show their paces here but lunch was overdue.

By this time food and drink was much needed and enjoyed, and sincere thanks and appreciation go to Virginia Phillips and Jeannie Smith who brought the chicken, hard-boiled eggs and salads, and Nigel Smith who supplied us with the excellent red and white wine.

When everyone appeared satisfied, a long convoy assembled and set of for Mr Platt's trout reservoir. 'All in' was the order of the day, and all in it was, even though one or two did not quite go out of their depths, nevertheless, confidence was built up by seeing so many of the others swimming and retrieving successfully. The highlight was one chap who did his utmost to catch the rising trout, a very sensible idea for a working dog, and it was quite a time before he could be persuaded to give up the hunt. By 4.30 pm we had all had enough, and as the dogs were being dried off the rain, which had miraculously kept away all day, came down in buckets. But I am sure, despite the long, wet drive home that many had to suffer, everyone enjoyed and benefitted from this get-together and it was agreed that it should be repeated if possible at the end of the summer.

A NOVICE STAKE AT LOTON PARK (1977)

Report

A novice stake was held at Loton Park on October 8th 1977. The ground worked consisted of stubble, hedges, grass and potato fields, game produced was pheasant and partridge. The weather conditions were good with a fresh wind all day. Scenting conditions were good.

1st Prize	Mr Parke's *Matai Pirok*	She worked her ground well all day. She had two very good points — a useful, steady gundog.
2nd Prize	Mr Farmer's *Waidman Bogar*	Very little to choose between this dog and the winner. He had good game finding ability, style and drive, also several good points. He lost marks on an untidy retrieve.
3rd Prize	Mr West's *Galfrid Gelert*	He worked well, good treatment of his ground but rather unsure of himself.
Conclusions		The standard of the first two placed dogs was well up to novice stake. The general handling has improved a lot. The average age was high for novice dogs. We would have liked to have seen them working with more drive confidence and speed.

Award Winning Dogs of 1977

The Vizsla Club held two novice stakes in the season, officially for Vizslas only, but they had to invite other breeds in order to fill the cards on both occasions. Over this year's trialling season, the following dogs were in the awards:

Mrs Auchterlonie's *Saline Cabal*	3rd open stake all breeds.
Major Wilkinson's *Galfrid Otis*	3rd novice stake all breeds.
Mr Farmer's *Waidman Bogar*	2nd novice stake Vizslas only
	Reserve novice stake all breeds.
	1st novice stake all breeds.
Mr West's *Galfrid Gelert*	3rd novice stake Vizslas only.
	1st novice stake all breeds.
Mr Parke's *Matai Pirok*	1st novice stake Vizslas only.

VIZSLA GATHERING AT INKBERROW (1978)

On Sunday June 4th 1978 the Society held their second annual get-together and training session at Lower Bouts Farm, Inkberrow, by kind permission of the Petrie-Hays. Much work was done by the organisers and this was well rewarded not only by an excellent turnout of 53 members, friends and visitors with their dogs but also by the improvement both of the dogwork and handling since last year. The president, Mrs Phillips, welcomed everyone and a short session of basic obedience followed ending with a simple test for dogs under 20 months — thirteen competed and Sylvia Cox with her ten month old puppy won by a whisker with a good performance.

Everyone then moved over the lane into the big field and there was a five minute playtime with Vizslas romping in all directions. Then came walking in line with gunfire and the dogs dropping to shot at heel and away from their handlers. On the return there was shot and also falling dummies to contend with and finally a stay — recall — and drop half way. After this all the dogs had a variety of retrieves — marked, memory, blind, double and over a jump. This ended with another test of a double retrieve, one thrown over the jump and the other launched across the field into thick hay. Nigel Cox pulled off a family double by winning this convincingly with his three year old dog. The line-up for the annual race was next, there was a couple of over keen early starters but Sheila Gray's *Emilio* just got his muzzle over the line first. Back in the yard Sheila Gray and Commander Val Hawes organised a beauty competition divided into dogs and bitches. Everyone sportingly entered and the judges made Mr Berry's dog puppy Best in Show with Mrs Young's bitch taking Reserve.

At last lunch and very much needed refreshment. At 2.30 pm Martin Jones gave a most interesting talk on falconry and the use of dogs. Question-time followed which proved the interest he had ellicited. A short walk up the little field where pigeon in release traps awaited to be pointed, flushed and shot at. This gave everyone the opportunity of seeing some excellent, staunch points and also some nice steadiness to flush and shot. Finally the grand exodus to the water, the convoy drove about five miles to Mr Richard Hocknell's trout lake where two Canada geese and their five goslings were waiting to watch the fun. The party walked down to the far end and the dogs had a short free for all, swimming and splashing happily. Then one at a time they completed a retrieve of a dummy, first thrown from the near bank and then from the far bank. The Canadas were totally unperturbed, in fact swam in line abreast to referee the proceedings and a common tern also joined in and gave a demonstration of a diving retrieve. With only two non-swimmers all the dogs completed both retrieves with ease. Styles of entry and swimming varied but the dogs' enjoyment and natural ability was very evident.

THE FIRST GROUSE TRIAL

In September the first grouse trial was held.

Field Trial Report

Everything augured well for the field trial this year. A good report from the moor, a satisfactory entry and fine weather during the preceding week. Saturday, September 16th dawned — grey clouds covered the sky; the wind, which had blown away the night's rain, decided to increase its force and although by 9.30 am conditions were not perfect, the trial started cheerfully. We were honoured by the presence of Mr G Sterne, president of the German Shorthaired Pointer Club who came to spectate as did Hilbre Smith, our ex-chairman of committee. Carol Auchterlonie reported for duty as chief steward. Out of the mist, and berry-brown from the deserts of Dubai, came Eric Greig, bringing his friend who now has charge of *Saline Caroline*. Mrs Lowis came from Montrose and a German Shorthaired Pointer owner with his wife from Glasgow. Nine out of the ten entries were present, Mrs Eppie Buist and myself were judging and our host Evan Young with two friends were shooting.

The first dog to run, Mr Farmer's *Waidman Bogar*, showed his inexperience of grouse at the beginning. Birds got up ahead of him and he made no effort to work round and draw on to where they had pitched. But as the day progressed this dog's work improved considerably and had the conditions been more favourable he would have undoubtedly shown us good sport. His quartering down wind was very professional and his handler knew better than to interfere with him. He dropped flat to flush and was 100% steady to hares. He retrieved a hare to hand but lost marks in an untidy pick-up.

The second dog, Mrs Nixon's German Pointer bitch *Quintana Tyr*, had the misfortune to have a hare shot in front of her, the temptation was too great and she was eliminated for running in.

Mrs Auchterlonie and *Saline Cabal* came next. This strong, sensible dog settled down to his work immediately, covering a lot of ground. He could be faulted by his use of the cheek wind but working into the wind no ground was left un-searched. He had a good point on a hare and was steady to shot. He was asked to retrieve an unmarked snipe in conditions where no scent was obtained. The bird had fallen in the lee of a stone wall, with the wind coming over the wall towards him. It was entirely a question of handling the dog onto the bird, after a good try, Mr Elliott was called into the line and achieved this with his German Pointer bitch. Mrs Auchterlonie got high marks for her handling which was quiet and effective.

Dog No.5 was Mr Elliott's German Pointer bitch *Inchmarlo Solas.* Her quartering was fast and efficient and she looked very pretty indeed as she covered the ground. She also showed a good sense of game and acquired top marks for steadiness. There was obviously a close bond between her and her handler and perhaps the only criticism might be that she was a little too reliant on him, but no doubt time and more experience will overcome this. She retrieved the wounded snipe to hand nicely.

Sheila Gray's *Abbeystag Bruna* started off well and her handler left her to get on with the job. After not many minutes she had a beautiful point which she held really well. She then worked this point out in copybook fashion, flushing a very young pheasant; a shot was fired at the bird and alas *Bruna* decided to chase, not far, but far enough to have to be eliminated — a great shame when she had found and flushed game so well.

The next dog down was Major Wilkinson's Wirehaired Pointer *Alphonse.* He started off with some indifferent quartering and some unsteadiness to a flushed hen pheasant. But as the day wore on, his groundwork improved and he seemed to be settling. Unfortunately just as he came into the line a second time, a hare got up behind him and was fired at. *Alphonse* was nothing but a hairy monster disappearing over the hill — a great pity but I am sure further training is all that is needed.

Mrs Auchterlonie then ran her bitch *Ella Elia of Saline*; a beautiful mover and an efficient worker, very thorough in her ground treatment. In her first round she was steady to fur and had a retrieve of a hare, but alas fell into temptation later when another hare was shot and she ran in, what a shame as she was in the lead in my book till then.

Mrs Nixon's other German Pointer bitch *Kirklade Tanzen* then started off well showing us how an experienced grouse dog should tackle a difficult wind, but a bird was shot and she overkeenly anticipated her retrieve and had to be eliminated.

Lastly came Major Wilkinson's *Galfrid Otis.* This little bitch worked well, covering her ground carefully though not always quite as thoroughly as she should and her handler made no effort to correct this. A hare was shot on one flank and supposedly wounded. The gun pointed this out and he was asked to shoot again before *Otis* was sent to retrieve. A shot was fired and as there was no movement *Otis* was sent to retrieve. As she approached, the hare got up and was off at full gallop. *Otis* stopped and returned to her handler; an extremely creditable performance in steadiness. She worked on well, despite her size and the fact that the heather was making a right mess of her under-carriage which was red and sore. Later on, after a snipe had been shot and *Otis* was coming over to retrieve it, an obviously wounded hare got up and went off across the heather and down along a narrow ditch out of sight. Major Wilkinson was told to send his bitch for this hare as it obviously had priority over what was supposed to be a dead snipe. He was a little bothered as he did not think *Otis* could carry a hare — 'try her' — was all the sympathy he got. She was put on the line and followed it well. The last we saw of her was way down the hill going towards a bit of woodland. A long pause — Major Wilkinson sensibly refrained from calling her as the wind was far too strong. In the distance the little Vizsla could be seen carrying the hare, head high and trying not to trip up over its legs. A very proud handler went to meet her and relieve her of her burden. It was an excellent bit of tracking and showed courage and determination.

That is an overall picture of the dogwork; the weather was far less pleasing. By lunch-time a gale force wind was blowing with intermittent rain. Plenty of birds were seen but none would hold long enough for the dogs to have the opportunity of a productive point. Evan invited us into a barn for lunch and this was a most welcome break from the roughening weather. Having sustained ourselves with liquids and some solids it was agreed to brave the elements again on the chance that it might clear — what a forlorn hope. Mrs Buist requested to be relieved as the pace and conditions had taken a heavy toll of her resources, and as she was due for an operation in the near future it would have been foolish to undergo further stress. Eric Greig, an experienced judge, agreed to replace her, with the agreement of the competitors. He strode into the teeth of the gale with that rear profile which fills us Sassenachs with envy! Our luck was right out and as we advanced the weather worsened. Nevertheless the dogs continued to work with style and pace. Eventually as we neared the reservoir it was agreed to call the competitors and report that owing to the conditions it was not possible to get a result. If they were game we proposed to give them the water retrieve and then assess the marks and award the cups on an unofficial basis; the trophies would not be awarded. It was felt that the dogs and handlers had acquitted themselves well enough to warrant a token of appreciation from the Society for their efforts.

Four dogs were in contention and the final placings were:

1st *Galfrid Otis*; 2nd *Inchmarlo Solas*; 3rd *Saline Cabal*; 4th *Waidman Bogar.*

A vote of appreciation and thanks to our host, the guns, the judges and the steward ended the day and despite the disappointment it would seem that those present really enjoyed themselves, which after all must be one of the main objects of any trial. I would like to mention that our vice-president, Mr Alec MacRae, was unable to attend but very kindly sent a donation as did Mrs Lowis who with—

drew her entry. Mr Hilbre Smith brought some very useful towelling materials which was sold at the end of the trial, for which a lot of very wet dogs were most grateful, the proceeds being donated to the Society.

The Hungarian Vizsla Society have held trials since 1973 under the rules and regulations of the Kennel Club; novice stakes at first and then non-qualifying open and all-aged stakes. The time has now come to apply to the Kennel Club for permission to run qualifying stakes. The winner of two such stakes becomes a field trial champion.

GET-TOGETHER — 10th JUNE 1979

Once again we were lucky with the weather and the Petrie-Hays much enjoyed welcoming so many Vizslas and their owners to Lower Bouts Farm. Among the new members were Mr and Mrs Armstrong, Mr and Mrs Hargreaves and Mr and Mrs Chaffe. The petrol shortage was responsible for a slight decrease on last year's numbers but the enthusiasm was as great. We sadly missed the presence of Mr and Mrs Hilbre Smith and extend the greatest sympathy to them for the loss of *Katy* who was killed on the road two days before. The tests were kept as simple as possible in order to encourage everyone to have a go and nearly everyone sportingly did.

PUPPY TEST For dogs of 12 months and under

1. Walk to heel on lead from A to B Stop and SIT.
   Continue to heel to C, Stop and SIT. Leave dog at C and walk back to B. Stand and count ten.
   Return to dog. Walk to heel off lead to A.
2. 25 yards marked simple retrieve with shot fired.
   Dog to be steady on or off lead.
3. 50 yards memory retrieve.

NOVICE TEST For dogs between the ages of one year plus or four years minus

1. Walk to heel from A to B, SIT. Leave dog and walk to C.
   Recall dog and SIT. Leave dog and walk to C. Walk to A recall dog and DROP at B.
   Recall dog and SIT.
2. 100 yards memory retrieve.
3. Blind retrieve placed in the same position as memory.
4. Two dummies launched left and right. Handler to select order of the retrieve of both dummies.

OPEN TEST For dogs over two years old.

1. Dog to quarter field up wind. Shot fired (no dummy) and dog to drop to shot then re-directed.
   Continue quartering dummy launched ahead and dummy dropped behind. Dog to retrieve
   both dummies, back one first (blind).
2. 200 yards L-shaped memory retrieve with diversion of running rabbit on return.
3. Seen retrieve over jump and blind retrieve to the side.
   Retrieves to be made in jump/blind order.

Dogs may enter one or more of the tests if eligible. The Marion Trophy will be awarded to the member with the highest placed dog in the Novice Tests. We can have a water test at the lake, but this will not be included in the marks as some people may wish to leave the party before we have finished.

The puppy test was won by Mrs Phillip's *Ibi*.
The novice test was won by Mrs Cox's *Barley Broth* with 88%
The open test was won by Mr Cox's *Hal* with 82%
Mrs Cox won the Marioni Trophy, many congratulations to her.
Mr Chaffe with *Anya* came a very close second both in the novice and open with 86% and 78%

The Grand Derby was won by 'Pasha' *Hambi*. Sheila Cox very kindly agreed to judge the dog show. Mr Berry came first with his dog and Mr Hargreaves owned the Best Bitch. Overall winner was Mr Berry.

FIELD DAY AT DONHEAD St MARY

The field day was held on the 13th of October and was kindly organized by Sheila and Jim Gray on ground that was generously provided by Mr Hall. Sheila had prepared a wonderful lunch and tea for everyone who attended this Vizsla gathering.

Figure 12.1 A Typical Get-together

Roger Phillips acted as judge and reported as follows:—

The intention of holding this field day was to give dogs and their handlers an opportunity to run their dogs on the lines of a field trial, without actually competing and those who attended certainly thought that it was well worthwhile and should be repeated if suitable ground could be found. It was unfortunate and nobody's fault, that the game was absent on the day. Six dogs with their owners were present, and most had driven a very long way so it shows how much enthusiasm there is.

The day was fine and damp after rain, ideal for scenting conditions, but alas no game could be found in the morning, so, apart from observing the dogs working and quartering, and the owners handling ability, nothing much could be learnt about the dogs.

After lunch, a water test was laid on with pigeons thrown into the lake and a shot fired. All the dogs entered the water and retrieved, though one only did so at the second attempt and with some persuasion!

We then went to a very tall kale field; a difficult test at the best of times for experienced dogs, and more so with inexperienced dogs especially if rabbits and game are moving about. It was here that the only two pheasants were seen departing unscathed at the end of the beat, by which time everyone was more interested in getting out of wet trousers and into dry ones.

EXTRACT from a letter from one of the competitors at the above field day:

As a 'competitor' may I say how interesting and rewarding my dog and I found the day and how helpful the comments from our very patient judge. I am not a great public performer and although enthusiastic, must admit approached the occasion with some apprehension. But, the atmosphere of work without the pressure of competition was such that with each run I gained more confidence and so therefore did the dog. I feel the day gave me a greater understanding of how the Vizsla works and it certainly gave my dog a very interesting experience which we very much hope can be repeated at some time.

FIELD TRIALS HELD BY THE VIZSLA SOCIETY

The Society organised and ran two field trials this year. On October 6th a novice stake was held at Loton Park by kind permission of Sir Michael Leighton Bt and on October 27th our first open stake carrying championship status was held at the Marshland Estate, by kind permission of Mr Alan Heyman QC.

The novice stake at Loton was judged by Sir Michael and Mr Peter Moxon. A very unfavourable report of this trial was published in the *Shooting Times* on October 25th. On the other side of the coin I think that the Society should feel pleased that this was the first trial to be held for Vizslas only with a full card of 12 runners and that all the competitors should be thanked for supporting the trial. I do not agree that the ground, which the dogs were expected to work during most of the day, was ideal. This consisted of sprayed potatoes, neither suitable nor conducive to any breed of dog in any stake. This was very noticeable when late in the afternoon we eventually came to grassland and roots, and the dogs called up to work this were awarded the certificates of merit. No dog was put out for hardmouth, no dog failed on the water retrieve. I think it was unfortunate that Mr Moxon did not even do us the minimum courtesy of spelling the name of the breed correctly.

Certificates of Merit were awarded to:
Mr Berry's *Galfrid Dali*
Miss Boy's *Galfrid Odo*
Mr West's *Galfrid Gelert*
Mrs L Petrie-Hay's *Waidman Crumpet*

We must thank Mrs Gay Gottlieb for acting as chief steward and also Mr Ron Martin for coming as picker-up.

The open stake in Suffolk was a much happier affair. This stake was open to all breeds which hunt, point and retrieve and the winning dog achieved one qualification towards the necessary two required by a field trial champion. Fourteen entries were received, eight Vizslas and six German Pointers. On the day seven Vizslas and five Pointers ran. It is interesting to note that four of the

Vizslas had run in the trial at Loton.

Juding this stake were Mr J Wylie (Kennel Club Panel 'A' judge for Pointers and Setters, Retrievers and Spaniels) and myself. It was a beautiful day with good scenting conditions and as usual really suitable ground, consisting of large areas of lucerne, stubble and roots. Partridges, pheasants, hares and rabbits were seen. The best report I can give of the Trial is to repeat what Mr Wylie had to say. He enjoyed judging the trial very much and thought the standard of work was very high. This is what he wrote to Mr Moxon:

> After reading your write-up of the Vizsla novice trial, I had my eyes open when I judged the open stake The hunting and quartering would put plenty of our pointers and setters to shame. The steadiness and retrieving was as good as plenty of labs. Several runners were collected first class. It was a very tough water test over a quite wide piece of water on a planted pigeon. It was a blind retrieve with no shot fired and the majority of the dogs went over with very little trouble. It was a very commanding performance all over. The trial was worth a lot of praise, I enjoyed every minute of judging.

One can assess from that and I can confirm that the dogs went well, with plenty of drive. The final results were:

1st — Mr Hale's *Trakevlyn Commanchero* (GSP)
2nd — Mr Musselwhite's Ft Ch *Fruili Asta* (GSP)
3rd — Mr West's *Galfrid Gelert* (Vizsla) handled by Mr Williams
Reserve — Mrs Nixon's *Quintana Tyr* (GSP)
Cert.of Merit — Mrs Stammer's *Moylock Maree* (GSP)

WORKING TESTS (1980)

The Vizslas get-together was held in June and in September the Society's working tests took place.

Figure 12.2 Gelert backing *Galfrid Gaspar,* 8 month old puppies

(Photo: Bruce Larner)

PUPPIES (Not under 6 months but born after January 1st 1979)

1. Walk to heel on lead — sit on command — sit and stay — handler to return to dog.
    Sit and stay — handler to recall dog.
    Walk to heel — off lead — sit and stay — handler to walk on — recall — heel.

2. (a) Seen retrieve in long grass with shot
    (b) Memory retrieve
    (c) Blind retrieve

3. Seen retrieve from water with shot.

NOVICES (Any dog under 5 years old)

1. Walk to heel — sit and stay — handler to walk on — recall — heel — sit and stay —
    recall and drop half way — recall and sit.

2. Quartering — dropping the dog twice and re-directing.
    Drop — launch dummy retrieve — continue quartering — shot fired and blind retrieve.

3. Double launched retrieve in order directed by judge.

4. Seen retrieve from water — shot fired — dog and handler 10 yards back from a bank.

OPEN (All dogs other than puppies)

1. Quartering to point caged pigeons. Shot fired — seen retrieve. Continue quartering to
    second point — 2 shots fired at (1) seen dummy (2) blind dummy.
    Blind retrieve *first* then the seen.

2. Retrieve over fence from cover — seen with shot.

3. Retrieve across water — no shot fired.

Report:

On Sunday September 7th the Society's first working test took place at Wotton Underwood near Bicester by kind permission of Mr and Mrs Mike Farquhar. It was a beautiful and ideal setting for the tests and the weather was perfect. The entries had come in well and we were very lucky to have John Gassman, Rosemary Jones and Sir Denis Smallwood to judge for us. John Gassman had presented a cup to the winner of the open test and the Cox's had presented the rosettes. There were 3 leather slip-leads as specials.

The puppy and novice tests took place in the morning and were judged by Mrs Rosemary Jones and Sir Denis Smallwood. There were seven entries in the puppy test:

The winner was *Juno* owned and handled by Mrs Sweetman
Second was Mr Greig's *Maggie* handled by Mrs Petrie-Hay
Third was Messrs Jones & Williams' *Alex* (*Maggie*'s brother)
Fourth was Mr Coller's *Jaffa* handled by Mr Coller
The special prize for the most promising puppy was awarded to *Freddie*
 owned and handled by Mrs Farquhar

There were nine entries in the novice test and the results were:

Winner — Mrs Cox's *Barley* owned and handled by Sylvia
Second was Mr Chaffe's *Anya*
Third was Mr Berry's *Bruce*
Fourth was Mr Bennett's *Miscka*
The special prize for the best handler was awarded to Mr Chaffe.

After a break for lunch Mr John Gassman started judging the open test. There were six entries and the results were:

Winner   — Mr Bennett and *Miscka*
Second   — Mrs Cox with *Barley*
Third   — Mr Cox with *Hal*
Fourth   — Mr Farquhar with *Vikki*

The special prize for the best water test was awarded to Mr Bennett and *Miscka*.

After the prize giving our host, the judges, the stewards and everyone who had helped organise this event were gratefully thanked.

Field Trial — Invitation Novice Stake for 8 dogs

Report:

Mr & Mrs Farquhar very kindly offered us part of their shoot for a field trial. Because we had not held a trial here before it was decided to limit the stake to 8 dogs. Myself and Mr Gerry Webb were invited to judge and Sir Denis Smallwood took a book. The weather was not good. There had been driving rain on the previous night and in the morning there was drizzle and a cold wind which did nothing to encourage the birds out of the coverts.

There were eight entries but only seven ran as number 8 failed to arrive. These dogs all had three or four runs each and were well tested for ground treatment and game finding, but conditions were severe for novices and at the end of the day despite all efforts, it was agreed that no awards could be given as not enough game had been shot to ensure that all the dogs had been tested fairly. Nevertheless, the competitors benefited greatly from the experience of running in a trial and the general standard of work and handling was good. No dog was eliminated for hardmouth and all the dogs completed the water test. The dogs which were submitted to temptation proved steady. The judges agreed that in many cases the dogs were over-handled owing to lack of confidence in the dogs by the handlers, but this will obviously improve with experience. It was good to see how all the dogs faced thick cover without hesitation.

Because of the number of field trials open to all breeds which hunt, point and retrieve organised by the other societies this year it was decided that the Vizsla Society would hold only this one.

Our congratulations to Mr Bil and Mrs Auchterlonie who came 1st and 2nd in a novice stake at Pitlochry for all breeds which hunt, point and retrieve run by the German Shorthaired Pointer Association.

Three Vizslas featured in the 1980 field trial awards. These were: Mr Bil's *Saline Gambler* which won a German Shorthaired Pointers Association's Novice Stake. Mrs Auchterlonie's *Saline Fulmarx Blue* which came second in the same trial and won a certificate of merit in a German Pointer Club's novice stake. Mrs Cox's *Calversam Barleybroth* came second in two novice stakes, one run by the Hungarian Vizsla Club and the other by the German Shorthaired Pointer Association. It would be nice to see a lot more dogs in the awards.

HUNGARIAN VIZSLA WORKING TEST 1981
(September 27th Piddington, Oxon)

Report:

It is very encouraging to find more Vizslas and their owners having a go at working tests, and this year's Society working test saw an increase in the entries to puppy, novice and open. We were very fortunate in having a lovely field loaned to us by Mr J Johns and arranged by Mr and Mrs Farquhar. We were also lucky in the weather, it was cold but stayed dry and the whole day was enjoyed by all. The judges were very patient and gave each dog every opportunity to do its best. The puppies were judged by Sir Denis Smallwood, novices by Mr Martin Gibbins and Sir Denis and the open tests were judged by Mr Martin Gibbins. I donated some leather slip leads for specials and Mr Peter Faulk presented the Society with a super trophy for the winner of the puppy tests in memory of his Vizsla puppy *Saddleglade Moni*. A plaque for the open winner was also donated by Mr Coller to be won outright. Many thanks for their generosity.

Results were as follows:

PUPPY	1st	*Viszony of Vallota*	Mr N Cox
	2nd	*Laser Duite*	Mr J Churchill
	3rd	*Abbeystag Josie*	Mrs S Gray
NOVICE	1st	*Czassa Camboge*	Mr M Coller
	2nd	*Viszony of Vallota*	Mr N Cox
	3rd	*Perdita's Puzzle of Szajani*	Mrs S Harris
OPEN	1st	*Calversam Barleybroth of Valotta*	Mrs S Cox
	2nd	*Waidman Brok*	Lady Smallwood
	3rd	*Galfrid Dali*	Mr E Berry

A Working Day in November 1981 at Piddington
Report by Jeanne Smallwood

There was an excellent turn out, with all the usual "suspects" plus several new faces, both canine and human. Was it my imagination or were one or two of the new dogs larger than the norm?

The tests for *Purdey*'s class were interesting, as the first one (split retrieve) was done in a paddock full of sheep. It was very satisfactory to note that not a single dog blinked an eyelash at the sight of them all day.

Figure 12.3 Champion *Peckers Perchance* (Mr Richard Houghton)

The pointing was done on a caged pheasant — very nice for the dogs, but somewhat disastrous for the poor victim, who departed this world before the day was over! I did not have a chance to watch the puppies but gather that there was quite a lot of potential about. The dog show was judged by Mr Elliott in a very professional style, and again, as far as I can remember, it was won by a very handsome large newcomer to the scene. The water test went well. A few reluctant candidates, but on the whole most dogs entered with enthusiasm and enjoyed themselves.

FIELD TRIALS

On Saturday October 17th the open qualifying stake was held on the Marshland Estate, Woodbridge by kind permission yet again of Alan Heyman. Chris Church and Eddie Hales were the judges and we had a full card of twelve runners. Sir Denis Smallwood was in the line taking a book. At the end of the day Mrs Marina Dumas, Alan's daughter, kindly agreed to give out the prizes. The winner was Mr Wagstaff's *Clara of Abberton*, a large Munsterlander, the first open win for this breed. Second prize went to Mr Street's German Pointer bitch *My Lady Belladonna*, third to Mr McErlean's international field champion *Orion Quaintways* and the reserve prize went to Mr Musselwhite's German Pointer dog *Friuli Cougar*. Mrs Kathleen Auchterlonie's Vizsla dog *Saline Fulmar x Blue* was awarded a certificate of merit. Two other Vizslas ran — Mr Bennett's *Waidman Chico* and Mr West's *Galfrid Gelert*. They both worked well and with enthusiasm but blotted their copy books alas! There was also a German Wirehaired Pointer running. With his usual generosity, Alan gave the officials an excellent lunch at the Oyster Bar in Orford.

On Thursday October 22nd we held a non qualifying All-aged Stake at Sansaw, Shropshire by kind permission of Major Thompson. Lord Joicey and Mr Graham Nixon judged and Maureen Nixon acted as Chief steward. Twelve dogs were entered with one reserve, but on the day there were only nine runners. Four of these were Vizslas. The winner was Mr Musselwhite's *Friuli Duchess*, German pointer bitch, she also won the **Waidman Brok Trophy** for the highest placed member. Second was Mr Hargreaves' Large Munsterlander bitch *Foxbrae Flora of Ghyllbeck*. No other awards were given.

On Saturday October 24th a Novice Trial was held at Apley Park, Bridgnorth by kind permission of Brigadier Goulburn and the Hon. James Hamilton. Here there was an entry of twelve dogs and five reserves but on the day due to withdrawals there were nine runners. The judges were myself and Geoff Sherring. Amongst our competitors was Mr Jim Pryke aged 76, which has got to be a record age for a competitor. On top of this he managed to gain a Certificate of Merit. He was congratulated by all. The winner was Mrs Harris' Vizsla *Perdita's Puzzle of Szajani*. Second Mr Hargreaves' *Foxbrae Flora*, third Mr Martin's German pointer bitch *Zhexe of Waidman*. The reserve and winner of the puppy cup was Mrs Cox's Vizsla, *Viszony of Vallota*. Certificates of Merit went to Mr Pryke's *Waidman Foxi* and Mrs Phillips' *Llewellyn Ibi*.

Other results this year were Mr Bennett's *Waidman Chico* won 1st prize in an All-aged stake and a Certificate of Merit in an Open stake. Mrs Cox's *Calversam Barley Broth* won 2nd prize in a Novice Stake.

THE 1982 ANNUAL GET-TOGETHER

Report

On June 13th this annual event was once again held at Inkberrow by kind invitation of the Petrie-Hays. Despite the date the weather was very pleasant and the turn out was even better than ever. Apart from all our old friends it was very nice to welcome Mr and Mrs John Gassman and also Gay and Sidney Gottlieb who had not attended before. Sidney clicked away with his camera and produced some really super pictures, capturing not only people and dogs but also the carefree atmosphere which pervaded.

The fun work this year consisted of a sponsored walk. Members, their dogs and families followed a trail round the fields taking part in various exercises at intervals. There were no judges, but any dog who failed an exercise requested his owner to report this to the steward who then penalised him 10p. Twenty dogs played this game and by the end of the day the Society was £10.00 better off. This included one or two kind donations or perhaps they were conscience money! There were three winners who amassed no penalty points at all, these were Jean Smallwood with *Purdey*, Sheila

Gray with *Katy* and Sylvia Cox with *Solly*. At lunch time Sheila Gray very kindly gave us a talk and demonstration on the art of showing your dog. As usual there was the annual Vizsla derby, won yet again by Sue Farquhar's *Freddie*, the fastest Vizsla in the south.

In the afternoon after some retrieving tests, the pigeons were put to good use again and some very nice pointing was achieved and good steadiness to flush. At five o'clock we returned to the house and everyone agreed that it was time to go home, so this year the water party had to be skipped. But despite this, everyone seemed to have really enjoyed themselves which makes the effort of laying it on all worth while. Very many thanks to the dummy launchers, dummy throwers and to John Dickinson who worked very hard as chief steward, also to Denis Smallwood our dead-eye-dick shot.

HVS WORKING TEST

Report by Sylvia Cox:

The Society held its first working test open to all hunt, point and retrieve breeds on Sunday 12th September at Little Ponton, near Grantham in Lincolnshire.

The weather was rather blustery but otherwise conditions were good. The ground was stubble and rough grass and was kindly given by Mr A McCorquodale who unfortuantely was unable to present the awards at the end of the day. However, he did come along to watch in the afternoon with his son and daughter-in-law Lady Sarah who is very fond of the 'ginger ones' — probably because she is ginger headed herself!

The entry of dogs was very encouraging with 13 Vizslas, 12 German Pointers, 1 Large Munsterlander and 1 Weimaraner. Even more encouraging was the amount of people who said they had enjoyed the day, for myself and Nigel it made all the work well worthwhile.

The judge for puppy and open was Louise Petrie-Hay and the judge for novice and open was Mr Gibbins.

Ged Leeson. The results are below:—

PUPPY
1st and winner of the Saddleglade Trophy was Mr M Gibbins GSP dog *Isara Kurzhaar Voyager*
2nd   Mr J Gatcliffe's GSP dog *Geramers Shannon*
3rd   Mr A Stammer's GSP dog *Lochpointer Mr Chips*
4th   Mr and Mrs Gray's Vizsla bitch *Abbeystag Katy*

NOVICE
1st and winner of the Ch Abbeystag Bruna Trophy was Mr J Churchill's *Laser Duite* Vizsla dog
2nd   Mr D Bennett's *Saddleglade Zoli* Vizsla dog
3rd   Mr & Mrs Horsefield's *Fineshade Quail Run* Weimaraner bitch
There was no fourth award

OPEN
1st and winner of the Braeville Award was Mrs M Simon's Ch & Ft Ch *Swifthouse Tufty* GSP dog
2nd   Mrs M Cox's *Trolanda Black Tern* GSP dog
3rd   Mr J Churchill's *Laser Duite* Vizsla dog
Certificate of merit went to *Fineshade Quail Run* Weimaraner bitch
There was no fourth place awarded

The best Vizsla puppy winner was *Abbeystag Katy* and the
Best Vizsla overall and winner of the Marioni Trophy was *Laser Duke*

Other Working Test Results 1982

Large Munserlander Club Sandpeck Park, 25th of March 1982
Open 4th *Viszony of Vallota*, owned by S Cox   Judge — Mr I W Sladden
Novice 4th *Laser Duite*, owned by J Churchill   Judge — J W Malesa

Large Munsterlander Club Hall Barn Beaconsfield, 16th April 1982
Open 2nd *Calversam Barleybroth of Vallota*,
  owned by S Cox   Judge — Mr C Church
Graduate 4th *Laser Duite*, owned by J Churchill   Judge — Mrs S Kuban

GSP Association, Lowdham Mill, Notts, 23rd April 1982
Open 4th *Viszony of Vallota*, owned by S Cox   Judge — Mr G Roberts
GSP Club, High Wycombe, Bucks 30th April 1982
Open 2nd *Waidman Chico*, owned by D Bennett   Judge — Mr E Hales
Novice 4th *Laser Duite*, owned by J Churchill   Judge — C Snelling
GSP Club (Eastern Counties Group)
Puppy 3rd *Dalegarth Gleam*, owned by Mr Newbury

FIELD TRIALS (1982)

The Society ran two field trials this year.   Both were well supported.

The Open Stakes

The open stake was held once again on Alan Heyman's ground in Suffolk and as usual supplied everything any field trial secretary could dream of to ensure success. Unfortunately our senior judge, Lord Joicey, was unable to come as he was still shooting in Denmark, so I replaced him and had great pleasure in judging with Roger Phillips.   Sheila Gray came and acted very efficiently as chief steward.

Fig. 12.4 Mr. D. Bennett's *Saddleglade Zoli* and *Waidman Chico*
resisting temptation on a dizzied pigeon (discussed in Chapter 13)

Report by Roger Phillips:

**Hungarian Vizsla Society open field trial held on Saturday 16th October
at the Marshland Estate by kind permission of Mr Alan Heyman, QC**

There was a full card for this trial, consisting of 4 Vizslas, 6 German Shorthaired Pointers, 1 Weimaraner and 1 Munsterlander. The weather forecast for the day was not promising, with rain spreading from the west; however it luckily remained dry all day — it was still in the morning, with increasing wind through the afternoon.

The land worked consisted of large tracts of stubble, kale and sugar beet. The first stubble field produced a surfeit of hares, which was indeed a severe test to all the dogs that were given a run at this stage. However, all but one survived and most proved to be rock steady. Several retrieves of hares were accomplished. All except one were large and heavy, and only *Mathams Goshawk*, (German Pointer) achieved a clean and efficient retrieve. The second large stubble field produced fewer hares, but sadly *Waidman Chico* (Vizsla) after some promising quartering succumed to the hare problem that most handlers have at some time experienced.

A field of kale showed a few pheasants, but *Fossana Blue John* (Weimaraner) developed a lack of interest in his handler, and so was withdrawn. Here, *Viszony of Vallota* (Vizsla) completed her run with some good work; a nice point, steady to flush — fall of bird, followed by a faultless retrieve. Earlier an inexperienced hare retrieve by this young dog cost her a few points.

There were nine dogs left at lunch and a picture began to emerge in the judges' mind as to what the final result might be. How wrong one can be! The promising dogs of the morning failed to improve on their position in the afternoon, and good work was put in by the other dogs to nudge them ahead.

All the remaining dogs achieved the water retrieve in an efficient manner and we then entered a large sugar beet field where there were plenty of pheasants. *Mathams Goshawk* did a useful blind retrieve from a wood, but failed after two runs to get a point and so had to be discarded. *Swifthouse Tufty* (German Pointer) a really strong looking dog who looked as if he would work for days without tiring, and who moved and quartered really well, failed to retrieve a wounded bird which unfortunately had fallen in or near a patch of wild mint. The same bird produced a negative retrieve by *Clara of Abberton* (Munsterlander) who subsequently retrieved an unseen bird efficiently. *Trolanda Common Tern* (German Pointer) a nice bitch not yet three years old improved on her morning run doing a good point and was rock steady, ending with a nice retrieve. More experience and she will be really good. Also in the same ownership *Feltimores Redpoll* (German Pointer) improved on the morning run but tended to be erratic when quartering, ranging too far ahead and returning on the same line. Birds could have been missed, but she was really steady to shot and fall and finished with a good retrieve.

At the end of the day the judges felt unable to award a first prize, the second prize going to Mrs Winser's *Trolanda Common Tern*, and the third to Sylvia Cox's *Viszony of Vallota*, handled by Nigel Cox. Both these dogs have great promise and with more experience will soon be in the winning positions.

If there is a general criticism to be made of most of the dogs, it is that the quartering was erratic; often the dogs were not going to the extremities of the line, and too frequently going directly away from the line and back again. Also when turning, even in a strong head wind, they would turn away from it rather than into it. It was a most enjoyable day, and we were sincerely thankful to our host, Alan Heyman for his hospitality.

THE NOVICE STAKE

The novice stake was held for the second time at Bridgnorth by kind permission of Brigadier Goulburn and again we were lucky to be supplied with ideal ground for the dogs to work on and to be seen working. This time Eric Greig had hoped to come down from Scotland to co-judge with Wing Commander Pat Godby but alas, Eila his wife, was not well enough for him to be away from home over-night. This occurred at the last minute which made it too late for me to try and replace him with an outside judge, so I withdrew my dog and judged with Pat. At the end of the day we compared our assessments of the dogs in order to place them in order of merit and found that our placings were identical. Pat sent me his critique after the trial which is below and in his covering letter he says, 'Mary and I thoroughly enjoyed the trial what a happy lot of people you have in your Society'.

Judges Report by Pat Godby

"I was very happy when asked to judge the Hungarian Vizsla Society's novice stake on Saturday November 6th as it was many years since I had seen them in action. And I must say I was very impressed with the general standard of work, particularly for novices.

The main weaknesses were failing to retrieve to hand, especially with pigeons at the water. Handlers must learn not to push forward as this will lose them marks as they move up to open stakes. The other failure was in not fully covering the ground allotted, a fault not always corrected by handlers.

The winner *Saddleglade Zoli*, was steady when a cock pheasant ran from a point in heavy cover. Later the handler accepted a retrieve on a hare though it was the first time the dog had been asked to do this. Though this was not a very clean one a later retrieve from rough cover was very sound. The dog entered water well and made a quick retrieve.

The runner up, *Calversam Barleybroth*, was slow to warm up, but picked up marks with a good point, and two very good retrieves. His water retrieve was sound.

Figure 12.5 Dog on Classic Point

Throphill Boss (German Pointer) earned his third place with a very good point although his quartering needs some attention. His retrieves were also not up to those of the dogs placed above him. The reserve, *Zhexe of Waidman* (German Pointer) covered her ground particularly well but missed a bird and was not too steady. Her retrieves were good.

I was very sorry that Eric Greig could not judge with me, but it was a pleasure to be joined by Louise Petrie-Hay with whom I had enjoyed judging at previous trials.

There was plenty of game to test the dogs and the field work was ably handled by the keeper, Mr Fred Cooke. Competitors and spectators were quickly and efficiently organised by the steward Mrs Sue Farquhar."

Major George Wilkinson makes this comment concerning a novice field trial held in Kent by the Large Munsterlander Club:

Two Vizslas completely outshone the other competitors. They impressed everybody with their tremendous drive and style. They were *Saddleglade Zoli* **1st and** *Viszony of Vallota* **2nd.**

At the very end of the season the GWP Club ran a novice stake and Mrs Cox's *Viszony of* Valotta came 2nd. The senior judge's comments on her work ran as follows:

"What a super little bitch this is, she finished her run with a fantastic retrieve of a wing-tipped cock pheasant that ran a long way into the wood before being caught up with. She was under very good control and besides being 2nd was awarded a prize for the best retrieve of the day and also a brace of pheasants by the guns as being the dog they would soonest take home."

THE 1983 VIZSLA GET-TOGETHER

Report by Sue Harris

"Major and Mrs Petrie-Hay kindly invited us to foregather at Inkberrow on Sunday 5th June, and made us most welcome on our arrival with a glass of wine — a lovely way to break the ice for new members. Personally I can still remember how nervous I was the first time I attended with my K9 accomplice, who was shaking like a jelly!

About 40 handlers set off with high hopes to the paddock. First to show their paces were the youngsters — walking to heel, sitting, staying and the recall. They had obviously been working hard at home, and the standard was very promising. They are certainly going to give the older dogs something to think about in a year or two if they continue to progress at this rate. The old hands were then put through their paces in basic obedience finishing up with the "Great Temptation" — a fur dummy on elastic which only enticed one victim. A great improvement on the last time it was used at a get-together!

We then progressed on up the track to try our hands — or should I say dogs — at some retrieves. The intention was to have a split retrieve, however, the dogs, being much more knowledgeable, had other ideas and thought the hedgerows needed closer investigation. It is terrible the way a dog can bring you down to earth — especially in public! The junior dogs did some very creditable retrieves. It was fun to see the senior class all going for their unseen retrieves at the same time — needless to say not everyone came back with their own dummy! Next it was the turn of the pigeons. The young entry showed great interest with their noses glued to the crate. After one or two came on point, the rest soon copied. What a lovely sight to see 4 Vizslas all on point together.

After a picnic we went to the lake for some water work. Sad to say there are still some non-swimmers in the Society, but they were given every encouragement and opportunity to take the plunge! And certainly enjoyed splashing around and getting muddy. Meanwhile at the other end of the reservoir some very competent water retrieves were demonstrated.

THE WORKING TEST

Report by Sylvia Cox

"The working test this year was held in the grounds of Little Ponton Hall, by kind invitation of Mr and Mrs A McCorquodale. We were very fortunate with the weather in that we had a short cool break in the morning, and then unfortunately, cooked again in the afternoon in the heatwave we were having. Due to the large novice entry, Brian Backhouse kindly agreed to myself judging the water test, and nearly all the dogs made light work of it. Over half the entries got 8 marks and over out of a possible 10 which made the novice competition very close all day. It was very rewarding to have so many Vizslas running. Mr Berry having 9 entered in the puppy out of an entry of 13. Mr Backhouse having 11 out of an entry of 24 and Mrs Layton having 6 in the open out of an entry of 14.

Puppy Results
1st and also best Vizsla puppy   Mrs S Harris's *Szajani Csipke*,
2nd   *Diela* (Vizsla) handled by Mrs Petrie-Hay,
3rd   Mr Bennett's *Saddleglade Kasa* (Vizsla)

Novice Results
1st   Mr Gibbins' *Isara Kurzhaar Voyager* (German Shorthaired Pointer),
2nd   Mrs Cowburn's *Peckers Penny* (Vizsla),
3rd   Mr Bucki's *Andesheim Clemmy* (German Pointer),
Certificate of merit went to Mr Gatliffe's *Geramers Shannon* (German Pointer)
and Mrs Harris' *Szajani Csipke* (Vizsla)

Open Results
1st and highest placed Vizsla overall was Mr D Bennett's *Waidman Chico*,
2nd   Mrs C Snelling's *Shaleward Esprit* (German Pointer),
3rd   Mr H Girling's *Monttaber Sparkel* (German Pointer)

WORKING DAY AT CLEARFIELDS FARM

Report by Sue Farquhar

"By kind permission of Mr and Mrs Johnie Johns, Sue Harris and I were able to hold a working day in ideal surroundings, luckily on one of the cooler days at the end of August. Many people travelled a long way to work their dogs. They were divided into two groups; one for beginners, the other for the more experienced dogs. The first group were involved in basic obedience, walking to heel on and off the lead, walking to heel bending in and out of other dogs, sitting, staying, recall and dropping to command, retrieving dummies seen and memory, also retrieving seen dummies over a fence.

After lunch we had an extremely interesting talk from Mrs Perkins on training puppies, outlining the basic do's and don'ts when first starting to train a new puppy. For the more experienced dogs there followed a working test kindly judged by Mrs Perkins. For the novice dogs a simple test involving the lessons learnt in the morning, also pointing at caged pheasants and a water test, ably judged by Air Chief Marshall Sir Denis Smallwood. Sir Denis said the standard of work was high considering that for many of the owners and their dogs it was a totally new experience."

FIELD TRIAL NEWS

The Society held three field trials this year — novice, all-aged and open qualifying stakes. We are greatly indebted to our kind hosts, Brigadier G Goulburn, Major Thompson and Mr Alan Heyman for once again inviting us to hold trials on their land. We would like to welcome our new honorary members Mr Fred Musselwhite and Mr D Layton who kindly judged for us and we would like to thank Mr G Nixon, Mr R Phillips, Mrs L Petrie-Hay and Mr E Hales for judging also — particularly those who so generously waived their expenses.

"The Society's three annual trophies which include work in the field were all won last year by Mrs Cox's *Viszony of Vallota*, it will be interesting to see if she clears the board again this year.

Judges' Reports and Observations:

In the all-aged stake at Hall Barn run by the Large Munsterlander Club, *Viszony* was awarded 2nd prize, the only award in the stake. In another all-aged stake in Kent, run by this club, Mr Bennett's *Saddleglade Zoli* came second. In an all-aged stake in Yorkshire run by the German Shorthaired Pointers Club, Mr Churchill's *Laser Duite* came third. In the novice stake at Clapham run by the German Shorthaired Pointer Association Mrs Cowburn's *Peckers Penny* was awarded a certificate of merit.

Novice Stake

Brigadier Goulburn has been host to the Society for many years and it is his kindness and hospitality which attracts the entries. The ground also is inviting. The judges were David Layton and Graham Nixon who proved understanding and helpful to the 11 Vizsla and 1 German Pointer handlers. Conditions at the start were not conducive to good scent as there had been a sharp frost which lingered till mid-morning, later the sun shone and the dogs had every opportunity of showing their paces. I was not in the line so cannot comment on the standards but regardless of results everyone had a happy and educative day and the spectators were well placed to watch all of the trial.

The winner for the second time on this ground was Mrs Sue Harris' Vizsla bitch *Perdita's Puzzle*, a great favourite with the Brigadier! Second was Mrs Cox's Vizsla dog *Calversam Barleybroth* and third was John Churchill's Vizsla dog *Laser Duite*. Two certificates of merit went to Mrs Harris' Vizsla puppy *Szajani Csipke* who also won the Touchie Quaish for best puppy. The Quaish was suitably christened with the correct lubrication which will delight the kind donor from Scotland, Mr Eric Greig. Roger Phillips handling his wife's Vizsla bitch *Llewelyn Ibi* won the other certificate of merit.

We reckon we held two records at this trial, one for the oldest handler, in his 80th year Mr Jim Pryke was once again handling his Vizsla bitch *Foxi*, and there were three generations of Vizslas running, *Starleypoint Victoria* was the dam of *Perdita's Puzzle* who was the dam of *Csipke*.

All-aged Stake

Roger Phillips co-judged with me — he was a successful Vizsla pioneer trialler in the early '60's. Of the 10 dogs on the card, 6 were Vizslas, 2 German Pointers, 1 Weimaraner and 1 Munsterlander. Seven of these were experienced dogs capable of competing in an all-aged stake and three were genuine novices, despite this those three ended up in the awards, the more experienced ones proving to be unsteady. In the morning one dog could have been put out for not hunting, he was keen enough but just did not seem to know what he was meant to be doing. Because there was the time and the game we gave him a second round in the afternoon. It was hard to believe it was the same dog. He got out well, hunted systematically, pointed, retrieved and completed the water retrieve. Roger muttered to me "must have had a double gin at lunch time!" Four dogs ran into shot, one of these John Churchill's Vizsla *Duke* proved himself to be a useful gundog if not a successful trialler on the day. He pointed and flushed a hen which was lightly hit and seen high-tailing down the far side of the hedge towards the covert. *Duke* went immediately down the near side to the bottom cutting off the bird's escape into the wood, then went through the hedge and worked his way back up, found the bird and had it back to hand, alive and undamaged. Had he not done this, that hen would have been in the cover amonst live birds and virtually irretrievable.

Mrs Cowburn's Vizsla bitch *Peckers Penny* won 1st prize. This novice bitch worked with style and pace but lacked experience in handling the wind and was not helped by her handler. However no game was missed and she had an excellent point at the end of her run on a cluster of young birds. Despite the temptation she remained quite steady until they had all been flushed. A bird was shot and fell over the road, apparently a dead bird, but not so when the dog got to the fall. She eventually worked out the line and picked the bird bringing it to hand. In the afternoon her quartering improved, a bird was shot and she completed another good retrieve her waterwork was good.

Second prize was awarded to Geoff Hargreaves' Munsterlander bitch *Foxbrae Flora of Ghyllbeck*. Only one mark separated this dog from the winner in my book. Her ground treatment was good, she pointed but failed to produce a bird and worked on, a cock then flushed back and was shot. She was steady and retrieved well. She had productive points on a rabbit, another cock and a waterfowl and did an excellent retrieve on a pigeon which dropped well ahead in the roots.

Third prize went to Mrs Cox's Vizsla dog *Calversam Barleybroth*. This dog must always be in contention. What he lacks in style and pace is amply compensated by the game he produces. His handler is unflappable. He deals with the wind as it comes, he points steadily and his retrieving is reliable. He gives the impression of a very experienced hunter who knows what he wants and where to find it.

Certificate of merit went to Mrs Gottlieb's Vizsla dog Ch *Russetmantle Troy*. This is the dog who benefited from his lunchtime tipple and impressed enough in the afternoon to gain a certificate. Another certificate to Mr and Mrs Gray's Vizsla bitch *Abbeystag Josie* handled by Mrs Gray. This was *Josie*'s first trial and she went with speed and style, very quietly handled. She made intelligent use of the wind on the stubble and in the roots. She had a good point and was steady but needed a lot of encouragement to retrieve. Experience will soon sort this out, she swam well and had no difficulty in finding and retrieving her pigeon. The third certificate was awarded to Brian Backhouse's *Throphill Boss* (German Pointer). His ground treatment was good but his handling of game running ahead was inexperienced. In roots, with a tail wind, he eventually got a good point on a pheasant and was steady. He had one good retrieve, but failed on two runners, only one of which was picked. His water retrieve was excellent.

Open Stake

At 4.30am on 29th October, 1983 I set off with my husband to steward the Vizsla Society's open qualifying stake on Mr Alan Heyman's Marshland Estate near Woodbridge. Alan has provided the society with this superb ground for nearly 10 years and as ever the judges Fred Musselwhite and Eddie Hales had the opportunity of testing the dogs as pointers. There were 7 German Pointers, 3 Vizslas and 1 Munsterlander running. They started in lucerne and then acres of stubble, giving all the dogs an opportunity of free hunting in varying wind conditions before going into kale and beet. Before the end of the day we had seen not only partridge, pheasant, snipe, woodcock, hares and rabbits but also a marsh harrier, geese, duck and fallow deer. Any dog unsteady to hares is wasting his time on this ground. By mid-morning 20 had been flushed, very few of which had been pointed although all those shot gave off sufficient scent for good retrieves. Not one dog was eliminated for chasing. Unlike pointers, hunt, point and retrieve breeds are expected to point and retrieve ground game. It is not the game they point, it is the scent, and it is accepted that if a hare has been laid up in its form for any length of time, no scent is given off. On one occasion in the roots a dog went on point, a hare flushed forward and was shot and a second hare flushed back from the identical spot. In the past on this ground I remember a dog pointing in stubble, a hare flushing and being shot and as the dog sat to shot another hare escaped from under him!

No 1st prize was awarded. Second went to Mike Street's German Pointer bitch *Cocklebrook Tamarisk*, third to Mrs Finan's German Pointer dog Ch *Geramers Sea Venom* handled by Mr Finan, reserve to Mrs Cox's Vizsla bitch *Viszony of Vallota*, handled by Nigel Cox and a certificate of merit to Dave Bennett's Vizsla dog, *Saddleglade Zoli*. Interesting to note that these four dogs were all born in 1980.

The fact that hosts at hunt, point and retrieve trials comment on the good sportsmanship is something to be proud of but some of the competitors would benefit by reading not only the Kennel

Figure 12.6   Ch *Russetmantle Troy*

Club rules for field trials but also the guide to judges which gives an insight into how and why the judges come to their decisions.

Thus over the last ten years there has been a considerable increase in the encouragement given to Vizsla owners by the Society, to enable them to train their dogs for work whether they have shooting facilities or not. The annual get-togethers aim to encourage owners to meet, talk and 'have a go' at simple exercises. The working tests give them an outlet to assess their success as handlers and trainers. The working days give courage to potential triallers and the trials give an opportunity to prove that the Vizsla can compete and win against the other hunt, point and retrieve breeds.

VIZSLAS AT THE GAME FAIR

The Game Fair is an annual event where sportsmen from all over the country meet. It is organised by the Country Landowners' Association and held at a different venue each year in order to give the maximum opportunity for people to attend. Once in five years it goes to Scotland.

Every year since 1973 Vizslas have been represented in the Parade of Gundogs and in the Gundog exhibition tent. Photographs and details of the breed are displayed and questions from the general public are answered by those Vizsla owners who are invited to attend with their dogs. This is an excellent shop window for the breed as a working gundog. It is only recently that it has been possible to demonstrate their working ability. In 1976 I was approached by the Game Fair Committee and asked to stage some sort of exhibition or competition which would help the general public to understand the work of the hunt, point and retrieve breeds. I gathered a committee and we decided as it was the first time such an exploit had been undertaken we would have a working competition between three German Shorthaired Pointers as these were the most numerous and best known of the hunt, point and retrieve breeds. Despite panics and set-backs during rehearsals, on the day the dogs put up a brilliant performance and have convinced a lot of people as to the value of these versatile gundogs. Proof of this was that I was invited again the following year to stage a similar show at Woburn. This time it was to be a match between a German Pointer, Vizsla and a Weimaraner in order to demonstrate that although the work of the breeds was similar their styles differed considerably. The dogs had to hunt, point caged pigeons, retrieve a dummy over a fence and then another from the lake. The fair was on Friday and Saturday and there was a match on both days. *Waidman Brok* represented the Vizslas. On the first day the German Pointer won with *Brok* and the Weimar tying for 2nd place. On the Saturday *Brok* won so there was a run off between the German Pointer and *Brok*. The German Pointer was declared the winner gaining 72 points out of 80 against *Brok*'s 69.

In 1980 at Welbeck we were again invited to demonstrate the work of these dogs and it was agreed that this should take the form purely of a demonstration. A German Pointer, Vizsla, Weimaraner, and a Large Munsterlander were represented and the fair lasted for three days.

The object of our demonstration was to cover the role of a pointer/retriever in the shooting field. The dogs would have to be seen to quarter the ground and hunt for game, to point steadily, to flush and to retrieve from land and lake. To do this in a controlled environment, on unnatural game, in public with an audience is quite a tall order for the most experienced of competitors — and it must be repeated for three days.

The hunting must be seen to be systematic and therefore the wind direction could not necessarily be used. The dogs would have to quarter as directed. The pointing would have to be on a caged pigeon, a scentless bird, probably partly visible. So the point had to be contrived as naturally as possible. The flush was definitely the most difficult obstacle. To persuade a pigeon to rise rapidly upwards can be achieved by a sprung trap, but sprung traps can fail to spring! The alternative is to tip the trap off the pigeon by pulling a piece of string. However, one can never guarantee the pigeon will feel like flying away. Some do, some do not, and those which do not are in considerable danger from an impatient, pointing dog whose next job is to retrieve. All credit to our dogs who remained statuesquely on point before a strutting dithering bird. Only one pigeon lost a few loose tail feathers!

The retrieving was the least of our worries, apart from the fact when a bird is flushed and shot fired, the dog's instinctive reaction is to mark that bird until out of sight, rather than to watch for a thrown dummy.

To make it more realistic we decided to use a dead pigeon instead of a dummy, and to incorporate a jump in the retrieve to make it more attractive to the spectators. The retrieve from water had to be a dummy launched into the lake. We now had to find suitable dogs to fulfil these requirements, dogs and handlers capable of coping not only with the work but also the artificial conditions. Speed, style and steadiness was essential.

I approached the breed clubs asking for volunteers and we held an audition in June on the ground. This proved difficult as "the ground" was covered in sheep but nevertheless we ran through the aspiring candidates and gave our commentator a vague impression of what we were attempting to achieve. This practice also gave us an idea of timings and the back-up team we would require — two guns, two pigeon replacers, one pigeon thrower, one water launcher and we were promised a military walkie-talkie gentleman. The plan was taking shape but we agreed a further meeting was necessary early in July to finalise the production.

Sylvia Cox was selected to represent the Vizslas with her dog *Calversam Barleybroth*.

We met on July 13th and, despite the date, were greatly heartened. The ground looked ideal, the grass had grown, it had been fenced off, the jump had been constructed and some offending reeds and rushes by the lakeside had been cleared, making it possible for the dogs to enter the water more spectacularly. We ran through the programme with the selected dogs and they went well. Jack Petit, the head keeper, brought us a couple of partridges to try in the traps to see whether this would produce a more effective point, it did, but the partridge flushed and flew very low, landing in the lake, where it had to be retrieved by one of the dogs and revived by one of the handlers inside his shirt! We decided to stick to unco-operative pigeons. Nothing more could now be done other than to pray for good weather. Our preparations were complete.

And what of the show? The weather was kind, the spectators were numerous and appreciative. Our arrangements and timing caused us no concern and every member of the team played their part without fault. If you had seen some anglers taking up their stations on the bank exactly where we had planned our water retrieve they had disappeared when you looked again. From the comments heard or overheard we got the impression that those who had seen our effort to increase the knowledge and under- standing of pointer/retrievers had been interested and entertained, and more than that we could not have asked.

In 1981 the fair was at Stowe School and again a demonstration was staged with the addition of the Wirehaired German Pointer. Sylvia was elected to show up the Vizsla in its true colours and put up yet another superb performance.

In 1982 the fair was at Totton Park and the same pattern was repeated. This time Sylvia and *Barley* did the first and second days and Nigel Cox demonstrated with *Viszony of Vallota* on the third day. This young bitch worked brilliantly. This is the sort of publicity which is invaluable to the breed.

In 1983 the fair was in Scotland and there was no demonstration.

Figure 12.7 Viszony of Vallota working on a Grouse Moor (Mr & Mrs N Cox)

CHAPTER 13

TRAINING

THE TRAINER'S OBJECTIVES AND THE DOG'S CAPACITY

Before going into the details of training a young dog for the gun it is essential to acknowledge your own objectives and the capability of your pupil. There are two very important basic rules involved in training Vizslas:

(1) **Mean what you say and say what you mean**
(2) **Trust your dog**

Vizslas take many roles in the field — a rough-shooter's dog who accompanies his master on forays up hedges, in woods, over stubbles and across water. Here he is expected to be a genuine jack of all trades. He must work as a Pointer over stubbles and open ground and, as a Spaniel when hedging and ditching and in cover. He must be prepared to retrieve rabbit, hare, partridge, pheasant and water fowl. His pointing on stubbles must be precise and staunch. To find and not miss game his ground treatment, i.e. his quartering must be methodical and expansive. Whereas in cover, although his ground treatment must be thorough, the pattern will vary with the density of the cover and when on point he must be prepared to get in and flush the bird bravely from the hedge, ditch or brambles in order that the bird springs into flight, thus giving his master a sporting shot. Where you have a dog that creeps into flush the chances are that the bird will do likewise and creep away rather than fly. This sort of shooting requires a dog that will adapt all the facets of his work to the conditions and be prepared to get after a wounded bird quickly in order, not only that time is saved searching for it, but also to ensure that it is in the bag and not lying up in the next county with pellets in its body.

As a non-slip retriever his role is very different and not really the ideal environment for a pointer/retriever, but nevertheless it is work and if that is all that is available it is certainly better than no work. But here the dog is used purely as a retriever and it is better in many ways not to encourage free hunting for live game but to confine his training to retrieving exercises only. On the other hand a dog can be used solely as a pointer, as would a falconer, and his retrieving ability actively discouraged as it is the hawk not the dog who picks up the game. Many Vizslas are also used on deer either as their main employment or as an adjunct to the general shooting scene. Here the training of such a dog must include some advanced training exercises and teaching the correct behaviour when stalking. It never ceases to amaze me how many dogs will take

201

to deer hunting who never had any specific training and how they will quickly differentiate between a rifle and a shot gun. Get out of a land rover with a shot gun and the dog is all ready to start searching for game, the sooner the better, take a rifle and he is at your heels, ears pricked and alert to the slightest smell or sound of the quarry ahead.

Some Vizslas never get any nearer to the shooting field than working tests, where a canvas dummy must take the place of the real thing, and dummy launchers simulate the gun. But here his innate instincts are given expression and being controlled and provided this gives the dog and his owner pleasure, a lot of enjoyment and sensible training can be acquired. The other extreme is the man who revels in the competition of field trials and keeps his dog solely for that purpose. This is a necessity if he is going to be a successful contender as very, very few winning field trial dogs will go on winning if they are used as regular shooting dogs. Why? Because in a trial the dog must be 100% attentive to his handler at all times. Admittedly he must find game, point it and then retrieve it when he is ordered to do so, but he must never use his own initiative whereas your shooting companion is the dog who will not bother to cover ground where he knows full well he is not going to find game, he is not going to hang around on point while the judges and guns all position themselves and the bird is already starting to creep away; and he is not going to wait one or even two minutes when he can see a wounded bird hot footing it for the nearest cover. Then there is the picking-up dog and the dog who is destined to be purely a family pet but who goes for long walks or out with the horses.

Every one of these dogs must have not only a basic education in manners but also advanced training if only in controlled obedience in order to prove themselves to be intelligent and co-operative companions as dogs and not as animals.

If you decide that it is for the shooting field that your pup is destined then before the intensive training which this involves you must be sure that he is neither gunshy nor has a hardmouth.

GUN-SHY

Many people think that if a dog is nervous of gunfire he is 'gunshy'. This need not be the case. With careful handing, many a pup that has shown disquiet on hearing a shot fired has turned into an excellent gun dog. There are two kinds of gun-shyness, inherited and man-made. A truly gun-shy dog will turn tail and GO, and I mean go, very far away from the bang when a gun is fired. If either of this dog's parents were also gun-shy then it is sensible to presume that it is inherited. I would say that this was comparatively rare in the breed.

It is extremely easy to make a dog gun-shy by insensitive handling particularly if the pup is gun nervous. Gun nervousness is not unusual; the noise of a gun, rifle or blanks from a launcher can be frightening, particularly if the pup has lived a quiet life with not many sudden noises to put up with. Many a young dog dislikes the sound of blanks whereas a cartridge will have no effect on him. The reason for this is the difference in the tone of the explosion, the blank is very much higher and sharper. A gun fired over the head of a young dog can damage its ear drums for life, as well as ensure that it is gun-shy because the noise has caused pain.

Obviously it is important to see that introduction to gunfire is gradual, careful and associated with pleasure. It is also important that if the dog shows a fear or dislike of blanks, then they should not be used and one must resign oneself to the expense of cartridges. The sound of gunfire can be associated with feeding time and, providing it is at a sufficient distance, little or no notice will be taken. Later on it can be associated with seeing dummies falling, thus the dog's interest is diverted from the noise to the pleasurable thought of a retrieve. This is the best way of overcoming any signs of nervousness when a shot is fired. Some dogs will also show timidity at the sight of a gun; this could have been caused by a variety of reasons, but in order to avoid it, it is important to get the dog used to the association with a gun. Carry one as often as possible even if you have no intention of using it, or carry a hefty stick or crook, which you can point skywards from time to time simulating the raising of a gun. It is also feasible to feed a dog with a gun lying beside his bowl on the floor.

Thus we have gun nervousness, which can easily be overcome by gentle and careful handling; inherited gun-shyness, about which very little can be done with any degree of certainty and man-made gun-shyness, which has been cuased by fear or pain due to thoughtless and careless handling, again almost impossible to overcome other than by a long, slow process of re-education with no certainty of success in the end.

HARDMOUTH

Just as in gun-shyness, a dog may inherit a hardmouth or have it thrust upon him. That

Fig. 13.1 A youngster retrieving a dummy (Mrs S. Harris' *Szajani Csipke*) — hardmouth should be detected as early as possible. (photo: Carlisle)

hardmouth can be hereditary is an accepted fact and anyone breeding from a dog that is known to have inherited this defect is very stupid indeed — unless you wish to live on pate all your life! A hardmouth in a gundog makes that dog a liability rather than an asset, not only as a field trial contender but also as a bag-filler. But if a hardmouth in a dog has been caused by human error then there is no reason why that dog should not be bred from and produce useful puppies.

It is not possible to recognise an inherited hardmouth from a man-made one by sight. An enquiry into the facts of parenthood and junior education however should prove the case. If it is known that either of the parents were rough on their game then, if the youngster also shows this fault, it would be sensible to presume it is inherited. If both parents have proven that they retrieve tenderly then it can be assumed that the fault lies with the trainer or his family.

The best way to ensure that a dog becomes hard-mouthed is to send it for a lightly wounded cock bird early on in its retrieving career. A good gash with a spur and a peck around the eye is virtually a guarantee that the youngster will give that bird such a squeeze as to ensure that no further pain is inflicted on him. It can also of course cure the dog for life of any further wish to retrieve. A loose feathered wood pigeon is also undesirable as a retrieve at an early age. Alternatively if the family is allowed to wrench or drag 'treasures' from the pup — albeit that they are favourite toys, hats or shoes — then this encourages a good hard grip in order to improve the odds of a fair tug of war. I have heard that bones encourage a hardmouth or rather I have been asked whether this is true — in my opinion it is not. Nor should the retrieval of any hard object necessarily be discouraged although I think it wise to ensure all dummies are well padded, as a soft mouthed dog not only means that he handles an object gently but also that his mouth is a soft and delicate orifice and should therefore be treated as such.

The cures for a hardmouth are various — extraction of the eye teeth being the most drastic I have heard of, winding barbed wire round a dummy, covering a dummy in gorse or other prickly substances so that when too firm a grip is taken pain is suffered. Of course this involves the co-operation of the dog in picking up that object which an intelligent dog is likely to jib at. Ordinary common sense is the most important asset for a gundog trainer. It is not difficult to assess the mouth of a young dog. Take careful note of how the pup handles an object, the pick up and the carry. It should be thoughtful, gentle and proud. A pup should be allowed to carry his treasure, be what it may, willingly and happily and encouraged to hand it over with confidence. But he should never be allowed to play with it or chew it. Reverence of a portable object both by dog and handler, be it a mouse or a pheasant, is essential. Care should be taken to ensure that dummies are attractive and retrieving exercises should neither be boring nor over-indulged in. Encouragement is often needed when progressing from the dummy to cold game to warm game, but sense and understanding by the trainer will ensure that the youngster understands that it is God's will that he should carry these objects and that, after all, is all the pup desires — to please and be pleased by his master.

And just a little more sense is again needed during the first season of work. Choose the retrieves a dog is allowed carefully, always dead birds, keeping a large cock pheasant till later in the season and retrieves from really tough, punishing cover till even later in the season. With birds coming to hand undamaged at this stage you should be set fair for many years of successful pot-filling. If not, find a happy retrieverless home for the dog and start again. The Kennel Club instructions to field trial judges concerning hardmouths is as follows:

All game should be examined for signs of hardmouth. A hardmouthed dog seldom gives visible evidence of hardness. He will simply crush in one or both sides of the ribs. Blowing up the feathers will not disclose the damage. Place the bird in the palm of the hand, breast upwards, head forward, and feel the ribs with finger and thumb. They should be round and firm. If they are caved in or flat, this is definite evidence of hardmouth. Be sure the bird reaches your co-judges for examination. There should be no hesitation or sentiment about hardmouth, the dog should be discarded. A certain indication of a good mouth is a dog bringing in a live bird whose head is up and eye bright. Superficial damage, if any, in this case can be ignored. At times the rump of a strong runner may be gashed and look ugly. Care should be taken here, as it may be the result of a difficult capture or lack of experience in mastering a strong runner by a young dog. Judges should always satisfy themselves that any damage done has been caused by the dog, not by the shot or fall, and in cases of doubt, the benefit should be given to the dog. Handlers should be given the opportunity of inspecting the damaged game in the presence of the judges, but the decision of the judges is final.

TRAINING A YOUNG DOG

Having proved your point that he is suitable material then let battle commence. But always remember that the dog is an emotive issue and should not be allowed to over-come man's sense of humour and proportion.

Training Equipment

Training equipment can be simple or complicated but a light slip lead is the first requirement. Choke chains, in my opinion, should never be necessary. If you put a slip lead on a 12 week old puppy and let him play with your hand as you walk along, within a week you will have that pup walking to heel on a lead.

A whistle is also essential if you are to control the dog at a distance. Man's voice is the last thing game likes to hear around the fields and the quieter you can be the more chance the dog will have of finding and producing fur or feather. I do not like the 'silent' whistle as I can never be sure that the dog has heard it. I would rather have an ordinary horn or bakelite one with a medium pitch which both dog and I can hear and understand. I also have at the ready a 'blaster' just in case things go wrong and I need to use surprise tactics. It is amazing how a really loud noise will affect a dog's behaviour if he is consciously doing wrong.

The third necessity is a dummy of one sort or another. It is best to have a variety in order to encourage the pup to get used to various sensations in his mouth My first 'dummy' is usually a glove, cap or slipper that a 12 week old can pick up and carry, I also use just a duck or pheasant's wing at this period. Then later I make canvas dummies and use them plain or with a rabbit skin tied round, and another with feathers stitched on. It is also a good idea to have one that will float but also have some weight. An empty 'squeezy' bottle with a little sand in it to give it weight and covered with canvas is very adequate. Be prepared to lose them, so make some spares! And lastly a gun and cartridges or blanks is necessary. You can go to the expense of buying a dummy launcher which is very helpful but not essential. It is also handy to have a loft full of homing pigeons or a pen with quail in and also an enclosed area where you can keep rabbits. But all these are refinements and not essential to basic training. Some training classes will supply them and some trainers will allow you to use theirs. The use of a rabbit run is obvious but it must be remembered that a dog will quickly learn not to chase the rabbits in that run but the wild rabbits up the fields are a whole new ball game. Treat them with respect and remember, however steady your pup is in the enclosure, he will need careful handling for the transition period to wild rabbits. Pigeons or quail can be used for pointing. Quail will behave like partridges, release the majority from the pen leaving one or two call birds inside. The released birds will go off into the surrounding fields but will return in the evening when they hear their mates calling. In this way you can be sure that there is game in certain fields for the dog to point. The only snag is that quail would far rather run than fly and at the beginning of the year, if you wish to use them, then it is necessary to release some and take an older dog who will be prepared to chase and chivy them around for 10 days in order to encourage them to fly. This works just as a good rousting does with the young pheasants at the beginning of the season. The alternative is pigeons who will return to the loft after use. Take two or three pigeons in a cage into a field. You can then do one of three things with them:

1. **Make a wire trap under which the bird can be placed.**
The trap must be strong enough to resist an impetuous snap and must have a cord attached to it which when pulled will tip the trap up and release the bird to fly away.

2. **Dig a small hole in the ground and into it place the bird, then put a tile on top to prevent escape.**
The tile can then be kicked away at the appropriate moment.

3. **You can 'dizzy' the bird.**
This is quite simple and involves putting it to sleep for a short period. It is done by tucking the head of the bird under one wing, holding it there and swinging the bird gently around or to and fro for a few seconds. On no account press the breast bone as this will cause the death of the pigeon, which is not the object of this exercise! Now place the bird on the ground and it should remain motionless for a matter of minutes. If it is not asleep then you have not rocked it sufficiently and it will need a bit more, I have found the older the bird the more time is needed to hypnotise it. Once 'out' you can leave it on the ground with a little grass over it and a twig to mark the place. When the dog comes on point you approach slowly and if the bird does not awake when you are ready then just tip it forward gently with one hand whilst the other ensures that the dog remains at a safe distance. But this is not normally necessary as the trance seldom lasts longer than 5/10 minutes.

Although almost all dogs will point quail some do not react to pigeons and, if this is the case, then it is possible to get a phial of concentrated pheasant, partridge etc. scent, which you can apply to the pigeon thus making it more 'pointable'; but I find these extras are not so much an aid for the exercise of pointing but to control the behaviour of the dog to flush. If you can produce a point when you want then you can be prepared to control the aftermath.

An area for training is necessary and also available water for swimming. Not everyone has these on their doorsteps but it is always possible to persuade a friendly farmer to let you use his land if he appreciates that you are genuine.

Training Schedule

Here is a simplified general schedule for training your dog between the ages of twelve weeks and eighteen months. It is not intended to be a full training guide or to replace the few good text books dealing with the subject. It will however answer the first questions a novice trainer usually has and I hope, encourage the training of your dog.

It must be stressed that every puppy's mental ability varies, as does the trainer's time and patience. Make haste slowly, never force the pace and always ensure that the dog is happy and that the trainer is in a kindly and relaxed mood during training sessions. Do not attempt to train a dog if you are in a hurry, irritated or if the weather is unsuitable. A high wind is never conducive to obedience, and both bleak and cold and hot, muggy weather adversely affects both dog and man.

Much basic training can be done in the house or garden and no pup should be allowed to run free on open ground where there is game until it is absolutely under control. One of the most important factors in training is that, by foresight, to prevent wrong doing rather than have to correct misbehaviour.

When it is from three to six months old the puppy should learn the following:

COME on command at all times.

SIT on command both when on the lead and when free; beside on the left, and in front of the trainer. Combined with word of command, use a hand signal and a whistle of your choice.

HEEL on and off a lead. Start training on the lead, then let the lead trail on the ground still attached to the collar, then remove the lead. Let the pup nuzzle your left hand and walk briskly. Use the word 'heel' frequently so that he associates the word with the action.
Combine COME, SIT and HEEL. When walking to heel encourage him to sit each time you stand still.

STAY either sitting or lying as you wish, on command. Start by sitting the pup with lead on and in your hand. Walk slowly round him and make him stay sitting, then take one pace backwards. Repeat this with the lead on the ground, repeat again with no lead. Once this is perfect then increase the circle and distance you step back. Always return to the pup at this stage. *Do not call him to you.* Once he is relaxed and confident that you will return you can begin to walk about 20 paces away, stand still, then a few seconds later say 'come'. Alternate this with returning to him, but always encourage him to come in at a gallop when you call him and to sit in front of you on arrival. Maximum distance to be aimed at now is 40 yards. Not more than this and do not go out of sight. During this period take him for frequent rides in the car to avoid any chance of car sickness. Always go out just *before* a meal, have plenty of air in the car. Drive carefully so he is not swung about.

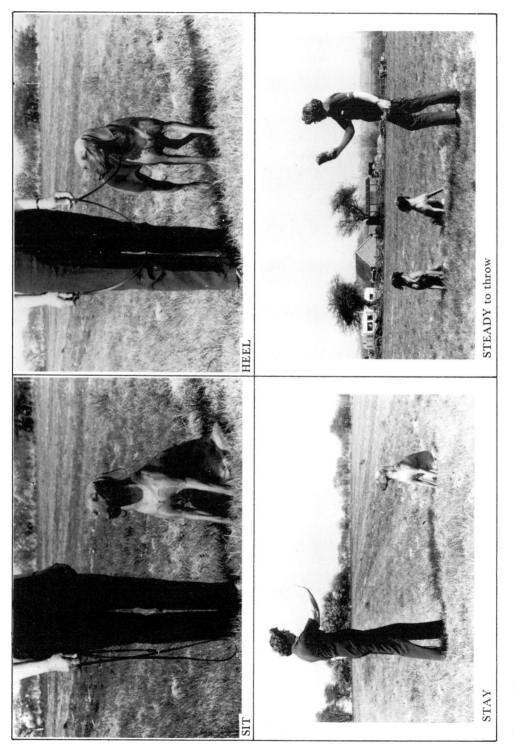

HEEL

SIT

STEADY to throw

STAY

Figure 13.2 Training by Mrs Louise Petrie-Hay I

POINTING A Caged Pigeon

HOLD

STEADY to Launch Dummy

Figure 13.3 Training by Mrs Louise Petrie-Hay II

When a puppy is from six to nine months old he should learn to cope with the following:

FETCH a simple retrieve. Start by throwing a dummy (weighing not less than one pound and at least one foot long) in sight and letting the pup run to retrieve it. Do this in a confined area and encourage him to bring it back to you either by bending right down to receive him or by running away. *Do not take the dummy from him straight away*, pat him and fuss him and let him hold it in his mouth. If he does not want to give it to you, slip his lead on and let him walk to heel carrying it. Then say 'sit' and remove it very gently from him. Once you know he will retrieve and bring it to you never throw the dummy where it lands in sight of the pup. In this way he will learn to use his nose and not his eyes to find it. Directly he is retrieving happily to hand, restrain him from running in by holding him gently at first, then insisting that he 'sit' on a lead, and then off a lead. Vary the type of dummy and never overdo this exercise. Two or three retrieves well done are quite enough.

There are three main types of retrieve from land. 'Seen', which is self evident, 'memory', which involves putting a dummy on the ground in sight of the pup and walking away a little distance then sending him back for it and increasing the distance as you progress, and thirdly 'blind', which means that he has not seen the dummy fall. This is best done by giving him an easy memory retrieve, and then placing the dummy in exactly the same spot but without him seeing it. Send him for it just as you did for the memory and preferably close enough and up wind for him to scent it. He will quickly learn in this way that the word 'fetch' means to go and look for the dummy regardless of whether he has seen it fall or not. If possible to every seen retrieve, give him two blind ones.

SHOT Ensure that he has heard gunshot by this age. Ask a friend to fire a gun at least 100 yards away from you whilst you are playing with the pup and watch his reaction. Providing there is no fear decrease the distance from the shot and combine it with playing or retrieving so that he is not in any way bothered by the sound. Once this is established, walk him to heel, sit him and fire a shot; repeat this but reverse the order to heel, shot and sit, when he will sit to shot combine it with throwing a dummy. *Do not* let him retrieve the dummy, leave him sitting and fetch it yourself for at least a week. Once he understands that he must sit to shot and stay steady to falling dummies you can combine shot and retrieving.

WATER Introduce your dog to water at an early age. Let him splash through brooks and streams or paddle into the sea or pond. Only do this on a warm day so that he is not discouraged by cold water. Directly he will enter water willingly encourage him to go deeper, either by the example of another dog or, if necessary, going in yourself. Never let him be frightened by the water. Throw the dummy into the shallows to begin with, and then into deeper water. He will quickly enjoy swimming for it. After this is achieved introduce steadiness, expecting him to sit and wait on the bank for the command to fetch.

THE DROP It is absolutely essential that your dog should drop instantly when commanded. Providing he understands your commands for sit, both by whistle and hand as well as word, this is quickly taught. Start by walking to heel and sitting him beside you, then encourage him to move a little away from you but within arm's length and tell him to sit. Ensure he sits immediately where he is and does not come to sit beside you, if necessary push him down with your hand, and step back. Continue to do this increasing the distance only when you are certain that he understands that you wish him to sit away from you. Never, at this stage, call him to you and stop him half way. Always drop him when he is going away or playing about never after the command to come. Practice this drop by word when he is close by, hand signal when he is looking at you, and by whistle when he is going away. Only after quite a period of time when you are certain that he will drop at a distance on command is it time to combine the commands of 'come' and 'sit' i.e., sit at a distance. If you try this too soon the pup will be puzzled, he knows that 'come' means to come to you and he does this happily and willingly so when you tell him to sit when on his way to you he will not understand. 'Come' means come and 'sit' means sitting beside or in front of you at this stage. Only when 'sit' also means sitting at a distance can you risk dropping him after having called him. Do not drop him too often on his way back to you or you will have a dog which comes in slowly expecting to be told to drop half way.

Once the drop is perfect then you can combine it with temptation, such as a falling dummy and a shot.

When a Vizsla is from 9 months to a year old the training should advance to the following:

QUARTERING This is the term used for the systematic hunting for live game. I have left it till now as this is about the time when you will be beginning to control this instinct. Up till now it is essential that there is no interference with the natural instincts of the pup when he sets off to hunt for game. You must be with him as a companion but not as a master. Some dogs need far more freedom and encouragement to hunt than others. There is only one taboo — never ever let a dog hunt for his own benefit and pleasure with no regard to his handler. This makes your dog a self-hunter, a fault which is almost impossible to correct once it has become established. The dog will be of no use as a shooting companion.

Your dog must discover for himself that only by quartering at a speed into the wind will his nose find scent. He may not point classically, he may chase, but he will show his instinctive ability as a hunter and pointer, you must foster and encourage this. Once this is established then you can introduce some discipline but not before. This should take place on ground where there are birds, but not ground game. The scent of birds is what he is learning to recognise and acknowledge at this stage. Try not to involve hares and rabbits, he can learn how to handle these at a later stage. Once you have established that he will hunt freely and point, introduce the discipline of dropping not only to flush but also to shot. Remember to do this or you will have a dog that associates the gun with retrieving only and as a result, he will be inclined not to hunt when you carry a gun.

Once you have established that he is a natural hunter it is time to control his quartering so that it is systematic and thorough. The easiest way to teach him to do this is to take him into a long narrow field of rough grass approximately 60—80 yards wide with the wind blowing either up or down the field but not across it. Stand at the end with the wind blowing towards you and then start running to the further hedge calling the dog and waving him past you. Let him continue either as far as the other side *or* until he looks at you. At this moment start running in the other direction calling him again and again waving him past you. Repeat this over and over again until you have arrived at the top of the field. When teaching a youngster to quarter always work him into the wind and very soon you will find that he will be zig-zagging in front of you naturally. You want to aim at walking in a straight line yourself with the dog working about 30 yards either side of you and about 10–15 yards ahead. If he diverts from this use your stop whistle, call him in and start again. It is useful to have a special whistle for the turn when you are working ground that is not bounded by a natural stop. I suggest two slow blasts and when in the narrow field blow them every time he turns. In this way he associates this whistle with changing direction. Initial quartering training should be done on ground where there is no game so that there are no distractions. Once he has got into a nice rythmic pattern and you are certain that he is reliable on the drop then you can take him where there is some game.

OVER Any time during these sessions you can introduce jumping. Start over low objects which he can jump easily, and use the word 'over' every time he jumps. If you use wire or sheep netting of any kind, put a sack over it so that he can see it easily. Throw the dummy over it, send him for it and as he approaches the jump say 'over'. Association of the word and action is important. Increase the height slowly and vary obstacles.

TRACKING This can be taught by trailing game down wind. Do not ever work up wind when teaching a dog to track or he will use the air scent and not the ground scent. Get a friend to help you lay a trail by stringing a freshly killed bird or rabbit between you and then dragging it along the ground. Your own foot prints must be far enough away for him not to be able to follow them and of course this must be done out of sight of the dog. When the trail is ready, place a small bit of skin or fur at the start, put the dog on a shortish lead and take him to smell the flesh. Then encourage him to get his nose down on the trail and to follow the *exact* track which you made, make him go slowly and exactly. If he diverts, pull him back onto the line. As he improves you can lengthen the lead and increase the speed, but on no account let him raise his head or cut corners. It will be quite a while before you can leave him to follow a line free from your assistance. Have a separate command for this exercise. 'Fetch' for a dead retrieve, and 'hie lost' for a runner which he must track. A young dog is puzzled when sent to retrieve a bird he has seen falling and has marked only to find that it has gone when he gets to the mark, but if you can encourage him to get his head down quickly and track the warm scent of the runner he will soon do this of his own accord.

Between one year to eighteen months it is time to start to control his pointing ability:

POINTING It is difficult to tell you when your dog should start to point. Some pups of three months will point anything from a sparrow to the family cat, others show no inclination before they are much older. The important thing is to know what to do when he does begin to point. Watch him carefully and when you notice him stiffening go quickly but quietly from the side — never from the rear — slip on his lead and stroke him, encouraging him to remain where he is for as long as possible. It matters not what he is indicating, but that you should impress on him that he is doing the right thing and that you are pleased with him. Once he has remained steady for any time up to five or ten minutes (providing the object he is pointing has not moved) go forward quietly and then flush the object yourself by a sudden movement. Sit the dog allowing him to watch the departure of the 'pointed'. Do not let him follow it. This procedure can start from three months upwards. As time goes by you will find that he gets more discriminating in his choice of objects to point. During this period good lessons may be taught in steadiness both to point and flush, so that by a year he should be auto-matically dropping to flush and watching the direction in which you will eventually be shooting. At no point should he be encouraged to flush his own game, still less to chase it once it has gone. It is essential that no other dog is allowed to interfere on these occasions.

When he is about a year old, if all has gone to plan, you can start combining quarter-ing with pointing. Take him onto ground where there is likely to be scent available for him to point. Allow him to quarter, point and drop to *your* flush of the game, then continue quartering. The next step is to introduce shot in combination with the flush. Again providing you have succeeded in your earlier lessons in keeping him rock steady to shot, no difficulties should arise, but still do not let him flush the game. And do not shoot to kill as yet. Go *slowly*, step by step. Once this is perfected then comes the moment when you will have to ask a friend to accompany you to do the shooting. It is important that your concentration should be on the pup and not on hitting the game. The game can now be shot but not retrieved. Either pick it up yourself or go elsewhere for ten minutes at least and then come back to the area and use it as a memory retrieve. It is important that the dog should not associate the point, shot and fall with retrieving at this time.

Now that he is steady to all facets of his pointing and retrieving job it is time for him to flush his own game. Game in the open will generally flush as he approaches but in cover it will sit tight. Teach him by allowing him to go forward with you and encourage him to 'get in' where you suspect the game to be. Do this by an excited movement of the hand and voice so that he bounces in — the sharper the flush the better chance of the bird rising for a sporting shot. If he has learned his lessons properly then as the game flushes he will drop. After half a dozen such flushes you can afford to shoot at the game providing you can rely on his steadiness. Continue in this way for two or three months and resist the temptation to allow him to retrieve after the fall. It will pay dividends in the years to come. After this time, and provided all is as you would wish, then you can allow him to retrieve but after a reasonable wait at the drop. A young dog in his first year should not be sent in for a runner.

Take things carefully, keep him steady and do your best to think ahead so that you can avoid mistakes. In this way he will gain experience and give intense pleasure and satisfaction. Sensible owners treat their dogs like their children and expect the same respect and obedience from them. Given these conditions a pup can grow up and mature in happiness and discipline to become a sound steady worker. Stick to the rules — playing is for fun, work is for real. Whether it is the man or woman of the house who does the training makes no real difference. A set training time and place should be arranged and only one person, one whistle and one dog should attend. All the rest of the day can be playing, sleeping and eating, but when the slip lead is put on, the whistle comes out and the game-bag goes over the shoulder, that is school time and nothing and no-one should interfere or alter the routine. Stick to one trainer until the pup has gone right through his basic education. Once that is well accomplished then is the time to introduce the shooting.

Should the owner lack both the time and patience to train his own dog then a resort to a professional trainer is indicated. Choose very carefully, Vizslas are not every man's cup of tea and with the wrong handling will be far worse than useless in the shooting field. If they are to be kennelled and trained by a stranger they will need a lot of understanding and kindness. When is the best age for the dog to go away? Trainers, like prep school masters appreciate youngsters whose brains are sufficiently developed to accept fairly intensive tuition and who have already had a modicum of the basic niceties — such as manners, cleanliness, and obedience to the normal requests demanded when living with a family. They do not welcome a wild, uncontrolled teenager with no knowledge of discipline. The age is normally around 8 or 9 months providing the owners can ensure that till then the dog has not been allowed to chase and catch fur or feather.

TRAINING CLASSES

Training classes and working tests begin in the spring. Vizslas are welcome to all the hunt, point, retrieve societies' sessions and it is far wiser to attend one of these than those organised purely for Retrievers or Spaniels. A letter to the secretary will produce full details of what is available in your area.

No sooner has the shooting season ended than the schools open and keen owners and reluctant pupils can be heard gathering all over the country with whistles, dummies launchers, rabbits on elastic and pigeons in cages. Societies for Retrievers, Spaniels, and the retrieving Pointers all arrange suitable pieces of ground and trainers in attendance for the weekly or monthly influx of aspiring super-dog owners. Training courses are interrupted by working tests which supply progress reports and finally end-of-term exam results. The non-gundog equivalents are the obedience classes up and down the country, held in village halls and playgrounds where with Barbara Woodhouse as their model, every shape and size of family pooch is shouted at and yanked about on choke chains until subdued into submission. As perhaps you suspect, I am in two minds as to the value of such behaviour and will probably be drummed out of the Brownies for saying so.

If the classes are well organised and if the trainer is efficient then they can be used as a means to an end. A lot of responsibility lies on the shoulders of those who organise gundog classes and tests, as many of the students end up in field trials, and if the standard of field trial drops where do you look for the reason? To the training- and those who aided and abetted it.

ADVANTAGES AND DISADVANTAGES OF CLASSES

Training classes have their advantages. The dogs become used to working in company, the owners realise they must take correction in public and a yard-stick is provided to judge progress against other dogs of the same age. For the hunt, point and retrieve breeds the classes try to cover three aspects of training — basic obedience, retrieving and hunting-and-pointing. Obedience is straightforward and the retrieving is similar to that taught in retriever classes, including waterwork providing there is a suitable river or lake on the ground. The advantage to the novice trainer is that the class provides not only instruction but also dummy throwers. The use of a dummy launcher is limited in that the dummy is always going away from the dog, whereas with assistance it can be thrown over a hedge towards the dog.

It is very much more difficult to provide suitable facilities for hunting and pointing. Do the Pointers or Setters have training classes or working tests? They do not for the very reason that not only is the "real thing" the best way to train a pointer, but to simulate it in training class conditions is impossible. Nevertheless, some help can be provided with pigeons and pheasants or even rabbits, to provide steadiness to flush, shot and fall of game.

Some dogs will point handled game quite happily, some will learn to point even the string of the release trap when no bird is in the trap! This cannot be recognised as pointing but it can be used (when the bird is inside) for steadiness. First the trap is sprung by the handler and the dog drops as the bird rises. Once that becomes automatic then a shot can be introduced as the bird flushes and again the dog must remain down. Lastly the shot can include a dummy thrown in the direction of the parting bird, or a dummy can be launched. But let the bird get well away before launching the dummy to avoid an accident!

In this way training classes can certainly help in the retriever training and in the training for steadiness on point, dropping to flush and also in teaching a dog to 'back' the pointing dog. But to train a dog to hunt and point there is no substitute for the effort you must make to find the real thing — i.e. suitable ground where there is a supply of birds and the permission to use it. This is not impossible; in fact if you want to train a Vizsla to work in its full role it is essential and if you are not willing to make this effort then do not expect the dog to work as it should. Training classes can only help you providing you accept their limitations.

WORKING TESTS

Working tests are the inevitable outcome of training classes, and as such are valuable in assessing the success or otherwise of the training. There are puppy, novice and open tests and if these are imaginatively laid out, they can give judges a fair appreciation of the stage of a dog's progress towards his debut on the shooting field.

Working tests should not be used to advertise a dog's potential as a worker. A proven worker must have a good nose and a soft mouth. Dummies give off a large amount of hand scent and are no proof of a nose for game, nor can a dog's mouth be judged by the manner in which it handles a dummy. Tests are an assessment only of the dog's ability to respond to commands (a very necessary part of the training) but no qualification for the inherent instincts necessary in a brood bitch or stud dog. Advertisements carrying the initials WTW (working test winner) are highly deceptive. The unsuspecting buyer accepts this as a prestigious field award. I would by no means denigrate the dog and handler who go through life entering and enjoying working tests (although I find this difficult to understand) but despise those who use the results as a genuine working qualification.

The working tests which take place at the Game Fair and other country events have a dual role; not only are they a competition but also act as guide to the general public who wish to see the ability of various gundogs. This is a valuable shop window for all breeds and the demonstration put on by the hunt, point and retrieve breeds at all the recent Game Fairs south of the border have proved of great value in educating the public.

Fig.13.4 A Retrieve to be proud of

CHAPTER 14

THE VIZSLA IN THE SHOOTING FIELD

As we have seen the work a Vizsla is capable of doing is manifold. He can be used for all purposes of shooting, stalking and falconry. But the ideal conditions where he is seen at his best and is most productive as a bag-filler is as a rough shooter's companion, where hunting hard for game and pointing it staunchly, is the order of the day. One must be prepared to give up time and energy to his training and have suitable ground for him to work over.

Is he any better than the other breeds which hunt, point and retrieve? To those who know and love the breed he is. Why? Because to succeed in training a Vizsla brings a very close relationship between man and dog and the character of the Vizsla makes this relationship more meaningful.

The work of the best Vizsla is equal to that of the best German Shorthaired Pointer both with superb noses, the softest of mouths and an urgent desire to hunt and find game. So the difference between them then lies in character and appearance. Anyone who has a good working Vizsla will never want to change to another breed.

ROUGH SHOOTING

As a rough-shooting companion the Vizsla must hunt according to the conditions of the ground, fast and wide on moorland and stubbles, close and systematically in roots, and even closer in woodland where an out-of-sight point causes problems. His pointing ability will then hold game, giving the gun time to approach and position himself before the flush and once game is shot he must mark the fall and retrieve it dead or wounded, from land or water. Hedgerows and ditches must be hunted. Also water meadows and marshy ground. Unlike Pointers and Setters the Vizsla must hunt in all these conditions and adapt his pace and style accordingly, he must point fur as staunchly as feather. Once dog and owner have worked together for a while the very stance of the dog will indicate to his owner what type of game he is pointing. Some say that with foreleg up it will be feather and hindleg for fur. I have not found this to be accurate, they raise the leg that happens to be spare at that time! It is more by a flick of the eye or twitch of the tail that you learn to read as meaning partridge or hare. How high he holds his head will indicate the distance between him and his quarry, the higher the head the further the game. Scent can be carried two or three hundred yards when conditions pertain. The high head will indicate this whereas weak scent clinging to the ground will not be located until the dog is almost on it and this will produce a very low headed point. When the shooter is ready he will go in and cause the bird to fly or rabbit to run and then remain steady so that a shot can be safely taken.

The difference between a Vizsla and a traditional English gundog such as a Pointer, Spaniel or Labrador as a rough shooting companion now becomes apparent. Instead of one dog for one job you have one dog that will take over the work of all three breeds.

ON THE GROUSE MOOR

No Vizsla can be more in his element than on the hill on August 12th. But after an idle spring and summer it is very necessary to see that he is fit and hard before that day arrives. Muscles have to be toned up and feet must be hardened if he is not to suffer.

Before the 12th, exercises should include galloping up and down steep slopes perhaps after a ball, strengthening his muscles and his heart and trotting behind a bicycle on hard roads for his feet. He will not want to be the dog that has to be left behind on the second day because he is too tired and stiff.

For Vizsla owners it does not matter whether the grouse are driven or walked-up. However the game is played your dog can take a leading role. Versatility is the slogan — grouse or pheasant, stands or walking up, duck or deer. A Vizsla is capable of making his presence appreciated whatever is asked of him. A pure British bird-dog is said to be spoilt if allowed to retrieve but I wonder why. Is it the training complications? This is a real teaser this for anyone who has owned a good Vizsla. I can see and understand the other chap's arguments and yet I can prove them to be wrong. An English Pointer must hunt and point, a Hungarian Pointer must hunt, point and retrieve game. An English Pointer must *not* retrieve game, whereas a Hungarian *must* retrieve game. Undoubtedly it is an extra temptation for the Hungarian to know he will be asked to retrieve but that is overcome in basic training.

Walked-up grouse shooting is the best experience a young Vizsla can have. The scent of grouse is strong and the terrain ideal for a long-legged, wide-ranging youngster full of enthusiasm and stamina. The hares are large and slow, just the temptation he needs to prove his steadiness to fur and the shot birds sometimes fall within sight of his keen eyes. What worse conditions could you have to test your training ability and how exciting when your dog proves himself!

Perhaps a few hints on training might be helpful here. Hares are the meanest thing God made for the downfall of dog. There are two schools of thought on training dogs to be steady to hares — I have tried both, with success and failure. The first method, which is widely used on the Continent, necessitates a plentiful supply of hares. Take a young dog into an area where you can guarantee to see 15 or 20 hares in a morning, release him and encourage him to hunt. When a hare gets up let him chase it; having chased, call him in and make a fuss of him, on no account reprimand him at this stage. Repeat this exercise until his energies begin to flag. Now is the time to alter the reception committee.

On his weary return after about the tenth chase, thump him and thump him hard;

a switch of some sort is ideal — hurt him but do not harm him. After this, walk him to heel, make friends again and then release him and encourage him to hunt. He may be unwilling, but insist until he flushes another hare.

According to the rules, this time, being both weary and sore not only will he not chase, but probably will drop to your whistle out of sheer exhaustion. Push on, and, if possible, work him on another five or six hares. By this time the drop should be automatic and your worries over. Familiarity and a stung backside does breed contempt and a lesson hard learnt is not quickly forgotten.

The second method is probably the more commonly used in this country as there are many areas where hares are scarce. In these conditions it is better that the dog is never allowed to chase. This is not difficult, but it is essential when working ground where there is a possibility of fur that no other dog is present to encourage competition or give a bad example.

Almost invariably when a pup encounters his first hare he does not chase it. The shock of a large furry creature dashing away from him is quite sufficient to make him check, watch and wonder. This unfortunately encourages the novice trainer to think he has a natural non-chasing dog. The dog will probably consider chasing the next hare he sees so it is important not to take him on to hare ground until he is reliable on the stop whistle. Once this is achieved take him where there are likely to be hares.

Fig.14.1 Champion *Abbeystag Bruna* the first Champion to be made up in the breed. (photo: C.M. Cooke & Son)

Send him out quartering on a check cord and when a hare gets up, drop him. If he should temporarily have become deaf you still have control with the check cord so use it sharply. I have found that most dogs chase hares because they are given the example of other dogs. If a dog is never allowed to chase the problem need not arise and by taking him, under control, where there are hares and stopping him from the beginning you will find that by preventing the pleasure of the chase, the wish to do so does not exist. This presumes that you can guarantee to find at least a limited supply of hares on your training ground. For the person who has to rely on a rabbit pen then anything other than instant, automatic obedience will make life difficult. Do not take a dog which is unsteady to fur on the moors — he will be damned and you will be very unpopular.

Equally do not take a dog which is unsteady to fall of game. This is absolutely essential when walking-up and the dog is working 80—100 yards away from you. His steadiness to point and flush will probably be trouble-free, but if game is shot and dropped within sight then a retrieve only on command is very important in case other birds are still to be flushed and shot. Shooting on ground other than moorland can make this aspect of training much simpler. Game shot over a pointing dog frequently falls the other side of a hedge or in a copse or down a valley. The temptation to run in to fall of game is infinitely less under those conditions. The moment of greatest temptation is the marked bird falling within sight and the handler, if not out of sight, certainly far enough away for threats to be impractical.

So if you want your Vizsla to be appreciated and invited to return, make certain that he is steady on point, steady to flush, shot and fall of game.

I remember one outstanding retrieve of a wounded bird which landed in rushes 200 yards below us. The dog had marked it and set off at a gallop down the hill. His nose went down where the bird had landed and he set off on the trail. A rabbit dashed across but he worked on regardless following the blood scent, another rabbit bolted and then a roe deer appeared and trotted away, all ignored by the tracker. A hare could be seen directly in front of him getting up and galloping away. He continued to persevere and flushed another deer and a pheasant. Then the rushes were too dense to see him but in another five minutes he was back up the hill with the wounded grouse in his mouth. That is the work of an experienced dog with the single minded perseverance you would expect from a Vizsla. A lot of pleasure can be had from a visit to the moors and it gives the dog valuable experience for the rest of the shooting season.

For a one-dog man 'backing' can be a problem. But if you have a number of dogs it is seldom necessary to teach them to 'back'. At the time of year when larks are plentiful, starlings are feeding or even an old 'woodie', who knows perfectly well that the stick I am carrying is not a gun is sitting tight in an open field, one of the dogs will stiffen and point, either on scent or sight, it does not matter — a second dog will look up from his play or whatever he is doing, will see this dog on point and immediately freeze — then another will look at the second dog and freeze, and so on in succession. You will have a number of dogs all pointing. None of them, other than the first, are connecting with scent; they are automatically taking up a pointing stance which indicates that somewhere game is present. The 'backing' dogs have only 'backed' the sight of a pointing dog.

You can teach your dog to do this if you are a loner and have no companion dog. Run your dog with an experienced dog, then when a point is achieved slip your dog on a lead taking him slowly towards the pointing dog. Directly he is aware of the point, hold him steady and encourage him to remain thus until the game is flushed and away. After repeating this for a number of times you will find it becomes a natural reaction. It is important that a dog should immediately 'back' a pointing dog because this avoids any interference when game is located. It also makes it much easier to train for steadiness when working in company.

Clothing

Clothing is an important consideration for any shooting day. Decisions are easily made later in the year when you can rely on it being both wet and cold, but in August it is different. There are four alternatives — hot and dry, hot and wet — cold and dry, cold and wet. Such is the charm of our English summer. Upper clothing must be waterproof and removable, underneath must be decent and cool. It is quite *a la mode* to tie removables around your waist, so too much is preferable to too little.

Colour is all important as for any type of shooting; it affects the presence of game just as noise does, and it is important that you should attempt to merge as closely as possible with the background.

The decision whether to wear shoes or wellingtons is not really a problem. I have found that walking long distances up and down moors can be rather exhausting if you are a Sassenach. Possibly one's feet suffer most and therefore it is very important that they should be as comfy as possible. From choice I wear light, completely waterproof ankle boots — now these dear things do not really stand up to the Trades Description Act, I only have to put my foot down one of those rather strange holes that crop up on moors and are filled with water. While watching my dogs obviously I cannot keep both eyes on the ground, so one foot goes down into a hole coming out very wet indeed. Now my feet, like my marriage vows, go on the principle, "in sickness and in health" or rather "in dryness and in damp" and they prefer to go squelch, squelch in unison, rather than alone and so I find it necessary to lower the other foot into the wee burnie that I happened to have encountered five seconds earlier. No 'waterproof' shoes that I have seem to be able to overcome the problem that when I immerse them in water they do not stay 'waterproof'.

The alternative is to wear wellingtons — these are waterproof — and if you do a silly thing like that the chances are you remain dry-footed and don't have to squelch around. Nevertheless, at the end of the day something very nasty happens when you remove a pair of these boots. Even the dogs recoil from the atrocious smell which cannot be avoided no matter what precautions are taken.

One further item, not to be worn but carried — a stick or crook. Recently I was presented with a very beautiful crook by some friends. Now, I am not normally addicted to walking with a stick but after a few weeks I discovered the joys of relaxing and resting my chin on both hands on the top of a crook. The old poem which says "what is this life if full of care, we have no time to stand and stare" hit me sharply on the head and I realised the pleasure I had missed over many years. But in fact a crook on the moors can help you up things, down things, stop things, like rather fast dogs running past you when they should not be, catching things and sometimes walloping things on the head. So a stick comes in very handy and like lead and whistle should be part of one's accoutrements.

221

R.I.P.

Finally let me say a word about cooking grouse. There are many ways of doing this and you only have to read a cook book to find out. A lot depends on the age of the bird but I think perhaps I will tell you the fairest and finest way of allowing a grouse to leave this world. See that he is dressed correctly, baste him well with whisky, garnish him with heather then cook in a moderate oven until ready to serve. In what finer array could a true Scottish grouse wish to enter the gates of heaven?

PICKING UP

This is yet another outlet for a workaholic Vizsla. A good picking up dog must not only be efficient at finding game and carrying it, i.e. good nose and soft mouth, but it must also be neither aggressive nor possessive. The back of a Land Rover stuffed with two or three pickers up and half a dozen mixed dogs is no place to be if there is a dog fight. Nor must it be a thief. It can be very embarrassing if you leave your dog with a brace of partridges in the back of the Land Rover to return and find only feathers.

I have two teams of dogs, the first XI and second XI. On big days when I know there will be a lot of work, the experienced older dogs come out, those who can be relied upon to get on with the job with the minimum of instructions and are safe to send after a runner into a covert with live birds. The second XI consists of one experienced dog and one or two youngsters. Young dogs have got to learn and, used in this way, birds are not lost and a fresh dog is preparing to take over from the old hand. My picking up career began twenty years ago and I quickly learnt my first lesson, which was to leave the work to the dogs. In my enthusiasm I would go bashing through the thickets with the dogs. The keeper asked me who was meant to be doing the retrieving! 'Stand still and send the dog — save your energy for commanding

Figure 14.2 Picking up a pheasant from across the water (*Zoli*)

your forces', he said. I use the dogs not only for retrieving but also walking up across the stubbles and sugar beet with the dogs working ahead. The guns thoroughly enjoy shooting over them as pointers. The dogs get a thorough experience of duck as a lot are reared and driven over the guns. The river is at the bottom of a steeply sloping wooded hillside and the wounded mallard take a lot of finding.

I learned the importance of watching my language. At the end of one morning I was asked by the Brigadier to look for a wounded partridge in some roots and also a dead bird, seen to fall in a copse beyond. The dogs covered the roots from end to end, getting points on live birds but no sign of the runner. We worked the surrounding hedges and ditches with no success, so went on to the copse and almost immediately found the dead cock pheasant. When I got back to the pub the guns were coming out and they asked whether I had found the birds, I reported that we had failed on the partridge but that I had found the Brigadier's cock! It took a long time to live that down.

We also came across woodcock. Not all dogs will retrieve these birds because of their slightly sour taste, but with the Vizslas I find that if they are hesitant to pick them at least they will point them, so provided I keep closely in touch with them when there is a woodcock down we seldom lose one. Over the years my eyes have got acclimatised to looking for them and I can now pick one out from amongst the camouflage of dead leaves.

A good picker up not only uses his dogs to find the birds but also uses his own eyes. I was inclined to watch and follow the working dogs and often the keeper would pick up a bird that I had actually walked over. When we went into the coverts after a drive to 'sweep up' I was watching the dogs working, while his eyes were on the ground. I learnt to let the dogs get on with their work of collecting the runners and the birds out of thick cover whilst I picked up the dead ones in front of me.

I also learnt the meaning and importance of "Watch that bird". If these words ring out from the line of beaters, I know that that is the one bird that will make my day. It will be a pricked bird that is possibly not visible to the pickers up and likely to carry on for quite a distance. If I can see, mark and collect it, it will be a memorable retrieve for the dog. *Brok*, my eldest Vizsla, is my star performer on this type of bird. When we are standing well behind the line of guns his instinct will tell him whether a bird is pricked or not and he will go and return with a bird that I could have sworn was untouched. At first I was cross with him not only for going without command, but also for possibly catching a live bird. But every examination proved him correct, a pellet in the thigh or wing, and it was not long before I appreciated that such behaviour, although not accepted in a field trial, was invaluable to a picker up. Many such birds land and given the chance, will go many miles only to die a lingering death. If a good dog is onto them quickly this is avoided, which is the prime object of picking up. There is much to learn about dogwork, game and guns which makes picking up such a fascinating sport on its own.

I am lucky in that I get quite a bit of partridge picking up at the beginning of the season and my experience here brought home to me the absolute necessity during the drives of either being in the line with the guns or 300 to 400 yards behind. Anywhere in between spoils the shooting and is dangerous. Up in the line one is in a good position for marking, but the dogs cannot be sent until the end of the drive. If well back, the dogs can get onto a wounded bird immediately. A lightly pricked partridge recovers quickly and then is away and out of the working area of the dogs, leaving little or no scent.

I remember *Crumpet* chasing a low-flying bird across a large field, over a hedge, up a bank and into a spinney — in all a distance of at least 300 yards. She returned with the wounded bird. I know we would have lost that bird otherwise because, a) there was no ground scent unto the spinney and, b) I would not have considered hunting in that area because the bird was shot 200 yards in front of us. This is an example of bad training for dogs, but sometime or other a picker up must decide whether he wants to field trial his dogs or to let them earn their keep picking up. There is a moderately happy medium between control and efficient picking up. In the above circumstances it was the dog which realised that the bird was wounded and that the situation was urgent. Most experienced pickers up will agree that dogs have a sense beyond ours which recognises a wounded bird in the air. A dog will seldom bother to behave in this way on an untouched bird.

It is well to remember that when working dogs in thick brambles their feet will suffer unless you apply something that will help to harden the pads. I recommend a liberal quantity of iodine and balsam rubbed into the feet two or three times a week for a while before the shooting season starts. And then repeat during the season if the pads appear to be softening. But for heaven's sake apply it before going out and not when bringing the dog into the house or you will have a lot to answer for when the persian carpets start looking a funny colour.

I can strongly recommend picking up as a winter occupation and although the money does not go far, the fun and enjoyment to be had for oneself and one's dogs is beyond price.

There are two golden rules for pickers up:

1. Never allow yourself or your dogs to distract the guns. Ensure they are aware of your position and once there do not move. Shooting someone is embarrassing and being shot is painful.

2. Always check with any gun who has his own dog whether or not he would like your help. Some bring their dogs for the work and others, believe it or not, bring them along purely for the beer and are only too grateful if your dogs will do the work. Prevention is always better than cure. A friend was badly bitten in the hand when he went to rescue his dog caught up on barbed wire. The pain will often make a dog automatically bite the hand that tries to help. NEVER attempt to lift a dog off wire until you have put a stick in its mouth which he can bite onto. Better still, prevent the dog jumping the wire until you have prepared it. I noticed a gun had fixed a piece of split hose round the shank of his shooting stick. This was easily removed and placed over the top strand of barb for the dog to jump over and then replaced round his stick. An antibiotic in the form of a 'puffer' is always advisable to have in your pocket as also a needle and thread. One friend of mine owned a bitch who was a compulsive jumper, she only had to see a fence or gate and she was over it quite regardless of whether they were going that way or not. She was an excellent jumper but nevertheless did get caught up on wire from time to time. When this happened her owner could be seen sewing up the offending gash, having powdered it first. The bitch died a natural death at the age of fifteen!

CHAPTER 15

FIELD TRIALS*

WHY HAVE FIELD TRIALS?

The objective of field trials? To find the best shooting dog on that day. And for what purpose? One presumes to assist in selective breeding, although no mention is made of this, and no check that the winner is a good specimen of the breed, free from hereditary defects and of good temperament. The accent is on the winning. A field trial is a competition, run under a set of rules and to a standard controlled by rules which the judge must adhere to. Under these conditions, is the dog which wins the trial necessarily the dog that should be used to improve and perpetuate the breed, or are we losing sight of this consideration? Is the winning dog the best shooting dog or is he the best trained dog? In which case should we not award the prize to the handler and breed from him?!

I am often not satisfied that the winning dog is the dog with the drive, initiative, perseverance and keenness that are the natural abilities I am looking for and that cannot be instilled into him or her if they are not inherited. The winner is the dog which works under the control of the handler, and if the handler is experienced, providing his dog has an average ability, then by the rules of the game, he could win. The dog with the burning ambition to find game, the instinct to point steadily and the keenness to retrieve the bird as quickly as possible in order to hunt on, more often than not will slip up by breaking one of the rules, not because he is out of control or purposefully disobedient, but because his keenness can at times overrule his schooling. Biddability and controllability are just as important as now; a wild dog is worse than a useless dog, but a dog which still has the courage to obey its instinct in the presence of game is a better game finder than the one which is fearful of stepping out of line.

Why do the Germans have the Derby and the Solms tests? These spring and autumn blood-line tests exist, not only to test the natural working abilities of the young dogs, but also the character and temperament, with a view to their future role in the shooting field, their potential as stud dogs or brood bitches and to assess the qualities inherited from their breeding. These dogs have only completed their basic training and it is possible to judge the truly natural qualities and capabilities of their work before these qualities are hidden by the final training. The classification of "Excellent" can only be awarded if the judges consider the work of the dog is attributable to its inherited

* A schedule of Vizsla winners is given in Appendix

natural ability and not to the training.

Thus we can see that it is accepted that a higher degree of training can inhibit natural ability. Controllability in a dog can be seen by the natural desire of the dog to keep in touch with its handler and willingly to take instruction from him. Obedience is instilled by training and is a vital part of a gundog's education. With this in mind, why am I, and some of my co-judges, not satisfied? The nit and grit of the matter lies in the fact that so often the best dogs must either be marked down or even eliminated by what I choose to consider is a minor indiscretion. The beginning of a chase on game, even though the dog is stopped, can prevent its name being put on the short list. A "run-in", although not listed in the Guide under eliminations (it is for Retrievers and Spaniels) is considered a major crime. Never have I known a dog that has run-in fail to be eliminated. This is surely an anomaly. A short chase, if corrected, cannot be described as "out of control" — quite rightly a reason for elimination — in fact to be able to control such behaviour should surely be marked up. The man who resists temptation has a far stronger character than he who is not tempted. And a run-in must surely be related to conditions. A run-in should only be a crime if it interferes with the sport. Only the finest margin separates it from a quick retrieve.

When does a normally steady dog run-in? On two occasions probably. If a bird is dropped within a few yards of it there is no way it can be blamed for picking it. It will not interfere with the shooting nor will it disturb other game. The dog could be said to be tidying up. If it is to be eliminated for this, then in all fairness, every other contender should be put in a similar situation and this is not possible in a trial. I maintain that it should be ignored. The other occasion when a useful shooting dog will commit a peccadillo is if a bird is seen to be winged, lands and then starts to run. In this case the dog may jump the gun. How many of our dogs when out shooting are not expected to collect that bird instantly? A pause of even a minute could make the difference between a quick death or a lingering one for the bird. On a poor scenting day that bird will leave little or no trail for even the best of dogs to follow unless it is close behind, and the best of dogs knows this from experience.

Surely the ultimate penalty should not be exacted in a trial when the dog is behaving as it would be asked to in the shooting field? This is the way a first-class shooting dog can be excluded from a field trial award and all that is associated with it.

Are field trials achieving their objectives when it is possible for a brilliant dog to be eliminated on such flimsy grounds?

I do not pretend that this happens all the time, but it does happen under our present system of judging. Is it in the best interests of the breeds that a dog with a mediocre nose but completely steady takes preference as the best shooting dog over a far superior natural worker whose keenness produces an error in steadiness? These dogs are not non-slip Retrievers nor are they close working Spaniels — they are wide, fast ranging pointers which must work hard and fast to find game, hold it and then retrieve it speedily and tenderly. Many genuine, honest working dogs are not entered in the trials because their owners are discouraged by this form of judgement. Yet, are not these shooting dogs the ones we want to see running in trials, showing the full potential of the breed and offering their services at stud to perpetuate the very qualities that are necessary to maintain and improve this group of multi-purpose pointer/retrievers?

If the objective of field trials is to produce the best shooting dog, then it is important that the result reflects the potential scope of the winner as the best shooting dog

Figure 15.1 Peckers Penny

rather than the best trained dog.

HOW TO RUN IN A FIELD TRIAL

When deciding to run in a field trial you must firstly be sure that your dog, be it a puppy or older, is ready for competition. By that I do not mean that there can be no possible chance of it not winning, but that you have proved that it will hunt on strange ground in front of strange guns; that it will point, and remain so, providing the game holds, and that it will actually pick up a warm bird or rabbit. (If you have a puppy competing then you can refuse a fur retrieve if you so wish.) And lastly, that it will swim not only your own swimming pool or lake, but in a strange one (this is particularly applicable to the writer!). It is also necessary that the dog should be under control, reasonable control that is, in order that it does not spoil the conditions for the other competitors. If a dog does not drop to flush, but moves to mark the fall of game and then stops that's alright. If it sees a hare or rabbit, and just cannot resist beginning to follow, but you have sufficient authority to stop him, that is alright too. If a bird is shot off the end of his nose and flaps in front of him, not many dogs will resist this ghastly temptation; and if it is tempted it is very bad luck. Luck, do not forget, is one factor which the organisers are totally incapable of eliminating if a trial is to be conducted as nearly as possible to a shooting day, and any competitors must be sporting enough to accept this. Nevertheless, should this happen and your dog be eliminated, which it must under Kennel Club rules, it is quite possible for the judges to award a Certificate of Merit, if they consider that in other respects the dog has worked well and proved that he can hunt, point and retrieve.

In a field trial a dog must also swim and, in a novice stake where possible, all the competitors are encouraged to do the water test. The last requirement, and possibly the most important from the breed point of view, is that he should be soft-mouthed. If your dog has a mouth like a gin-trap and consistently mangles game, then do *not* enter him in a field trial, no matter how efficient a game finder he is — there is no use in game finding if you cannot eat the produce, and great harm can be done to the breed if such dogs run at trials.

After reading this, you will realise that any self respecting Vizsla who is used for shooting is eligible to enter a trial. If you decide to enter your dog in a trial, the next step is to note the date and venue, and to apply for an entry form, and the regulations. Then you must remember to send off the entry form with the required fee by the required date; in fact as early as possible in order to make the work of the secretary as easy as possible. You should also write to the secretary of the Kennel Club, and ask him to send you the Kennel Club *Rules and Regulations for Field Trials* i.e. *R1,R2* and *R3*, in order that you will understand the procedure that governs all trials held on live game. This will include the *Guide to Field Trial Judges*, which will give you an insight into how the judges assess the performance of your dog.

HANDLERS AND HANDLING

Handling is a special field trial word which describes the waving of arms, blowing of

whistles, leaping around, falling over and the general apoplectic actions of a competitor at a field trial whilst attempting to control his dog. When out shooting with his
dog you would describe him as a normal, sane, balanced person, but once in the line
under the judges' orders he may become terrified and hysterical. His dog reacts just as
one would expect an intelligent animal would. Out shooting he knows his owner and
his job and gets on with it accordingly — in a trial he becomes perplexed and excited.
His owner, obviously temporarily insane, must be pandered to in the hopes that he will
revert to his normal, healthy state of mind as soon as possible. This is an extreme example of field trial nerves which affects many handlers. With time and experience they
usually get over this, if not, it either kills them or their efforts to continue trialling.
One could spend many happy days at trials never looking at the dogs, just watching
the antics of the handlers. It has an amusing fascination all of its own. I can recall
one handler who imitated a policeman on traffic duty to perfection — another who
was constantly winding and unwinding his arms in a sort of Cordon Bleu sauce-making
exercise and yet another who never stopped blowing noises on his whistle till finally
the pea got stuck and he was right up the proverbial gum tree, completely purple in
the face.

A competitor must think about what are judges expecting when they have to consider their marks for handling and what do they mean when they report that a dog
was well handled, or over-handled or did not respond to handling? In a nut-shell,
handling is the final outcome of training and almost every mistake a dog makes can be
attributed to bad handling, i.e. lack of training — all, that is, except a true hard-mouth,
and in this case it should not be entered in a trial anyway. The very best handler is
seen and not heard, the worst is heard and seen to be totally ineffective.

There is no doubt that nerves, like luck, play a great part in trials and are difficult
to overcome. Much good dogwork is spoilt by a nervous handler losing his confidence
in front of the gallery, or by a handler who is under the mistaken impression that by
proving his dog is obedient to every instruction interferes with his natural working

Figure 15.2 Champion *Galfrid Tara* retrieving a duck

ability. In the judges' opinion a good handler is the man who listens carefully to the instructions given him regarding his beat, who checks the wind and ground conditions intelligently and who controls his dog with the minimum of noise and actions. But this obviously can only be achieved with a steady dog with good gamefinding and re-trieving ability and applies to an experienced handler and dog.

Help can be given to a novice if he considers the following points. The judges in-dicate clearly to the handler the ground to be covered by his dog and every effort is made to ensure that this will be upwind. The position of the guns should be noted and the dog then sent off in the direction which will give him the maximum benefit of any available scent. Handler and dog dictate the speed at which the line advances. At this stage it is most important to keep the dog working within his beat and this can be done by word, whistle or hand signals — obviously the quieter the better — and good marks will be given if the dog responds quickly. Directly the dog comes on a firm point it is up to the handler to see that the judges are aware that a point is being claimed. A good handler knows better than the judges whether his dog is on a pro-ductive point and he must go quickly and quietly up to his dog ensuring there is no flush until the guns are in position and the judges tell him that he may send his dog in to flush the game.

Steadiness to flush, shot and fall of game is required and this is far easier to ensure if the handler is close to his dog, it may be necessary to steady or drop the dog on command and a handler will get good marks if this is done quietly and effectively. If the game is shot then the handler must wail until told by the judges to send his dog for the retrieve. At this stage good marking by the handler is helpful as at least he then knows where he should send his dog if the fall was blind to the

Handling onto a blind retrieve is naturally necessary but the quieter the better. If the dog is in the area of the fall and is using his nose, then do not interfere with him. Handling at the water retrieve again should be kept to the minimum. Keep your dog sitting whilst the shot is fired and pigeon thrown, then, when told by the judges, send the dog and wait quietly for him to return. If encouragement to enter water is needed, give it quietly, and once swimming leave him alone to get on with the job. If the dog has been trained for the test then it should be quite unnecessary to whistle or call him in once he has the bird.

Over-handling is almost always the result of nerves and lack of confidence in the dog — try to relax and leave the dog to get on with the work as if it was an ordinary shoot-ing day. Under-handling is the other extreme, where a dog blatantly works off his beat and the handler makes no effort to check this, or when a dog is pointing the handler stays rooted to the ground, neither claiming the point nor going forward to help en-sure steadiness. Another example of under-handling is when a handler is given a retrieve and sends the dog in a vague fashion towards the fall, allowing it to gallop in all directions in the hope that he may be lucky and stumble across the bird. A good handler appears to be doing very little, but the little he does is effective. A final word — remember the one thing a handler may not do is *handle* (i.e. touch) his dog!

GUIDE FOR HANDLERS
(With kind permission of GSP Club)

All stakes organised for breeds which hunt, point and retrieve are run in accordance with Kennel Club *Rules and Regulations*, copies of which may be obtained from the field trial secretary of the Kennel Club. These comprise:

R 1) a. *Kennel Club Field Trial Rules*

  b. *General Regulations for the Conduct of Field Trials*

  c. *Field Trial Rules for Various Breeds* (in our case breeds which hunt, point and retrieve)

R 3) *Guide to Field Trial Judges* issued by the Kennel Club Field Trials Committee (in our case breeds which hunt, point and retrieve)

Those who read these will see that R 1) are mandatory, and judges are bound by them just as much as handlers; whereas R 3) is a guide only to judges who may exercise discretion in their interpretation of the recommendations made therein.

The notes below are designed to convey the spirit of field trials rather than the chapter and verse of rules and regulations, which may be found in the above, and which should be read by all handlers prior to competing.

General Rules

The essential thing to remember is that the handler and his dog along with the gun are a game finding team.

The handler must consider the ground, wind direction and cover, and decide how best to work the dog.

The dog must run across the wind to scent game, point game when winded, and remain on point until the gun is ready for the shot.

On command, the dog should find and retrieve game shot.

The above four paragraphs set out what is required of a handler and his dog in the shooting field or at a field trial.

The judge at a field trial only imposes himself upon the team by:

1. Defining the area of ground for the dog and handler to work.

2. By signalling when the dog can work out its point, the judge having instructed the guns and made them ready for the shot.

3. By signalling if and when the dog may retrieve.

This makes it clear that the handler of a dog is responsible for ground treatment once the judge has defined the area, and the direction he requires the line to proceed. It is the handler's responsibility to read his dog and signal when it is pointing game.

Field trials should approximate as closely as possible to an ordinary shooting day, and handlers should therefore remember at all times that their main object is to find and produce game.

Guns, both on a shooting day and at a field trial, do not want to stand about idle. In either event, therefore, an efficient handler and dog is one which gets on with the job and finds game for them quickly. In field trials, this is what the judges are looking for, and should give the prize to the most efficient at this, provided that the dog behaves himself properly and in accordance with the rules.

On arrival at the Field Trial meeting place

Competitors are expected to arrive half an hour before the scheduled time of starting. They should immediately report to the steward, collect their number, find out where they can exercise their dog and learn what arrangements are being made for transport and lunch during the day.

Competitors are advised to take this opportunity to give their dogs as much exercise as possible, as they will have to be on the lead for the rest of the day, except when under the judges.

Before the start, one of the judges will introduce the host for the day, the guns and the officials, and will brief the competitors on the task planned for the day.

On being called to perform

Competitors must be ready to come quickly into the line when called to do so by the steward.

They should immediately report to the judge, who will indicate to them the general direction of advance, the limits to which a dog may be allowed to quarter and any other general instructions of cautions eg the proximity of a road or railway etc. It is now up to the handler, within the scope of these instructions to find game on the ground as quickly as possible. As soon as he is sure of these instructions, he should remove the collar and lead and command his dog to quarter in search of game. When his dog indicates game, he should signal by raising his hand. When the judges are ready, the game should be flushed, but if it is shot, the dog should not be sent to retrieve until the judge's permission has been given.

Handlers should be aware that pointers rely for pointing largely on air-borne scent, and that therefore the dog which quarters across the wind and into it is most likely to give itself the best chance of finding game. Judges also will recognise this and do not expect to see a dog conform slavishly to the line of guns regardless of the direction and vagaries of the wind. It is up to the handler to decide how to tackle the allotted ground and to control the pace of advance. This should be as fast as will allow the dog to cover the allotted ground adequately, without the likelihood of missing the game.

Remember that game will probably be running on quickly all the time away from the sight and sound of the line of guns. A very slow line will probably never catch up with it. On the other hand, on a bad scenting day, it is easy for an inexperienced dog to go too fast.

Note: It is generally accepted that when hares and rabbits are clapped tight in their form, they may not give off any scent. A dog failing to point a hare or rabbit in these circumstances cannot be regarded as having missed game.

At all times, handlers must be aware of the judge's problem of testing thoroughly twelve dogs during the course of a fairly short day. They must not therefore waste time.

The handler should expect to continue quartering his dog even after a successful flush and retrieve, until told by the judges that they have seen enough for the moment. When told to put his dog on the lead, the handler should do so immediately.

Handlers can normally expect to have two 'runs' in the course of the day, as well as the water test, unless the dog is eliminated for any reason.

Water Test

The water test at field trials is semi-artificial, in that each dog is required to perform a set test, retrieving a previously shot bird.

In novice stakes, a shot is fired and a bird is thrown into the water in view of the dog. The dog should remain sitting and steady until given the command to retrieve.

In all other stakes, a bird is concealed on the other side of a stretch of water. No shot is fired, and the dog is expected to swim across and find and retrieve the bird, re-entering the water with the bird on the return journey where practicable.

Handlers and dogs still to be tested are not permitted to watch the performances of previous dogs, and will be directed by the steward where to stand.

Queries and Complaints

Handlers must remember that judges are under considerable pressure, both to get through the day's programme during a short winter day, and to produce a definite and fair result at the end of it. Nevertheless, judges should always be ready at the end of the day to discuss with the handler concerned any decision regarding his or her dog, or any other problems; they should not, of course, discuss the merits or demerits of other competitors' dogs.

Conclusion

At the end of the day, when the prizes have been awarded, it is customary for the winner to thank the judges.

FIELD TRIAL JUDGING

In an article on field trial judging I read that the handler, if he is to train his dogs effectively, must know and be aware of the judging factors involved to be competitive in the sport.

The qualifications for a Pointer/Retriever judge are that he must be conversant with the Kennel Club *Field Trials Rules and Regulations* and must have gone through the procedure for judges, i.e. taken a book at a field trial under two or three different judges. If well reported by those judges and they consider his assessment of the dog-work to be fair and reasonable then he may be invited to judge a novice stake as a learner judge. If again no adverse report is made either as to his conduct or decisions then his name can be considered by the Kennel Club for addition to their Panel B of field trial judges. After this, if he has co-judged two open or all-aged stakes his name may again be presented to the Kennel Club for promotion to Panel A. Once a judge is qualified he must be prepared to stand by his decisions and opinions and as far as is possible ensure that during a trial he can see all things at all times.

A field trial judge is only one of us ordinary people who has accepted a judging appointment regardless of journeys and weather because he enjoys watching dogs work. A good judge should be impartial and friend to none, he is no good if he lacks the respect of officials of competitors. He should give no award unless in his opinion a proper standard of performance has been achieved. There is no way of telling how a judge comes up with the best dog on the day because each judge has his own concept and subjective opinions in the situations that are met at a field trial where conditions are constantly changing. Some mistakes by a dog can be overlooked because they are unseen. The judge is trying to evaluate the total work of the dog not the individual performances of hunting, pointing, retrieving etc. A judge appreciates that neither handler nor dog are machines. It is possible at a trial that the best dog is not in the awards owing to the conditions of his particular run and that the winner was only the dog who did no wrong. Since judges too are human their judgement must be personalised. Judging calls for good personal and physical qualities, but it is a tough, thankless task. There can be only one winner — eleven losers, and the elements, availability of game and poor shooting can also be against the judge. Most judges use some form of judging system and certainly a memo book, but there are times when a judge is so cold, wet and miserable that the only thing on his mind is a roaring fire and a large drink.

A good judge will help the competitors to the best of his ability. He can do this by briefing them kindly and carefully at the beginning of their run, by remaining calm when things go wrong and by explaining his assessment of their dog in confidence at the end of the day. This will help to give the competitor confidence and an insight as to how the judge evaluates the good and the bad. At every trial there are two judges, one of these must be a Panel A judge who takes responsibility for the trial and makes the final decision should there be any disagreement between them. Otherwise the two judges assess the dogs independently and both should see everything that occurs on the day. At the end of the morning they discuss their assessments and decide which dogs they wish to be brought into the line after lunch. At the end of the day they make their final decisions and place the dogs in order of merit, deciding then whether they consider the quality and standard of work merits the premier award. It is wise to remember that at times a first prize may not be given, *not* because the work of the dog placed first was unsatisfactory in any way, but because the situations pertaining to the availability of game and retrieves were too simple to be able to test the dog's ability. The dogs must run in the order of the draw at the start of the trial and there is no way that the luck of the draw, ground and game can be eliminated.

GUIDE TO FIELD TRIAL JUDGES ISSUED BY THE KENNEL CLUB FIELD TRIALS COMMITTEE

Breeds which Hunt, Point and Retrieve
1. Trials should be run as nearly as possible to an ordinary day's shooting. Judges are responsible for the proper conduct of the trial in accordance with the Kennel Club Regulations and with the schedule for the stake. They should co-operate with the host and the steward of the beat to achieve the best results in an atmosphere of friendliness and confidence. If conditions force them to depart from usual practice They should explain the reasons to handlers and spectators. Guns and handlers should be briefed at the start.

2. Judges at open and all aged stakes should ask the guns to shoot everything, except DIRECTLY over a dog out working. In other stakes judges should ask the guns to shoot only over the 'Point' and when the handler is beside the dog, unless otherwise directed.

3. The first round should be taken as drawn. For subsequent rounds judges may call forward dogs at their discretion, so that those showing merit will be thoroughly tested and given every opportunity in roughly comparable conditions of wind, scent and ground. Dogs which are not forward within 15 minutes of being called may be disqualified.

4. Judges should so position themselves that they can see every move of the dogs while in the line. They should regulate the pace of the line to the handler and dog to avoid game being flushed on a part of the beat not yet covered by the dog. Game so flushed should not be counted as missed by the dog.

5. Judges should accede to a request from the handler of a puppy in a novice or puppy stake who asks to be excused from retrieving fur.

6. If a dog catches game and the judges are satisfied that the game was unwounded and undamaged, the dog should be eliminated. When it appears that game will not flush for the dog, the handler may ask permission to take up his dog, and should only be marked down for handling if subsequently shown to have been wrong.

7. Judges must confirm the arrangement for the collection of unretrieved and un-wanted game.

8. Judges may discuss situations that arise and must agree that actual marks they award as these represent their opinions and should be kept strictly to themselves. The marks should represent the work seen on the day, and should not be influenced by past performances.

9. The standard of work in open and all ages stakes carrying field trial championship status should be higher than for other stakes. A prize should not be awarded unless the dog has had a productive point, a retrieve in the field and has completed the retrieve, whatever the conditions of the day. Other stakes may be judged more leniently, but a prize should not be given unless the dog has proved himself a pointer, and a retriever on land or at the water, and has swum. Certificates of merit are not prizes and may be awarded at the judges' discretion to dogs showing all round qualities and that they swim.

10. Judges should mark the following categories:—

(i) **Ground Treatment** The dog has to hunt the beat allotted thoroughly, making good all ground, missing no game and using the wind correctly. A dog that deliber-ately runs into game up wind should be discarded, but if he drops to birds rising down wind of him, this is a credit.

(ii) **Pointing** The dog should point game staunchly, and work out only on word of command. He must be steady to flush, shot and fall, Persistent false pointing should be severely penalised, but an unproductive point, where the dog indicated by nose down and wagging tail where departed game lay should not be marked, but may be credited as a 'point' for the award of certificate of merit. It is accepted that hares and rabbits in their forms may not give off scent for the dog to point. Judges should not penalise dogs for failing to point in such conditions.

(iii) **Retrieve** The retrieve must be on command. If game is shot over the point, and is marked, the dog should go straight to the fall, and any diversion marked down. With blind retrieves, judges should indicate to the handler where the game fell. The dog should go directly as indicated by the handler and any diversion from that line, with consequent waste of time and risk of disturbance of game, should be marked down. On a long blind retrieve, the dog should be taken towards the fall. A handler should be allowed to position himself where he can see to direct the dog according to conditions, but he should be beside the judges for the delivery.

In the case of a strong runner, the judge should give the immediate order for a dog to be sent. Wounded game should be retrieved before dead game. The seen dead game lying in the open does not really test a good dog, should not be highly marked and should be avoided except in stakes other than open and all aged. Not more than two dogs should be tried on the same bird. When a judge goes forward to locate the game, no further dog should be tried on it. If more than one bird is down, and the dog changes birds on the way back, he should be severely marked down.

The pick up should be clean with a quick return and delivery to hand. A dog that puts game down to take a firmer grip should not be severely marked down as he may have had a gruelling stint quartering, but sloppy retrieving and finishing should be penalised.

All game should be examined for hard mouth. A hard mouthed dog seldom gives evidence of hardness. He will simply crush in one or both sides of the bird. Blowing up the feathers will not disclose the damage. Place the bird on the palm of the hand, head forward, and feel the ribs with finger and thumb. They should be round and firm. If they are caved in or flat, this is definite evidence of hard mouth. Be sure the bird reaches your co-judge and the handler for examination. There should be no hesitation or sentiment with 'hard mouth' — the dog should be eliminated. A certain indication of a good mouth is a dog bringing in a live bird whose head is up and eye bright. Superficial damage, if any, in this case can be ignored. At times the rump of a strong runner may be gashed and look ugly. Care should be taken here, as it may be the result of a difficult capture, or lack of experience in mastering a strong runner by a young dog. Judges should always satisfy themselves that any damage done has been caused by the dog, not by the shot or fall, and in cases of doubt the benefit should be given to the dog. Handlers should be given the opportunity of inspecting the damaged game in the presence of the judges, but the decision of the judges is final.

(iv) **Game Finding Ability** This is of the highest importance. The judges will be looking for it throughout the dog's work by the manner in which he works his beat, finds his game and responds to scent generally, and by the degree of sense of purpose and drive that he displays.

(v) **Steadiness** The dog must in all cases be steady to flush, shot and fall. He may move to mark the fall, and this may be a credit. A dog that runs in to retrieve and is stopped, and then retrieves on command should be marked down according to the extent of the break, but the dog that does not stop should be eliminated. Dogs should be steady to fur and feather going away.

(vi) **Facing Cover** There are occasions, eg on a grouse moor, when this category cannot be marked. Unless all dogs can be marked, none should be. In general the dog should go boldly into reasonable cover when ordered, either to push out game or to retrieve it. The judges should agree what is reasonable.

(vii) **Style** This embraces grace of movement, stylishness on point and of the retrieve, and the general appearance of keenness, competence and happiness in what he is doing.

(viii) **Handling** Noisy, ineffective and over handling should be severely marked down. Usually the best dogs seem to require the least handling, but the dog should be responsive to his handler's signals.

(ix) **Water Retrieve** This should be fully assessed, with special attention to direct, courageous but not suicidal entry, strong swimming, direct emergence and speedy delivery to hand.

In open and all aged stakes the water retrieve is blind across water and should be judged accordingly, including the re-entry into water carrying game.

Eliminations Whining or barking, out of control, chasing; failure to hunt, point, retrieve, enter water and swim, face cover; hard mouth; deliberately catching unwounded game (myxamatosis rabbits excluded).

Major Faults Not making ground good, missing birds, unsteadiness, stickiness on point, not acknowledging game going away, failing to find game, disturbing ground, sloppy work, noisy handling, changing birds.

Credits Game finding ability, style on point, drive, good marking speed and efficiency in gathering game, good waterwork, quiet handling.

KENNEL CLUB SCHEDULE FOR BREEDS WHICH HUNT, POINT AND RETRIEVE

1. Dogs shall be run singly under two judges.

2. Dogs shall be required to quarter ground in search of game, to point game, to be steady to flush, shot and fall, and to retrieve on command.

3. Water Retrieves — Dogs shall be required (1) in puppy, novice and non-winner stakes to retrieve from or across water a seen bird which has been thrown and shot at whilst in the air, (2) in all other stakes to make a blind retrieve of a bird from across water re-entering the water, where practicable with the bird and with no shot fired

4. Dogs must not wear any form of collar when under the orders of the judges. All dogs must be kept on a lead when not competing.

5. Any dog which in the opinion of the judge fails to hunt, point, retrieve tenderly, complete the water test, is gun-shy, or is out of control shall not receive any prize. Any dog in any stake must have been tried at least twice in the line, excluding the water retrieve, before receiving a prize.

6. Eliminations — Whining or barking, out of control, chasing, failure to hunt, point, retrieve, enter water and swim, face cover; hard mouth: deliberately catching unwounded game.

APPENDIXES

GLOSSARY

Angulation   Angles formed by the joints, specifically applied to the shoulder with the upper arm (front angulation). Also to the angles of the stifle and hock (rear angulation).

Balance   Symmetry, no part too big or too small in relation to another part.

Bite   The way the teeth meet when the jaw closes.

Bossy   Superfluous muscular development over the shoulder (fault).

Bowlegged   Front or back legs curving outward (fault).

Briskit   The base of the rib section, lower part of the chest in front of and between the forelegs. Thus the term "depth of chest" or "shallow".

Cannon Bone   Section between the hock joint and the foot of the back legs.

Cat-Foot   Neat round arched compact foot.

Cloddy   Thick-set, lacking elegance (fault).

Chest   The front area of the body at the terminus of the breast-bone.

Conformation   Shape and form of the body.

Coupling   Loin, connecting the forehand to the hindquarters.

Cowhocks   Hocks pointing inward to one another (fault).

Covering the Ground   The amount of ground covered by the spread between front and back legs compared to the height from the ground to briskit, question of measurements and ratio of the parts.

Crabbing   The dog moves diagonally, thus the hindlegs do not follow the track of the forefeet, and the back legs move sideways (fault).

Croup   Part of the back line above the pelvis, from loin to 'set on' of the tail.

Daylight   The distance from the lowest point of the body to the floor, shows too much or not enough daylight.

Dewclaw   The fifth claw on the inside of the foreleg.

Dewlap   Throatiness, excess fold of skin from lower part of neck (fault).

Down in Pastern   Showing an angle forward or sideways which is abnormal, due to faulty bone structure, weak tendons or muscles (fault).

Drive   Impetus — 'to move with drive'.

Dudley nose   Liver coloured nose.

Ewe-neck   Concave topline of neck, resembling the neck of the ewe or camel (fault).

Fiddle front   Combination of curved forearm, elbows out, pasterns close together and turned out feet. (Fault)

Flank   Sides of the body below the loins.

Flew	Pendulous lips and cheeks.
Forearm	Section of front legs, between the elbow and pastern joint, composed of the radius and ulna.
Foreface	Part of the head in front of the eyes.
Front or Fore-hand	The entire aspect of the dog except the head when seen from the front.
Gait	Movement, action.
Gaskin	Lower thigh,
Gay Tail	Tail carried over the back (fault).
Gene	One of the many thousands of determinants concerned with the development in the offspring of hereditary characters and contributed in equal number by the parents.
Goose rump	Steep croup, sloping more than 30 degrees to the ground (fault).
Hackney	To lift the forelegs high under the chin when moving (fault).
Hare-foot	Elongated foot, with long third digits (fault).
Hawk eye	A yellow eye (fault).
Hock	The joint between the 2nd thigh and the pastern of the hindleg.
Knuckling-over	Forelegs bent forward at the knee (fault).
Leathers	Ear Flaps.
Length of neck	The first seven vertebrae (cervical) of the spinal column, from head to withers.
Level Bite	When the teeth meet edge to edge.
Level topline	An even backline from neck to tail.
Light in Eye	Eyes light in colour or yellowish (fault).
Light Boned	Inadequate frame. (fault)
Loaded Shoulder	The muscles under the top half of the shoulder blade have been over-developed so that the blade is pushed outward from the body and cannot occupy its natural position. (fault)
Loin	The section between the rib and the croup.
Long in the Back	The total length of the back is too long compared to the height of the dog. (fault)
Long in Leg	Legs too long in proportion to the rest. (fault)
Muzzle	The fore-face.
Occiput	Protuberance at the middle and rear of the skull.
Out at Elbow	The elbows turned outward from the body due to faulty front formation (fault).
Overshot	The upper incisors protrude beyond the lower teeth leaving a gap (fault).

242

Pace	A gait in which the legs move in lateral pairs (fault)
Padding	Throwing the font feet sideways in action. (fault)
Pastern	The bones between knee and foot (foreleg), & hock and foot (hindleg)
Pigeon Toes	Toes pointing in (toeing in). (fault)
Pin Toes	Toes pointing in. (fault)
Plaiting	Placing one forefoot in line with the other.
Quality	Denotes refinement, degree of excellence, a distinguishing characteristic.
Quarters	The two hindlegs together.
Rangy	Long and loose limbed (fault).
Roach Back	Excessive convex curve of back line from the 8th rib over the loin and the croup (fault).
Scissor bite	Upper incisors just overlap.
Second Thigh	Lower thigh, gaskin.
Set of Tail or Tail Set On	Placement of tail.
Shelley	Narrow, with little depth to chest (fault).
Short Coupled	Short and strong in loins.
Short in Body	Total length of body being short compared to the height (fault).
Shoulder	Region created by the shoulder blade and supporting muscles.
Sickle Tail	Tail carried high in a semi-circle (fault).
Sickle Hock	The hock joint is bent so that the cannon bone is at an angle rather than vertical to the ground creating a curve suggesting a sickle (fault).
Slab Sided	Flat in the ribs (fault).
Snipey	Tapering face, narrow and shallow in muzzle (fault).
Sound	Free from malformation.
Splay Foot	A foot with toes spread wide apart and lacking arch (fault).
Spring of Rib	Roundness of the ribs.
Stifle	Joint between the upper and second thigh in backleg corresponds to the knee in man.
Stilted	Short restricted stride (fault).
Stop	Depression between the forehead and eyes.
Straight Hocks	Hocks lacking angulation or bend at the joint (fault).
Straight Pasterns	Pasterns with little or no slope to the bones between the joint and the foot. (fault).
Straight Shoulder	Insufficient angulation between shoulder and upper arm (fault).

Straight Stifle	Insufficient angulation of the joint (fault).
Stride	Distance from one padmark to the next of the same foot in any gait.
Substance	Body weight, power.
Swayback	Dipping back line. (fault)
The Trot	Two time movement, right front, left rear, and left front and right rear, when the foot is placed on the ground.
The Walk	Four time movement.
Tendon	Band of elastic tissue joining the muscle to the bone.
Terrier Front	Normal shoulder angulation with short upper arm, showing little fore-chest (fault).
Throaty	Excessive loose skin under the throat (fault).
Tighten Up	To develop more muscle.
Topline	Profile of upper outline from the back of the skull to the tail.
Tuck-up	Upward curve under belly — too much (fault), too little (fault).
Turn of Stifle	Angle of the joint.
Type	The sum of those parts that make the dog look a particular breed.
Undershot	The lower teeth project beyond the upper ones (fault).
Upright Shoulders	Shoulders too nearly vertical (fault).
Weedy	Lacking in bone (fault).
Whelp	To give birth to, noun — a newly born puppy.
Whelping	Giving birth to puppies.
Withers	The highest point of the shoulder where the blades meet. The point from which the dog is measured.
Wry Mouth	The lower jaw does not line up with the upper jaw (fault).

Appendix II

VIZSLA FIELD TRIAL WINNERS from 1973–1984
ACCORDING TO KENNEL CLUB STUD BOOK RECORDS

Owner	Dog's Name	Year	Sire	Dam	Breeder
Berry	Windover Ripp	1973	Waidman Fules	Atlanta Lass of Zelten	Dr O. Maxim
Heyman	Matai Vica	1974	Matai Serle	Helvecia Alfa	M Farkashazi
Parke	Matai Pirok	1975	Matai Lurko	Matai Panni II	M Farkashazi
Parke	Matai Pirok	1976	Matai Lurko	Matai Panni II	M Farkashazi
Parke	Matai Pirok	1977	Matai Lurko	Matai Panni II	M Farkashazi
West	Galfrid Gelert	1978	Matai Lurko	Matai Sari of Galfrid	A Boys
Farmer	Waidman Bogar	1979	Waidman Nagi	Bella vom Wurmbrand-park	L Petrie-Hay
Powell	Galfrid Csaba	1980	Galfrid Gaspar	Galfrid Mia	A.Boys
Bil	Saline Gambler	1980	Saline Achilles	Elia Alia of Saline	K Auchterlonie
Bennet	Waidman Chico	1981	Waidman Brok	Timashar Zamarra	L Petrie-Hay
Harris	Perditas Puzzle	1981	Waiman Brok	Starleypoint Victoria	S Farquar
Harris	Perditas Puzzle	1983	Waidman Brok	Starleypoint Victoria	S Farquar
Bennet	Saddleglade Zoli	1982	Waidman Chico	Oroshaza Lynx	S.Aldridge
Bennet	Saddleglade Zoli	1984	Waidman Chico	Oroshaza Lynx	S Aldridge
Cowburn	Peckers Penny	1984	Swanside Little Trooper	Peckers Perchance	R Houghton
Cox	Viszony of Vallota	1984	Waidman Brok	Calversam Amber	R Andrews

CHAMPIONS AND SHOW CHAMPIONS UP TO 1984
ACCORDING TO KENNEL CLUB BREED RECORD SUPPLEMENT

Owner	Dog	Date of Birth	Sire	Dam	Breeder
Boys	Windover Ondine of Galfrid	1970	Waidman Fules	Atlanta Lass of Zelten	Dr Maxim
Boys	Galfrid Jade	1973	Galfrid Gaspar	Matai Sari of Galfrid	A Boys
Boys	Galfrid Mia	1973	Galfrid Gaspar	Saline Coire of Galfrid	A Boys
Cox	Calversam Braeville	1977	Penkevil Zauber	Kenstaff Gay Sadie	A Coupe
Douglas-Redding	Wolfox Fabia	1969	Wolfox Saline Attila	Wolfox Kinford Rica	B Douglas-Redding
"	Abbeystag Claudia of Wolfox	1972	Sh Ch Futaki Lazslo	Abbeystag Wolfox Flavva	S Gray
Finch	Dutch, Lux & Bel Ch Prins	1975	Kamp Mild Cinnamon Magyar V Beaulaker	Luizza	S Middleton
Foster	Kinford Zsuzsi	1968	Waidman Ficko	Kinford Vlada	L Petrie-Hay
Gottlieb	Waidman Remus	1969	Waidman Fules	Kinford Vlada	L Petrie-Hay
"	Galfrid Sofia of Russetmantle	1975	Sh Ch Waidman Remus	Saline Coire of Galfrid	A Boys
"	Russetmantle Troy	1976	Galfrid Odo	Galfrid Leda of Russetmantle	G Gottlieb
"	Russetmantle Sage	1979	Ch Russetmantle Troy	Sh Ch Galfrid Sofia of Russetmantle	G Gottlieb
"	Russetmantle Paris	1980	Ch Russetmantle Troy	Sh Ch Galfrid Sofia Russetmantle	G Gottlieb
Gray	Abbeystag Wolfox Flora	1969	Wolfox Saline Attila	Wolfox Kinford Rica	B Douglas-Redding

Owner	Dog	Date of Birth	Sire	Dam	Breeder
Gray	Futaki Lazslo (USA Import)	1971	Janos V W Come Lately	Futaki Lenke	B Hadik
Gray	Abbeystag Bruna	1972	Sh Ch Futaki Lazslo	Sh Ch Abbeystag Wolfox Flora	S Gray
Gray	Abbeystag Emilio	1974	Sh Ch Futaki Lazslo	Abbeystag Wolfox Flavia	S Gray
Hurst	Russetmantle Bronze	1981	Russetmantle Crisp	Russetmantle Ash	G Gottlieb
Houghton	Swanside Zsigmund	1972	Bingo vom Wurmbrand-park	Sh Ch Swanside Czarina	R Simkin
"	Galfrid Tara	1976	Galfrid Pej	Matai Sari of Galfrid	A Boys
"	Peckers Perchance	1979	Sh Ch Swanside Zsigmund	Ch Galfrid Tara	R Houghton
"	Peckers Parody	1981	Sh Ch Swanside Zsigmund	Ch Galfrid Tara	R Houghton
Islip	Russetmantle Seth	1979	Ch Russetmantle Troy	Sh Ch Galfrid Sofia of Russetmantle	G Gottlieb
Larner	Galfrid Hugo of Yelreta	1982	Matai Bitang Tucsok	Faradpustai Charlott of Galfrid	A Boys
Larner	Yelreta Gemini	1973	Sh Ch Galfrid Hugo of Yelreta	Halstock Fairmaid of Yelreta	D Larner
McCabe	Chantilly Jester	1972	Saline Szeppataki Csaba	Saffron Flora	H McCabe
McCabe	Russetmantle Kushba	1978	Sh Ch Swanside Miklos	Sh Ch Galfrid Sofia of Russetmantle	G Gottlieb
Mills de Hoog	Swanside Miklos	1972	Bingo vom Wurmbrand-park	Sh Ch Swanside Czarina	R. Simkin
Neill	Saline Judi	1981	Sh Ch Chantilly Jester	Saline Grote	K Auchterloni
Perkins	Russetmantle Grebe Gardenway	1982	Ch Russetmantle Troy	Sh Ch Galfrid Sofia of Russetmantle	G Gottlieb

247

Owner	Dog	Date of Birth	Sire	Dam	Breeder
Perkins	Gardenway Bula	1980	Galfrid Sean	Galfrid Erica	J Perkins
Rankin	Arctic of Zelten	1967	Joram de la Creste	Kinford Lidi	P Rankin
Rice	Gamelands Zorro	1972	Sh Ch Waidman Remus	Sh Ch Zsuzsi	M Foster
Rice	Gamelands Zekkie	1971	Waidman Flook	Kinford Nora	M Foster
Rice	Swanside Czorna	1975	Waidman Brok	Sh Ch Swanside Czarina	R Simkin
Swindell	Czassa Calista	1979	Duicke Lorange	Goldenclaret of Czassa	J Swindell
Seward	Galfrid Anya of Annadale	1979	Kenstaff Zavier of Galfrid	Saline Coire of Galfrid	A Boys
Simkin	Swanside Czarina	1969	Waidman Flook	Bonnie Robin	M Maloney
Webster	Russetmantle Jake of Asquanne	1979	Sh Ch Waidman Remus	Galfrid Leda of Russetmantle	G Gottlieb

CHAMPIONS UP TO THE END OF 1983

Breeder	Dog
Gray	Abbeystag Bruna
Gray	Abbeystag Emilio
Houghton	Galfrid Tara
Houghton	Peckers Perchance
Gottlieb	Russetmantle Troy

APPENDIX IV
LIST OF VIZSLA IMPORTS INTO BRITAIN
AND SOME OF THEIR PEDIGREES

Year	Dog	Sex	Origin
1953	Ernest	Male	Hungary
	Agnes	Female	Hungary
1956	*Tardosi Gyongyi*	Female	Hungary
	Adalyn v Hunt	Female	USA
1962	*Sibriktelepi Tigi*	Male	Hungary
1963	*Joram de la Creste*	Male	France
1969	*Saline Szeppatki Csaba*	Male	Hungary
1970	*Warhorse Lwow*	Male	USA
	Bingo vom Wurmbrandpark	Male	Austria
	Bella vom Wurmbrandpark	Female	Austria
	Starleypoint Komlosreti Atok	Male	Hungary
1972	*Futaki Lazslo*	Male	USA
	Matai Sari of Galfrid	Female	Hungary
	Farad Pusztai of Galfrid	Female	Hungary
1973	*Matai Vica*	Female	Hungary
	Matai Pirok	Female	Hungary
1977	*Mocsarkereso Vac of Galfrid*	Female	Hungary
1981	*Prins*	Male	Holland

The Imports listed are those that have played a significant role in increasing the potential of the breed in Britain up to 1984. The pedigrees included are those Vizslas who feature in most pedigrees of today, or would be of interest for future breeding programmes.

APPENDIX V

PEDIGREES OF IMPORTS

The pedigrees which follow indicate the origins of the new blood lines brought into the U.K.

Name of Dog   *Ernest* and *Agnes* (Hungarian Imports)

Sire	Sire	Sire
Puschi	Bogar	Dam
	Dam	Sire
	Lady	Dam
Dam	Sire	Sire
Vlada	Ficho II	Dam
	Dam	Sire
	Canky Racer	Dam

Name of Dog   *Tardosi Gyongyi* (Hungarian Import)

Sire	Sire	Sire Canki Pajtas
Betyar	Betyar	Dam Bijou
	Dam	Sire Betyar
	Zsuzsi	Dam Rica
Dam	Sire	Sire Csibesz
Csikcsikoi Ari Nora	Ripp	Dam Lidi
	Dam	Sire Puschi
	Kati Jutka	Dam Panni

Name of Dog   *Adalyn V Hunt* (USA Import)

Sire	Sire	Sire Heros Povazio
Morho Z Povazio (Import Hungary to Austria)	Trysk Z Povazio	Dam Herta Povazio
	Dam	Sire Fakir Z Povazio
	Bystra Z Povazio	Dam Bojka Z Povazio
Dam	Sire	Sire Rex V Povazio
Astra Z Povazio (Import Hungary to Austria)	Rex Z Pod Devina	Dam Alena Vido
	Dam	Sire Lord Brok Selle
	Astra Selle	Dam Zsuszu-Selle

Name of Dog *Saline Szeppataki Csaba* (Hungarian Import)

Sire	Sire	Sire
	Hargitai Dani	*Cinkos*
		Dam *Hargitai Reka*
Kisujfalui Dani	Dam	Sire *Harry*
	Mari	Dam *Szolnoki Kitty*
Dam	Sire	Sire *Harry*
	Szolnoki Picki Muki	Dam *Szolnoki Kitty*
Arokparti Erzsok Ledi	Dam	Sire *Cinkos*
	Kati	Dam *Kicsi*

Name of Dog *Warhorse Lwow* (USA Import)

Sire	Sire	Sire *Gingo V Schloss Loosdorf*
	Miclos Schloss Loosdorf	Dam *Jill V Schloss Loosdorf*
Warhorse O'Jay	Dam	Sire *Nikki's Arco*
	Duchess of Shirbob	Dam *Mic of Shirbob*
Dam	Sire	Sire *Gingo V Schloss Loosdorf*
	Miclos Schloss Loosdorf	Dam *Jill V Schloss Loosdorf*
Warhorse Bella	Dam	Sire *Miclos Schloss Loosdorf*
	Warhorse Cindy Bea	Dam *Duchess of Shirbob*

Name of Dog *Sibriktelepi Tigi* (Hungarian Import)

Sire	Dam	Sire *Harry*
	Szolnoki Picki Muki	Dam *Szolnoki Kitty*
Edenkerti Csibesz	Sire	Sire *Hector Pick*
	Gyongyi	Dam *Kati*
Dam	Sire	Sire *Ficko*
	Csibesz	Dam *Zsuzsi*
Sibriktelepi Maca	Dam	Sire *Szikra Ficko*
	Fruzsi	Dam *Panna*

251

Name of Dog   *Joram de la Creste* (French Import)

Sire	Dam	Sire *Bor*
Schan Von Trutzhoff	*Rheingold Von Trutzhoff*	Dam *Reri Z Povazia*
	Sire *Reri Z Povazia*	Sire *Rex Z Pod Devina*
		Dam *Bystra Z Povazia*
Dam	Sire *Pipas Stuller*	Sire *Ficko*
Kobraz Povazia		Dam *Szidi Vacduka*
	Dam *Bora Zaborkreky*	Sire *Tapolcai Koma*
		Dam *Bystra Z Povazia*

Name of Dog   *Bingo Vom Wurmbrandpark* (**Austrian Import**)

Sire	Sire *Faun V Ovar*	Sire *Sieg V Trutzhof*
Bodo V D Dopplerhutte		Dam *Barbi V Sumeg*
	Dam *Rexya V Arany*	Sire *Arany V Gromback*
		Dam *Doly Olca*
Dam	Sire *Szolnoki Picki Mucki*	Sire *Harry*
Tormaspusztai Zsa Zsa		Dam *Szolnoki Kitty*
	Dam *Vica*	Sire *Ogy Betjar*
		Dam *Dorka*

Name of Dog   *Futaki Lazslo* (USA Import)

Sire	Sire *Kiraly Rokuvar*	Sire *Wilsons Pal Joey*
Janos V W Come Lately		Dam *Princess of Cadlstadt*
	Dam *Whitselle Miska*	Sire *Brokselle Son of a Gun*
		Dam *Gold Star Kandi*
Dam	Sire *Caesar*	Sire *Gypsy's Brandy*
Futaki Lenke		Dam *Kay's Katezala*
	Dam *Futaki Lincsi*	Sire *Brok Selle*
		Dam *Piri*

Name of Dog	Matai Sari of Galfrid (Hungarian Import)		
Sire Matai Bitang Tucsok	**Sire** Pisti	Sire Sibriktelepi Pisti Csibesz	
		Dam Rita	
	Dam Dardai Cil I	Sire Csikcsicsoi Aprod	
		Dam Dardai Zsuzsie	
Dam Matai Boske	**Sire** Irsay Camill	Sire Pisti	
		Dam Zsoka Mici	
	Dam Matai Bori	Sire Matai Tucsok	
		Dam Kati	

Name of Dog	Farad Pusztai Charlott (Hungarian Import)		
Sire Matai Legeny	**Sire** Rabakozi Tisza Ripp	Sire Viranyosi Pufi Ficko	
		Dam Rabakozi Lili	
	Dam Matai Bori	Sire Matai Tucsok	
		Dam Kati	
Dam Allatkerti Dorka	**Sire** Kenyermezti Pikk Dani	Sire Szolnoki Picki Muki	
		Dam Miss	
	Dam Allatkerti Cil Zsoka	Sire Annavolgyi Szittya	
		Dam Hogyeszi Sylvia Zsoka	

Name of Dog	Mocsarkerso Vac of Galfrid (Hungarian Import)		
Sire Matai Vadasz	**Sire** Helvecia Alfa	Sire Borvi Deki Nimrod	
		Dam Zagyvaparticsurka Cinkapanna	
	Dam Matai Gerle	Sire Matai Lurko	
		Dam Matai Sari of Galfrid	
Dam Morcos-Pusztai Bori	**Sire** Lucaszeki Kope Ficko	Sire Kistalyai Lux	
		Dam Ushartyani Betty	
	Dam Durcas Arankca	Sire Kisujfalui Dani	
		Dam Nadorvardosi Myra	

Name of Dog	*Prins*				
Sire *Kamp Milo-Cinnamon Magyar V D Beulaker*	Sire *Kamp Gerecsei Elias Ezsaias*	Sire *Irsay Camill*
		Dam *Rakos-Varosi Csilla*
	Dam *Anouschka V Chariten*	Sire *Siksagi Burkus*
		Dam *Frissic V H Land V Ravenstein*
Dam *Luizza*	Sire *Pajtás*	Sire *Siksagi Burkus*
		Dam *Asta V H Land V Ravenstein*
	Dam *Siksagi Bogyo*	Sire *Kamp Siksagi Csatt*
		Dam *Siksagi Csilla*

APPENDIX VI
LIST OF PRE-POTENT VIZSLAS UP TO 1984

Pre-Potent Dogs

Dogs producing 2 or more show champions in the breed shown in Britain:

	Number of Sh Champions
Ch *Russetmantle Troy*	4
Sh Ch *Waidman Remus*	3
Sh Ch *Futaki Laszlo*	3
Wolfox Saline Attila	2
Bingo Vom Wumrbrandpark	2
Sh Ch *Swanside Zsigmund*	2
Galfrid Gaspar	2
Waidman Flook	2
Waidman Fules	2
Waidman Ficko	1

Widman Ficko is included here because it is interesting to note that three dogs out of the same litter sired five show champions.

Sire	Dam	Sire *Joram de La Creste* (French Import)
Waidman Flook *Waidman Fules* *Waidman Ficko*	*Waidman Bor*	Dam *Strawbridge Czinka*
	Dam *Tardosi Gyongyi* (Hungarian import)	Sire *Betya*
		Dam *Csikcsiksoi Ari Nora*

Pre-Potent Bitches

Bitches producing 2 or more show champions in the breed shown in Britain up to 1984:

	Number of Sh Champions
Sh Ch *Galfrid Sofia of Russetmantle*	5
Saline Coire of Galfrid	3
Sh Ch *Swanside Czarina*	3
Matai Sari of Galfrid	2
Sh Ch *Abbeystag Wolfox Flora*	2
Kinford Vlada	2
Wolfox Kinford Rica	2
Ch *Galfrid Tara*	2
Galfrid Leda of Russetmantle	2

APPENDIX VII

FIVE FULL CHAMPIONS IN THE BREED
AND THEIR PEDIGREES

Ch *Abbeystag Bruna*   Ch *Galfrid Tara*   Ch *Russetmantle Troy*
Ch *Abbeystag Emilio*   Ch *Peckers Perchance*

There are now five champions in the breed, it is not many, but those who have managed it should feel justly proud. Looking at the pedigrees there seems no common denominator except that out of thirty nine show champions, Sheila Gray and Richard Houghton have produced two full champions from their kennels, and out of the five, three are bitches and all have had litters:

Sh Ch *Futaki Lazslo* sired both of Sheila Gray's champions, when put to litter sisters Sh Ch *Abbeystag Wolfox Flora* and *Abbeystag Wolfox Flavia*.

Ch *Galfrid Tara* when put to Sh Ch *Swanside Zsigmund* produced a champion daughter.

Abbeystag Bruna	Sire Sh Ch *Futaki Lazslo*	Sire *Janos V W Come Lately*
		Dam *Futaki Lenke*
	Dam *Abbeystag Wolfox Flora*	Sire *Wolfox Saline Attila*
		Dam *Wolfox Kinford Rica*

Abbeystag Emilio	Sire *Futaki Lazslo*	Sire *Janos V W Come Lately*
		Dam *Futaki Lenke*
	Dam *Abbeystag Wolfox Flavia*	Sire *Wolfox Saline Attila*
		Dam *Wolfox Kinford Rica*

Galfrid Tara	Sire *Galfrid Pej*	Sire *Galfrid Gaspar*
		Dam *Farad Pusztai Charlott*
	Dam *Matai Sari of Galfrid*	Sire *Matai Bitang Tucsok*
		Dam *Matai Boske*

Peckers Perchance	Sire *Swanside Zsigmund*	Sire *Bingto von Wurmbrandpark*
		Dam *Swanside Czarina*
	Dam *Galfrid Tara*	Sire *Galfrid Pej*
		Dam *Matai Sári of Galfrid*

Russetmantle Troy	Sire *Galfrid Odo*	Sire *Galfrid Gaspar*
		Dam *Windover Ondine of Galfrid*
	Dam *Galfrid Leda of Russetmantle*	Sire *Galfrid Gaspar*
		Dam *Starbeater Phoenix of Galfrid*

APPENDIX VIII
CHALLENGE CERTIFICATE AND BEST OF BREED WINNERS, CRUFTS 1971 — 1984

1971
Judge — Mrs V C Yates

Bitch C C & BOB	Sh Ch *Kinford Zsuzsi*	owned by M Foster bred by L Petrie-Hay
Dog CC	Sh Ch *Waidman Remus*	owned by G Gottlieb bred by L Petrie-Hay

1972
Judge — Mr W E Foster

Bitch CC & BOB	Sh Ch *Swanside Czarina*	owned by R Simkin bred by M. Maloney
Dog CC	Sh Ch *Waidman Remus*	owned by G Gottlieb bred by L Petrie-Hay

1973
Judge — Miss G Broadley

Bitch CC & BOB	Sh Ch *Kinford Zsuzsi*	owned by M Foster bred by L Petrie-Hay
Dog CC	Sh Ch *Arctic of Zelten*	owned & bred by P Rankin

1974
Judge — Major J Houghton

Bitch CC & BOB	Sh Ch *Swanside Czarina*	owned by R Simkin bred by M Maloney
Dog CC	Sh Ch *Gamelands Zorro*	owned by M Rice bred by M Foster

1975
Judge — Mr R J Gadsden

Dog CC & BOB	Sh Ch *Arctic of Zelten*	owned & bred by P Rankin
Bitch CC	Sh Ch *Gamelands Zekkie*	owned by M Rice bred by M Foster

1976
Judge — Mrs M Lyndesay-Smith

Dog CC & BOB	Ch *Abbeystag Emilio*	owned & bred by S Gray
Bitch CC	Sh Ch *Abbeystag Wolfox Claudia*	owned by B Douglas-Redding bred by S Gray

1977
Judge — Mrs J. De Casembroot

Dog CC & BOB	Sh Ch *Chantilly Jester*	owned and bred by H. McCabe
Bitch CC	*Sh Ch Swanside Czorna*	owned by M Rice bred by R Simkin

1978
Judge — Mr D L Page

Bitch CC	Sh Ch *Swanside Czorna*	owned by M Rice bred by R Simkin
Dog CC & BOB	Sh Ch *Galfrid Hugo*	owned by D Larner bred by A Boys

1979
Judge — Miss L Turner

Dog CC & BOB	Ch *Russetmantle Troy*	owned and bred by G Gottlieb
Bitch CC	Sh Ch *Russetmantle Kushba*	owned by H McCabe bred by G Gottlieb

1980
Judge — Mr J Cartledge

Dog CC & BOB	Ch *Russetmantle Troy*	owned and bred by G Gottlieb
Bitch CC	Sh Ch *Galfrid Sofia of Russetmantle*	owned by G Gottlieb bred by A Boys

1981
Judge — Mr W Parkinson

Bitch CC & BOB	Ch *Peckers Perchance*	owned and bred by R Houghton
Dog CC	Sh Ch *Calversam Braeville*	owned by J Dickinson bred by A Coupe

1982
Judge — Mr R Finch

Dog CC & BOB	Sh Ch *Russetmantle Paris*	owned and bred by G Gottlieb
Bitch CC	Ch *Peckers Perchance*	owned and bred by R Houghton

1983
Judge — Mr F G Waring

Dog CC & BOB	Sh Ch *Russetmantle Paris*	owned and bred by G Gottlieb
Bitch CC	Ch *Peckers Perchance*	owned and bred by R Houghton

1984
Judge — Mrs M Lyndesay-Smith

Dog CC & BOB	Sh Ch *Russetmantle Bronze*	owned by M Hurst bred by G Gottlieb
Bitch CC	*Galfrid Rosa*	owned and bred by A Boys

APPENDIX IX
FIELD TRIALS
Vizslas featured in field trials from 1964 to 1983*
according to Kennel Club Stud Book Records

Date	Society	Stake	Name & Owner		Place
1964 Aug	GSPC	Novice	*Sibriktelepi Tigi* MacRae		2nd
Oct	GSPC	Novice	*Creagan Anya*	Phillips	2nd
1965 Sept	GSPC	Novice	*Creagan Anya*	Phillips	3rd
1966 Oct	GSPC	Novice	*Creagan Anya*	Phillips	2nd
Oct	GSPC	All-aged	*Kinford Ficko*	Phillips	Res
1970 Oct	LBGA	Novice	*Saline Achilles*	Auchterlonie	3rd
1971 Nov	GSPC	Novice	*Saline Achilles*	Auchterlonie	Res
			Saline Czeppataki Csaba	"	CofM
1972 Oct	LBGA	Novice	*Saline Caroline*	Greig	CofM
1973 Nov	HVS	Novice	*Windhover Ripp*	Berry	1st
	(Vizslas Only)		*Saline Caroline*	Greig	2nd
			Starleypoint Ulles	Maitland-Smith	3rd
			Capeland Cascade	Anthony	CofM
			Saline Achilles	Auchterlonie	CofM
1974 Oct	GSPC	Novice	*Waidman Brok*	Petrie-Hay	3rd
	HVS	Novice	*Matai Vica*	Heyman	1st
	(Vizslas Only)		*Saline Caroline*	Greig	2nd
			Mintaka	Van Helfoort	3rd
	HVC	Novice	*Galfrid Gerda*	Gottlieb	CofM
			Matai Sari	Boys	CofM
Dec	HVC	Novice	*Waidman Brok*	Petrie-Hay	CofM
1975 Jan	GSPA	Novice	*Waidman Brok*	Petrie-Hay	3rd
Sept	HVS	Novice	*Matai Vica*	Heyman	Res
			Saline Achilles	Auchterlonie	CofM
Oct	HVS	Novice	*Matai Pirok*	Parke	1st
	(Vizslas Only)		*Matai Vica*	Heyman	2nd
			Galfrid Gelert	West	3rd
	WCGB	Novice	*Matai Pirok*	Parke	1st
1976 Sept	GSPA	Novice	*Saline Achilles*	Auchterlonie	Res
Oct	HVC	Novice	*Galfrid Gelert*	West	1st
	(Vizslas Only)		*Galfrid Gerda*	Gottlieb	2nd
			Galfrid Odo	Boys	3rd
			Ch Abbeystag Bruna		CofM
	LBGA	Open	*Saline Achilles*	Auchterlonie	CofM
	GSPC	Novice	*Galfrid Otis*	Wilkinson	3rd
	HVS	Open NQ	*Galfrid Gelert*		CofM
Nov	GSPC	Novice	*Saline Cabal*	Auchterlonie	3rd
1977 Aug	GSPC	Open	*Saline Cabal*	Auchterlonie	3rd
Oct	HVC	Novice	*Galfrid Otis*	Wilkinson	3rd

Date	Society	Stake	Name & Owner		Place
	HVS	Novice	*Matai Pirok*	Parke	1st
	(Vizslas Only)		*Waidman Bogar*	Farmer	2nd
			Galfrid Gelert	West	3rd
Nov	GSPC	Novice	*Waidman Bogar*	Farmer	Res
1978 Jan	GSPC	Novice	*Waidman Bogar*	Farmer	1st
Jan	HVC	Novice	*Galfrid Gelert*	West	1st
Oct	HVC	All-aged	*Galfrid Gelert*	West	Res
1979 Oct	HVS	Novice	*Waidman Crumpet*	Petrie-Hay	CofM
	(Vizslas Only)		*Galfrid Odo*	Boys	CofM
			Galfrid Gelert	West	CofM
			Galfrid Dali	Berry	CofM
	HVC	All-aged	*Galfrid Gelert*	West	3rd
	HVS	Open	*Galfrid Gelert*	West	3rd
Dec	HVC	Novice	*Calversam Barleybroth*	Cox	CofM
1980 Jan	HVC	Novice	*Galfrid Csaba*	Powell	1st
			Waidman Crumpet	Petrie-Hay	3rd
Aug	GSPA	Novice	*Saline Gambler*	Bil	1st
			Saline Fulmarx Blue	Auchterlonie	2nd
Nov	GSPC	Novice	*Saline Fulmarx Blue*	Auchterlonie	CofM
Dec	HVC	Novice	*Calversam Barleybroth*	Cox	2nd
1981 Jan	GSPA	Novice	*Calversam Barleybroth*	Cox	2nd
Oct	WCGB	Novice	*Calversam Barleybroth*	Cox	2nd
	LMC	All-aged	*Waidman Chico*	Bennett	1st
	HVS	Open	*Saline Fulmarx Blue*	Auchterlonie	CofM
	HVS	Novice	*Perdita's Puzzle*	Harris	1st
			Viszony of Vallota	Cox	Res
			Waidman Foxi	Pryke	CofM
			Llewelyn Ibi	Phillips	CofM
Nov	GSPC	All-aged	*Waidman Chico*	Bennett	CofM
1982 Jan	GSPA	All-aged	*Viszony of Vallota*	Cox	3rd
Sept	GSPA	Novice	*Viszony of Vallota*	Cox	2nd
			Laser Duite	Churchill	Res
			Calversam Barleybroth	Cox	CofM
Oct	GSPC	Novice	*Viszony of Vallota*	Cox	2nd
			Calversam Barleybroth	Cox	3rd
	LMC	Novice	*Saddleglade Zoli*	Bennett	1st
			Viszony of Vallota	Cox	2nd
	LMC	Novice	*Calversam Barleybroth*	Cox	CofM
	WCGB	Novice	*Viszony of Vallota*	Cox	3rd
Nov	HVS	Open	*Viszony of Vallota*	Cox	3rd
	HVS	Novice	*Viszony of Vallota*	Cox	CofM
			Laser Duke	Churchill	CofM
			Llewelyn Ibi	Phillips	CofM
			Calversam Barleybroth	Cox	2nd
			Saddleglade Zoli	Bennett	1st

Date		Society	Stake	Name & Owner		Place
	Nov	WCGB	All-aged	*Viszony of Vallota*	Cox	CofM
		GSPC	Novice	*Saddleglade Zoli*	Bennett	Res
	Dec	LMC	All-aged	*Calversam Barleybroth*	Cox	CofM
1983	Jan	GWPC	Novice	*Viszony of Vallota*	Cox	2nd
		GSPA	All-aged	*Viszony of Vallota*	Cox	Res

Provisional Results (to be KC Stud Book certified)

	Oct	LMC	All-aged	*Saddleglade Zoli*	Bennett	2nd
		CSPC	All-aged	*Laser Duite*	Churchill	3rd
		LMC	All-aged	*Viszony of Vallotta*	Cox	2nd
		HVS	Open	*Saddlegalde Zoli*	Bennett	CofM
				Viszony of Vallota	Cox	Res
		HVS	Novice	*Perdita's Puzzle*	Harris	1st
				Calversam Barleybroth	Cox	2nd
				Laser Duke	Churchill	3rd
				Szanjani Csipke	Harris	CofM
				Llewelyn Ibi	Phillips	CofM
		GSPA	Novice	*Pecker's Penny*	Cowburn	CofM
		HVS	All-aged	*Abbeystag Josie*	Gray	CofM
				Ch Russetmantle Troy	Gottlieb	CofM
				Pecker's Penny	Cowburn	1st
	Nov	LMC	Novice	*Pecker's Perchance*	Houghton	CofM
				Ch Russetmantle Troy	Gottlieb	CofM
		GSPA	All-aged	*Saddleglade Zoli*	Bennett	Res
				Viszony of Vallota	Cox	1st
		GSPA	Open NQ	*Viszony of Vallota*	Cox	CofM
1984	Jan	GSPC	All-aged	*Saddleglade Zoli*	Bennett	CofM
		WCGB	Open NQ	*Saddleglade Zoli*	Bennett	3rd
				Viszony of Vallota	Cox	Res

GSPC	German Shorthaired Pointer Club
GSPCA	German Shorthaired Pointer Association
HVC	Hungarian Vizsla Club
HVS	Hungarian Vizsla Society
LBGA	Lothian and Borders Gundog Association
LMC	Large Munsterlander Club
WCGB	Weimaraner Club of Great Britain
GWBC	German Wirehaired Pointer Club

APPENDIX X
HUNGARIAN NAMES

Ablak	Dacos	Fal	Ideg	Majus	Szag
Adui	Dal	Falu	Igiret	Maradek	Sjag
Ado	Del	Faradt	Ima	Mennyi	Szaj
Agy	Delelott	Farkas	Imas	Mertek	Szerda
Ajto	Delutan	Feg	Ipar	Mikor	
Alak	Dio	Felett	Iaras	Mojott	Tanito
Alatt	Divat	Felso	Iras		Tars
Allam	Dohany	Festek	Iro	Noveny	Tartos
Allas	Dragor	Fesu	Iskola	Novar	Tavasj
Alma	Durvar	Fui	Ismet		Tehat
Almos			Isten	Okos	Tej
Angol		Forras		Ora	
Arc		Forro	Jarni	Orr	Tenni
Azutan	Edes	Fosni	Jatek	Ota	Tilos
Azert	Egesz	Friss	Jobb	Oreg	Tiuta
	Eladni	Furdo	Jovo	Otven	Titok
Baj	Eleg	Fust	Kem		Tojas
Bekes	Elet		Kep		Torok
Belso	Elni	Gos	Kerek		Tudas
Ber	Elott	Gyar	Kerni	Palack	Tudo
Beteg	Elso		Kert	Piros	Tukor
Betu	Eli	Haj	Kes		Turni
Boritni	Elvesni	Hajo	Keso	Ravasz	
Bors	Ember	Hamar	Ketes	Regen	Udvar
Borso	Enek	Hamis	Ketto	Resz	Unokar
	Erdek	Hatea	Kusi	Rittia	Usni
	Erret	Haj	Kim		Utan
Cikk	Eryno	Haz	Kor	Sajt	Utolso
Cim	Ero	Haza	Koran	Sarok	Ulni
Cipo	Eros	Huzvet	Kutyia	Senki	Uveg
Csak	Esset	Husz		Sietni	Vaj
Csepp	Eso	Huzi		Sovany	Vajjou
Csendes	Eszak	Huzn	Lassam	Sult	Vack
Csor		Huzni	Lecke	Szabo	Valaki
Cukor	Ezust		Lalek	Szaj	Vallas

A few Hungarian names taken from a phonetic
Hungarian—English Pocket Dictionary.

263

GENERAL INDEX

Your Vizsla (Strauss & Cunningham) 54—5, 56

Z
Zay Family of Zaycegroe 4
Zelton, M.J. 21

INDEX OF DOGS' NAMES

*** Dual Champion
** Champion
* Show Champion

270